DEVELOPMENTAL LEADERSHIP

ALSO BY DAVID L. GOETSCH

Quality Management for Organizational Excellence

Effective Teamwork

Effective Customer Service

Effective Strategic Planning for Competitive Advantage

Effective Leadership

Effective Change Management

Effective Supervision

Occupational Safety and Health

The Basics of Occupational Safety

Construction Safety and Health

Construction Safety and the OSHA Standards

Establishing a Safety-First Corporate Culture in Your Organization

Building a Winning Career in a Technical Profession

Building a Winning Career in Engineering

Economic Development 101

DEVELOPMENTAL LEADERSHIP

Equipping, Enabling, and
Empowering Employees
for
Peak Performance

By

David L. Goetsch

ISBN: 978-1-4269-5909-7 (sc)
ISBN: 978-1-4269-5910-3 (hc)
ISBN: 978-1-4269-5908-0 (e)

Library of Congress Control Number: 2011905499

Trafford rev. 04/06/2011

 www.trafford.com

North America & International
toll-free: 1 888 232 4444 (USA & Canada)
phone: 250 383 6864 ♦ fax: 812 355 4082

TABLE OF CONTENTS

Introduction: Equipping, Enabling, and Empowering Employees for Peak Performance

This book presents best practices in 20 key areas for helping executives, managers, and supervisors become developmental leaders who can equip, enable, and empower employees for peak performance and continual improvement.

Introduction

Equipping, Enabling, and Empowering Employees for Peak Performance

Even in the age of high technology, no single factor is more important to organizational excellence than the human factor. People still make the difference between excellence and mediocrity in organizations. This book is about best practices for meeting one of the most difficult challenges faced by executives, managers, and supervisors in every kind of organization: getting the absolute best performance from employees every day, week after week, month after month, and year after year. A corresponding and equally difficult challenge is ensuring that an organization's personnel continually improve their performance. Enhancing the performance of people at work has been the focus of my career for more than 35 years, a period during which I have worked simultaneously as a professor of business, corporate trainer, and business consultant.

In my role as a college professor, enhancing the performance of people at work has been my principle area of research and the subject of most of my books. As a corporate trainer it has been the main focus of my seminars and workshops. As a business consultant and management coach it has been the driver behind the bulk of my contracts. This book is the result of what I have learned over the past 35 years from research, investigation, experimentation, and actual practice concerning what works best for equipping, enabling, and empowering employees to achieve peak performance and continual improvement.

One of the most enduring lessons I have taken away from my many years of working as a college professor, corporate trainer, and business consultant is that you cannot have a high-performance organization without a high-performance workforce. Even in this age of high technology, the most important factor in an organizations performance is still the human factor. Stated simply, organizations that perform at peak levels are able to do so because their employees perform at peak levels. Of course, the performance of processes is also a critical factor, but it is determined in large measure by the performance of people. The performance of individual employees and work teams is still the key factor in determining how well the overall organization performs. Organizations in the private, public, and non-profit sectors are just like baseball, football, and basketball teams. It matters how well their players perform. Organizational excellence requires workforce excellence which, in turn, requires individual employees to consistently perform at peak levels and to improve continually. Ensuring that this happens is one of the most important responsibilities of executives, managers, and supervisors.

DEVELOPMENTAL LEADERSHIP AND PEAK PERFORMANCE

Organizations excel in a competitive environment by consistently providing superior value for their customers. Superior value is a combination of at least three key factors: superior quality, superior cost, and superior service. Achieving superiority in these critical areas requires that an organization have a peak-performing workforce. An organization cannot achieve a competitive edge in any of these key areas unless its employees consistently perform at peak levels and continually improve. Since this is the case, one might reasonably ask, "How does an organization turn its employees into peak performers who continually improve?" Answering this question is the purpose of this book. Although many factors go into creating and maintaining a peak-performing workforce, the one irreplaceable factor is what I call *developmental leadership*.

DEVELOPMENTAL LEADERSHIP DEFINED

Leaders are individuals who can inspire others to make a whole-hearted commitment to achieving an organization's mission and goals. Developmental leadership takes this concept to an even higher level. Like all good leaders, developmental leaders inspire people to make a total commitment to the mission, but they do not stop there. They take the next logical step: equipping, enabling, and empowering employees to carry out their commitment to the organization. It is one thing to make a commitment. It is quite another to be able to keep it. When a football game is tied at the end of the fourth quarter with just seconds remaining on the clock, the field goal kicker is probably the most committed individual in the stadium. Nobody wants to see the field goal score the winning points more than the placekicker. But it will require more than commitment to get the ball through the goal posts. It will require steady nerves, focused concentration, finely-honed talent, good coaching, and the help of teammates. In other words, the field goal kicker must be more than just committed. He must be equipped, enabled, and empowered to carry out his commitment.

The same rule of thumb applies to employees in an organization. In order to carry out their commitment to helping the organization accomplish its mission, employees must be willing and able to consistently perform at peak levels and to continually improve. The developmental aspect of leadership is about teaching, mentoring, coaching, counseling, and role modeling to equip, enable, and empower employees to perform at peak levels and to continually improve. Showing employees the vision and saying follow me are important aspects of leadership but they are not sufficient to produce peak performance and continual improvement. Organizational leaders—executives, managers, and supervisors—must take the next logical step and do what is necessary to equip, enable, and empower employees to help the organization accomplish its mission and goals. In other words, executives, managers, and supervisors must become developmental leaders. Helping you become a developmental leader is the purpose of this book.

DEVELOPING A PEAK-PERFORMING WORKFORCE

In studying and interacting with peak-performing organizations in the private, public, and non-profit sectors over more than three decades, I have concluded that they have several things in common. One of the most important of these is that executives, managers, and supervisors in these organizations tend to be developmental leaders. These developmental leaders are committed to being good teachers, mentors, coaches, counselors, and role models for their personnel. They understand that transforming employees into peak-performing producers is a developmental task. Executives, managers, and supervisors who want to be developmental leaders must learn to do certain things themselves and, in turn, help employees learn how to do these things as appropriate. Specifically, developmental leaders are executives, managers, and supervisors who have learned how to use the following best practices to equip, enable, and empower employees for peak performance and continual improvement:

- Provide consistent, effective, inspiring teaching, mentoring, coaching, counseling, and role modeling for employees.

- Establish a corporate culture that encourages, supports, and rewards peak performance and help employees accept, adopt, and internalize that culture.

- Understand the organization's big picture and help employees understand where they fit into it.

- Help employees become proficient at doing their part in executing strategic and operational plans.

- Exemplify a positive work ethic and help employees develop one.

- Become proficient at motivating employees and helping them become self-motivated.

- Maintain the highest standards of integrity and ethics and help employees emulate this example.

- Become proficient at communication and, in turn, help employees become effective communicators.

- Become an effective team builder/team leader and help employees become good team players.

- Become proficient at change management and help employees become positive change agents.

- Use the performance-appraisal process to actually improve performance.

- Become proficient at time management and help employees develop time-management skills.

- Become a customer-service champion and help employees develop good customer-service skills.

- Maintain a positive can-do attitude and help employees emulate this example.

- Become proficient at decision making, problem solving, and critical thinking and help employees develop skills in these critical areas.

- Become proficient in conflict management and help employees learn how to prevent and resolve conflict.

- Use employee complaints as opportunities for improvement and help employees learn how to solve their own problems.

- Mentor employees to continually improve their performance.

- Set an example of persevering in times of adversity and help employees learn to follow this example.

- Become proficient at working well in a diverse environment and help employees learn to do the same.

To transform employees into peak performers, executives, managers, and supervisors must become developmental leaders. You become a developmental leader by applying the 20 best practices listed above. This book was written to help executives, managers, and supervisors become developmental leaders capable of transforming employees into competitive assets by equipping, enabling, and empowering them to become peak-performing producers who improve continually.

NEW AND INNOVATIVE CONCEPTS INTRODUCED IN THIS BOOK

In addition to the concept of developmental leadership, this book introduces numerous concepts or new twists on old concepts that will help executives, managers, and supervisors become developmental leaders capable of transforming employees into peak-performing producers who continually improve. These concepts are:

- A ten-step model for transforming "entitled employees" into peak-performing producers.

- A five-step model for helping employees understand the organization's big picture as well as where they fit into it.

- A ten-step model for establishing a peak-performance corporate culture in any kind of organization.

- Tailored-Improvement Plans (TIPs) for individual employees that are used in conjunction with performance appraisals.

- Team charters.

- The "Eight Cs of Developmental Leadership."

- The concept of reluctant compliance from poorly led employees and how to overcome it.

- The "Personal Dream Sheet" as a motivational tool for employees.

- A five-step model for overcoming resistance to organizational change.

- The roadblock analysis for identifying factors that might inhibit the effective execution of a plan.

- Using assignment sheets in executing plans.

- Upward mentoring (employees helping supervisors improve their performance).

- Personal Motivation Plans (PMPs) for overcoming the one-size-fits-all syndrome when trying to motivate employees.

- The "Five-Minute Rule" to help executives, managers, and supervisors maintain an open-door policy without getting bogged down in employee complaints.

- Strategies for dealing responsibly with the extenuating circumstances that can cloud judgment when making ethical decisions.

- Using the development of a "Team Charter" as a teambuilding exercise.

- Strategies for eliminating unintentional bias in organizations.

- Seven-step model for tying organizational change to improved performance.

- Strategies for ensuring that performance appraisals actually improve performance.

- A new customer service philosophy that will have more credibility with employees than the old maxim, "The customer is always right," and will bring better results.

- A model for establishing a customer-service infrastructure for any kind of organization.

- Strategies for maintaining a positive attitude during times of adversity and for overcoming negative attitudes.

- Checklist for identifying root causes in problem solving.

- How to avoid applying $100 solutions to $10 problems.

- How to factor in ethics, morale, and public relations considerations when conducting a cost/benefit analysis as part of the problem-solving process.

- Six-step process for encouraging creativity in decision making.

- Strategies for becoming a critical thinker.

- A conflict resolution model that includes how to disagree without being disagreeable.

- Strategies for preventing workplace violence.

- Strategies for transitioning angry people from "anger mode" to "solution mode."

- Strategies for staying calm when dealing with angry people.

- Strategies for handling habitual complainers.

- Strategies for persevering during times of adversity.

- Strategies for overcoming "learned prejudice."

- Strategies for making diversity an asset in an organization.

Each of the 20 best practices listed earlier in this Introduction is the subject of one successive chapter in this book. Each chapter is based on a corporate training seminar I have presented many times over the years for private, public, and non-profit organizations. Over the years the material in each chapter has been refined, revised, updated, and improved on a continual basis as new information has become available through both research and practice. The material in all chapters has been field tested in hundreds of organizations and found to be effective. My hope is that it will help executives, managers, and supervisors become developmental leaders and, in turn, use developmental leadership to transform employees into peak-performing producers who improve continually.

A NOTE ON TERMINOLOGY

For convenience, the term "organizational leader" is used sometimes in this this book as a collective substitute for the terms "executive," "manager," and "supervisor." Whenever you read the term "organizational leader" or "organizational leaders" it is intended to encompass all three of these titles.

One

DEVELOPMENTAL LEADERSHIP

Best Practice Number 1: *Become a developmental leader who not only inspires employees to perform at peak levels and continually improve, but also equips, enables, and empowers them to do so.*

Whenever people come together to accomplish a specific mission and shared goals, leadership is needed. In any kind of organization—business, government, military, or non-profit—the difference between excellence and mediocrity is often determined by the quality of the leadership provided. Consequently, executives, managers, and supervisors should commit to becoming effective leaders. However, just becoming an effective leader is not enough for those who want to equip, enable, and empower employees for peak performance. Organizational leaders who want peak performance and continual improvement from employees must become *developmental leaders*.

DEVELOPMENTAL LEADERSHIP DEFINED

To understand the concept of developmental leadership, one must first understand leadership in general because developmental leadership is leadership taken to a higher level. Leadership in the workplace can be defined as follows:

> *Inspiring employees to perform at peak levels and continually improve.*

It is significant that the term *inspiring* is used here rather than *motivating*. While it is true that leaders must be good motivators, inspiring people is a higher level undertaking than motivating them. Human motivation is fleeting. Like the gasoline in the tank of a car, it burns up quickly and must be replenished constantly. Inspiration, on the other hand, can be permanent. People who can inspire employees to make a total commitment to peak performance are leaders, but they are not necessarily developmental leaders. To become a developmental leader, one must take the next step and equip, enable, and empower employees to fulfill the commitment they have made to peak performance and continual improvement. Employees making a commitment is one thing, but being able to fulfill the commitment is quite another. With this distinction stated, developmental leadership can be defined as follows:

> *Inspiring employees to perform at peak levels and continually improve, then equipping, enabling, and empowering them to do so.*

Being an effective leader is about consistently providing an inspiring example. Being a developmental leader is about consistently providing an inspiring example and then teaching, training, coaching, mentoring, and otherwise developing employees so that they are fully equipped, enabled, and empowered to follow that example.

THE EIGHT Cs OF DEVELOPMENTAL LEADERSHIP

Many people think that leadership is about image, dressing for success, and charisma. I can no longer count the number of times—but the number is high—that I have shared the podium at a professional conference with another speaker whose central theme was: *If you want to be a leader, you must look like one.* These image consultants typically focus on such topics as dressing for success, how to look taller, compensating for baldness, developing charisma, how to shake hands, and various other image enhancement strategies.

If you can believe image consultants, the contents of a book do not matter as long as the cover is attractive. It is certainly true that an attractive cover is more likely than an unattractive cover to convince someone to open a book, so I do not discount the importance of image. However, I believe the concept is over sold. After all, once a book is opened it must have substance. No amount of glitzy artwork on the cover will convince people to read a book that has no substance, is poorly written, or is just plain boring. It is the same with leadership. No matter how polished one's outer appearance is, the inner substance—or lack of it—will eventually show through.

In fact, when people are asked what characteristics they want to see in leaders, a much different picture emerges than the one painted by the prophets of charisma and glitz. I conducted such a survey as part of the research for my book *Effective Leadership* (Prentice Hall) and the results were revealing. They showed that people are more inclined to follow those who consistently exemplify several specific characteristics that I call the *Eight Cs of Developmental Leadership:*

- Caring

- Character

- Communication

- Clarity

- Commitment

- Courage

- Credibility

- Competence

Each of these characteristics is important to executives, managers and supervisors who are committed to becoming developmental leaders capable of equipping, enabling, and empowering employees for peak performance and continual improvement.

CARING AND DEVELOPMENTAL LEADERSHIP

There are executives, managers, and supervisors who care only about the work their teams are responsible for. They care nothing for the employees who do the work. Then there are those who care greatly for their employees but little about the work they are responsible for. In both cases, these organizational leaders have their priorities out of balance. To inspire employees to peak performance and continual improvement, leaders must care about them as well as the work to be done.

The importance of caring for the work as well as the employees who do it cannot be over emphasized. Employees will not wholeheartedly follow organizational leaders who do not care about them. Of course, executives, managers, and supervisors may be able to coerce employees into carrying out their demands, but coercion is not leadership. In fact, coercion is more likely to result in *reluctant compliance* than a commitment to peak performance and continual improvement. Reluctant compliance means doing just enough to get by but not enough to excel. It is the opposite of the wholehearted commitment organizational leaders need from employees if they hope to see them achieve peak performance and continual improvement.

The best leaders are those who can inspire employees to make a total and willing commitment to peak performance and continual improvement; to put their hearts and minds into doing the best job they can possibly do. This is important because well led employees who put their hearts and minds into their work will outperform those who just reluctantly comply out of fear of coercion. Because of this, executives, managers, and supervisors must show that they care about not just the work to be done, but the employees who do the work. If organizational leaders do not care about employees, why should employees care about them or the work they are responsible for doing.

Caring leaders exemplify several important traits that make employees more willing to follow them. These traits are: 1) honesty, 2) empathy, 3) sincere interest, 4) patience 5) a participatory approach to decision making, and 6) servanthood/stewardship. To become developmental leaders, executives, managers, and supervisors must recognize the importance of these traits, internalize them, and apply them consistently when interacting with employees.

Honesty and Caring

Leaders who care about their followers are honest with them. Whether the message they have to convey to followers is good news or bad, effective leaders care enough to tell the truth. When communicating with an honest leader, followers can take comfort in knowing that the message—whether good news or bad—is the truth. This is important because employees will not be inspired to perform at peak levels by someone they do not trust, and nothing dampens trust faster than lies, prevarication, and deceit. Employees who think they are being lied to or are having information withheld from them will not be inspired to perform at peak levels and continually improve.

Employees want organizational leaders to keep them informed. Further, they want to know that when they are informed they can trust the message. Whether the news is good or bad, employees want to know the truth. They want to be able to trust that what they are told is accurate, complete, and up to date—especially when it comes from those they look to as leaders. Employee expectations of organizational leaders are always higher than those applied to peers, and they should be.

Consequently, to become good leaders, executives must commit to being honest with employees at all times. Having made this point, a caveat is in order. Being honest—especially when the news to be conveyed is bad—does not mean being tactless. Leaders who care about their followers make a point of being tactful. Using tact means driving in the nail without breaking the board or making your point without making an enemy. It does not mean withholding information that might be unwelcome or hurtful. Rather, it means being empathetic while fully and honestly delivering an unwelcome or potentially hurtful message.

For example, leaders in the workplace are often called upon to give constructive criticism to employees as a necessary step in helping them improve. This is one of those situations in which driving in the nail without breaking the board is crucial. Assume that two supervisors need to give corrective feedback to two employees who have fallen into the habit of coming to work late. Supervisor A tells employee A, "When I told you that we start work at 8:00am, it wasn't a suggestion. If you can't manage to get to work on time, I will find someone who can." Supervisor B tells employee B, "John, you are doing a good job on the XYZ account. Your work so far has been exceptional. Now let's talk about how you can do equally well at getting to work on time."

Both supervisors made the point that that tardiness is unacceptable, but supervisor A did so in a tactless manner; a manner likely to break the board. Supervisor B, because he cares about the employee in question, was firm but tactful. Rather than just chastise the employee, he acknowledged something the employee was doing well before offering the constructive criticism about tardiness. Put yourself in the shoes of these two employees. Which approach—that of supervisor A or supervisor B—would you prefer?

Empathy and Caring

Empathy means identifying with and understanding another person's feelings, motives, and circumstances. Caring leaders are empathetic. They try to put themselves in the shoes of those they lead when making decisions that will affect them. Empathy is not sympathy or feeling sorry for someone. Rather, it is about putting yourself in the shoes of the other person and trying to see things from his or her point of view. The following story illustrates the concept of empathy as applied by a developmental leader.

John worked for a waste management company I will call ABC, Inc. He was the company's best and most popular driver. John was respected by his supervisor and liked by his fellow drivers for doing a good job himself, and for pitching in to help other drivers whenever the need arose. ABC's drivers dumped their loads in a landfill about ten miles outside of town. To encourage productivity, the company awarded an incentive bonus in each pay period to drivers who exceeded their dumping quota for that period.

John was a no-nonsense worker who hustled from the moment he clocked in until he clocked out. In addition, because he was so efficient at the collection and compacting aspects of the job and because he knew his routes so well, John earned the incentive bonus more often than any other driver. In fact, in recent months he had earned a bonus every payday; an unheard of accomplishment. One pay day, while congratulating John on receiving yet another cash bonus, his supervisor observed some discomfort in his star driver. As they talked, John squirmed uncomfortably in his chair and avoided making eye contact. After observing this reaction on several paydays, the supervisor began to sense that something was wrong.

When he looked into the situation, the supervisor learned that his intuition had been right. Something was wrong—very wrong. In order to surpass his dumping quota, John was skipping the compacting step on several loads every week. This was a serious procedural breech because it violated an important municipal statute. The city's landfill was fast reaching capacity, a fact that made the compacting step a critical part of the overall waste management process. The city council and John's company shared a common interest in putting off, as long as possible, the expensive development of a new land fill. Consequently, John and his fellow drivers were trained to compact their loads as tightly as possible before dumping them in the landfill.

The supervisor was disappointed in his star driver to say the least. However, he had also learned that there were mitigating circumstances that complicated what, on the surface, had looked like an open-and-shut case of cheating and greed. While investigating the situation, the supervisor had learned that John's motive for cheating on his quota was neither productivity nor greed; quite the contrary. John was ignoring standard operating procedures as a way to increase his income; there was no doubt about that fact. But his reason for doing so was need not greed. With a critically ill son in the hospital, John had taken to cheating on his dumping quota as a way to help pay the rapidly mounting medical bills that were accumulating. John's son was suffering from a serious and extended illness, and his treatment was so expensive that even with his health insurance, the bills were piling up faster than John could pay them. Clearly, John was acting not out of greed or self-gratification but fear and desperation. The mitigating circumstances of the situation created a heart-wrenching dilemma for the supervisor.

On one hand, he knew the procedural violations were serious and had to stop. In fact, he planned to put a stop to them right away. But he feared that this action alone would not be sufficient to satisfy higher management. In fact, once the violations became known, it was likely that John would lose his job. The supervisor, a developmental leader who cared about his employees, did not want this to happen. He saw John not as a bad person, but as a good person caught in a bad situation and making bad choices. Aware of how higher management was likely to react when informed, the supervisor thought hard about how to handle the situation. An idea finally emerged that he thought might allow him to turn a bad situation into something good. His first step was to develop a plan to preempt any hasty action from higher management. The supervisor proposed a plan to higher management in which he would do the following:

- Meet with John privately and put an immediate end to the procedural violations. Further, he would ask John to cooperate in determining how many times he had received an undeserved bonus and to agree to forgo that many future bonus payments as an alternative to paying back the unearned funds. If John agreed to this step in the plan, the supervisor would proceed to the next step.

- Convene a team meeting of all of ABC's drivers in which John would openly admit his violations and apologize.

- Require John to work weekends until the uncompacted material in the landfill had been fully retrieved and properly compacted.

- Personally organize a companywide fund raiser to help defray the costs of John's out-of-pocket medical expenses.

- Limit the punishment John received to a written reprimand placed in his personnel file.

Higher management accepted this plan, but made it clear to the supervisor that it better work. In other words, the supervisor was putting his credibility with higher management at risk on behalf of his wayward driver. When the supervisor confronted him that evening, John was contrite, embarrassed, and remorseful. He made a full confession, accepted responsibility, apologized, and even offered to resign. However, when the supervisor informed him of the proposal he had made to higher management, a vastly relieved John gladly accepted. He made a full admission without excuses to his fellow drivers, never once mentioning his son's illness or the resulting medical expenses. At the end of the meeting, John promised his fellow drivers and the supervisor that he would be at the landfill every Saturday morning at 7:00am until he had retrieved all of the improperly dumped materials and run them through the proper compacting process.

John was as good as his word. The following Saturday, he showed up at the landfill at 6:45am, but upon arriving found that his supervisor and several other drivers had been there since 6:00am and had already made a good start on the clean up. Further, the companywide fundraiser the supervisor organized really caught on and soon became a community-wide event. In just weeks, the company and community raised more than enough money to ensure that John would not have to worry about his son's medical care or the corresponding expenses.

This supervisor in this case showed empathetic leadership in a situation in which he had to put his credibility with higher management on the line. Because he cared enough to take an empathetic approach to solving a problem, everyone involved—John, his sick son, and the company— benefitted; a fact noticed by higher management. Less than a year later, a management position opened up and John's supervisor was promoted into it. By exemplifying the traits of caring and empathy, this supervisor turned a bad situation into something good.

Sincere Interest and Caring

Leaders who care about their followers take a sincere interest in them. Effective leaders take the time to ask people about their families, career aspirations, and well being. In short, they get to know employees well enough to understand what is important to them and how to help them achieve it. This is an important aspect of being a developmental leader because the better that executives, managers, and supervisors know their employees the better they will be at helping them match their personal goals with those of the organization. Further, by caring enough to get to know employees, leaders put themselves in better positions to equip, enable, and empower them for peak performance and continual improvement.

A leader I will call Wanda worked as an office manager who supervised a staff of eight insurance agents and an administrative assistant. Wanda's team was typically the most productive in the company. One of the hallmarks of Wanda's leadership style was showing a sincere interest in her team members. Wanda got to know her team members by consistently taking the time to talk with them. At the beginning of every day, she made a point of greeting her team members individually and asking how they were doing. Many people ask "How are you doing?" in a perfunctory way, but Wanda's team members soon learned that when she asked this simple question, she sincerely wanted to know. If a team member was having trouble, Wanda tried her best to help—even if that meant just listening.

One of Wanda's most effective ways of showing interest in her team members was what she called her "Personal Dream Sheet" or PDS. Once a year Wanda met with each of her team members to develop or update his or her personal dream sheet. The PDS is a single-page document that contains the employee's most important career goals and/or personal needs. Most of the entries for Wanda's employees were career oriented, but some were not. For example, one year Wanda's administrative assistant said that what she really needed for that year was a more flexible work schedule during baseball season so she could attend some of her son's after-school ball games. As a single mother, it was difficult for the administrative assistant to spend as much time with her son as she wanted. Consequently, the goal of having a flexible schedule during baseball season of his senior year in high school was important to her. It took some convincing on Wanda's part, but higher management eventually approved the flexible schedule she proposed for her administrative assistant.

Wanda made a point of doing everything within reason to help her team members realize their dreams. As a result, they were uncompromisingly loyal to her. They gave their best every day. In addition, they tried hard to improve continually. This combination of consistent peak performance and continual improvement on the part of her team members is what made Wanda's the highest performing team in the company.

Patience and Caring

People who care about others are patient with them. Patience is a willingness to tolerate human differences, frailties, quirks, opinions, and personality traits that differ from yours and to do so while maintaining a positive frame of mind. For many people, patience comes hard if at all. Patience can be a difficult state of mind to maintain. For example, do you ever honk your horn at a slow-to-react driver when the traffic light changes from red to green? Do you get fidgety when you have to stand in line? Do you become frustrated when you want something now but can't get it until later? All of these are signs of impatience.

Employees who are treated with patience are more likely to make a wholehearted commitment to peak performance and continual improvement. Patience is crucial to organizational leaders who want to help employees continually improve. Leaders who are impatient with employees are not likely to help them improve because employees who are treated this way will either resent it or become flustered and actually do worse.

Participatory Decision Making and Caring

Leaders who care about employees care about their opinions. In fact, there are few higher compliments than to sincerely ask for a person's opinion. Asking for an employee's opinion encourages him and gives hope. It shows that he matters. Every time organizational leaders make a decision, others have to help implement it. The employees who must implement decisions are known as stakeholders because their involvement gives them a stake in the decisions. Decision makers who care about stakeholders learn to take a participatory approach to decision making.

Participatory decision making is an approach in which the employees who are closer to the problem in question and who will have to implement the eventual decision are given a voice in the decision-making process. This does not mean that organizational leaders just take a vote or let the employees make the decision for them—far from it. Rather, it means that organizational leaders set the stage for making better decisions and for gaining buy-in from those who will carry out the decisions by involving them in the decision-making process.

People who are given a voice in making a decision—even if the decision is not the one they would have made themselves—are more likely to buy into the decision and commit to its implementation than those who are given no voice. This is an interesting aspect of participatory decision making; it shows stakeholders that organizational leaders care about their opinions while at the same time gaining their commitment to successfully implementing decisions. Another advantage of participatory decision making is that it benefits from the perspective of employees who are closer to the problem in question it than the decision maker. Organizational leaders are typically farther removed from the hands-on aspects of the problems they have to deal with than are frontline employees. Bringing employees who are closer to the problem in question into discussions of how to solve it can only strengthen the eventual decision.

My favorite example of participatory decision making occurred while I was serving in the United States Marine Corps. I had only a couple of months left in the service and was playing football at Camp Pendleton, California. Our coach was a crusty old gunnery sergeant who was the walking personification of the non-participatory decision maker. In fact, one of his favorite sayings was, "If I want you to have an opinion, I'll give you one." We were playing a Navy team and the score was tied six to six. Navy had scored two field goals. We had scored a touchdown, but missed the extra point. We were strong at most positions, but weak in the kicking game. In fact, to say that our kicking game was weak is a gross understatement. It was nonexistent. Our kicker had been injured early in the season and we had no backup at that position. There was nobody on our team who could kick a field goal or an extra point.

It was fourth down with just four seconds left in the game, the score was tied, and we had the ball on Navy's one yard line. Either we scored on the next play or the game would end in a tie and put an end to our ten game winning streak—an unacceptable result. As our quarterback glanced over at the sideline for guidance before calling the final and most crucial play of the game, our coach called a timeout and signaled the entire offensive team to join him on the sideline. That's when he did something we had never seen him do. Our coach, possibly the least participatory leader I had ever met, asked our opinions concerning what play he should call.

Our first reaction to the coach's request was dead silence. Not sure we were hearing clearly, nobody was bold enough to venture an opinion. Finally, when the strained silence became too much to endure, our right tackle took a tentative step forward and said: "Coach, their defensive tackle on my side is the best player on their team, but he is practically out on his feet. He has been going both ways for the whole game, and he is beat." As the team's tight end, I was in a position to verify what our right tackle said, and did so.

Then, based on our input, the coach called a play that had the right tackle and me double-team Navy's faltering defensive tackle while our fullback blasted through the hole we created and turned Navy's defensive end to the outside. Our halfback scampered quickly though the hole, head faked the Navy linebacker, and went into the end zone standing up. The clock ran out and we won the game by a touchdown. Later, in the locker room, our coach told the team that without our input he would have called a different play—a play that in retrospect probably would not have worked.

We did not call the play that won the game, our coach did. But he made a better call because before making his decision, he asked for the input of those of us who would have to implement it. As a result of being asked to participate, we put everything we had left into making the play succeed because it was not just the coach's call—it was ours too. This is the essence of participatory decision making. Because our coach cared enough to ask our opinion, we went the extra mile to successfully carry out his decision.

Servanthood/Stewardship and Caring

In today's fast-paced, pressure-packed workplace, those who lead best serve best and they are good stewards. Servant leaders put their employees, customers, and organization ahead of their personal needs and agendas. Leaders who are good stewards take care of the resources entrusted to them—human, physical, and financial. In fact, when leaders who are good stewards are promoted, resign, or retire, they pass on the resources entrusted to them in better condition than when they received them.

Nothing shows employees that a leader cares more than being a good servant and a good steward. I saw an excellent example of these concepts when I served in the Marine Corps. Our company had been commanded by an officer whose motto was "Rank has its privileges." He treated the enlisted Marines in our company like his personal serfs. In the field, while we ate cold C rations out of a can, he brought along a pack full of fresh vegetables and other delicacies that he required an enlisted Marine to carry for him. He also required an enlisted Marine to prepare and serve his meals. Whenever we had been on patrol long enough that our supplies were running low, this officer made sure that he ate before anyone else did so as to get the best of whatever was left.

Our loyalty to this officer was less than zero and our performance for him was mediocre at best. As a result, he was soon replaced by another officer; one who, as it turned out, had a servant's heart and was a good steward. By contrast, our new company commander made a point of pitching in and helping do the dirty work. If, while on forced marches, one of our men began to fall behind, our new company commander would lighten his burden by carrying his pack for him until he was sufficiently rested to carry it himself. Whenever we took a break to eat, he made sure that everyone else had plenty of food before he would take even a bite for himself. If he had goodies from home—what we called pogey bait—he distributed it among the men rather than eating it himself.

Our new company commander was the kind of officer more commonly found in the Marine Corps; one who would carry your pack and cover your back. His servant's heart and stewardship quickly turned things around in our company. Morale and performance quickly improved. He took care of us so we made a point of taking care of him. The same thing will happen in the workplace for organizational leaders who are good servants and good stewards.

CHARACTER AND DEVELOPMENTAL LEADERSHIP

One of the most fundamental aspects of effective leadership is trust. Employees will not follow organizational leaders they do not trust. Employees trust organizational leaders who consistently demonstrate that they have a trustworthy character. Character is the sum of an individual's moral and ethical composition. Character is what allows leaders to recognize the right thing to do in a given situation and what gives them the courage to actually do it regardless of pressure or temptation to do otherwise. Character traits that are important for organizational leaders include honesty, integrity, dependability, trustworthiness, compassion, courage, diligence, respectfulness, fairness, optimism, persistence, selflessness, tact, and tolerance.

COMMUNICATION AND DEVELOPMENTAL LEADERSHIP

To be developmental leaders, executives, managers, and supervisors must be good communicators. Communication is one of the most important leadership skills. In fact, it is an essential skill for those who want to equip, enable, and empower employees for peak performance and continual improvement. Communication is so fundamental a leadership skill that it has an entire chapter devoted to later in this book (Chapter 8).

CLARITY AND DEVELOPMENTAL LEADERSHIP

Employees are just like people who are going on a long trip—they want to know where they are going. Imagine calling several of your best friends and saying, "Let's take a vacation. We can leave tomorrow morning." The first thing your friends will ask is, "Where are we going?" Employees are the same. They want to know where organizational leaders are trying to take them. Only when they know where they are supposed to be going can employees get a sense of whether they are making progress, and people like to know if they are making progress. Consequently, executives, managers, and supervisors who want to be developmental leaders must have a sense of purpose and be clear about what that purpose is. In other words, they must have clarity.

Employees need to feel that their work has meaning. They need to know that their work is important and why it is important. In short, they need to know that their work matters because if it does not, they will begin to wonder if they matter. Organizational leaders who develop a sense of purpose about their work and can convey that purpose to employees are going to have loyal followers because people are more inclined to follow leaders who have a clear sense of purpose. The effect a sense of purpose can have on people was illustrated for me in an informative way when I was studying for my first Masters degree.

I was taking a course on leadership from a professor whose teaching methods were unorthodox to say the least, but effective none the less. It was a night class. At the beginning of each class meeting we discussed what we had learned from the previous week's assignment. Then we were given our assignment for the current week. Our assignments all had to do with some aspect of leadership. On the evening in question, our assignments had to do with the need for leaders to have a sense of purpose.

My assignment was as follows: Go to the regional airport in our town and sit in the waiting area near the boarding gates. This was in the early 1970s when security at airports was nonexistent by today's standards. I was to wait until a flight was either cancelled or delayed at which point I was to stride to the head of the line of disgruntled passengers and announce, "I know where a flight leaves for this same destination in 10 minutes." Then, without another word, I was to walk confidently away from the boarding gate and see what would happen. What happened is that more than half of the passengers holding tickets on the now cancelled flight quickly picked up their belongings and fell in line right behind me. I understood immediately the point my professor was making: look like you know where you are going—have a clear sense of purpose—and people will follow you. They did.

In fact, they followed me right out the front door of the airport before beginning to sense that they had been duped. The professor had given me excellent instructions on how to carry out the experiment, but no instructions concerning what to do if it worked. From the angry comments I heard, it was clear that letting the duped passengers in on the details of my assignment would be a bad idea. In fact, discretion being the better part of valor, I decided to solve my problem in the simplest and most practical way possible. I ran. My every step was accompanied by a chorus of insults, but I had completed the assignment and learned the intended lesson. If you want people to follow you, have a clear sense of purpose. Be clear concerning what you are trying to accomplish.

COMMITMENT AND DEVELOPMENTAL LEADERSHIP

Commitment is an essential aspect of developmental leadership. Effective leaders must be committed to doing what is necessary to equip, enable, and empower employees for peak performance and continual improvement. Commitment means more than just trying hard. It means that within the boundaries prescribed by ethics and the law leaders will do everything possible to get the job done.

There is a joke about commitment that has circulated over the years in leadership circles that makes the point about the difference between just being involved and being committed. It goes like this. With a breakfast of eggs and bacon, the chicken is involved but the pig is committed. This joke makes the important point that commitment is more than just getting involved. Commitment implies a willingness to sacrifice, if necessary, to get the job done. This is an important distinction to grasp because mediocrity results more often from a lack of commitment than a lack of talent.

When organizational leaders commit to peak performance and continual improvement, there will be sacrifices. You might have to sacrifice time you would rather spend doing something else or resources you would rather use for another project. Organizational leaders who are not willing to sacrifice will be ineffective at equipping, enabling, and empowering employees for peak performance.

People who refuse to commit because they think it will require too much of them are common in organizations. Uncommitted people like to sit back and let others do the heavy lifting associated with leading for peak performance and continual improvement. Not only will such people be ineffective as organizational leaders, they are wrong about their assumptions concerning commitment. When you commit to something, there is a sense in which everything actually gets easier not harder. For example, committed leaders have no problem making decisions. In fact, decisions practically make themselves. This is because their commitment eliminates uncertainty and narrows the range of choices. If you are committed to peak performance and continual improvement, you will know exactly what must be done in most cases. There will be no stress producing ambiguity to deal with when making decisions.

For example, assume that you have decided to go on a healthy diet and exercise program to lose 30 pounds. If you commit to this program, you no longer have to decide whether you are going to eat "just one little donut" or cheat on your exercise program. These decisions have already been made for you by your commitment. In both cases, the appropriate decision is to simply say "no" and do what you know is right. If you are not willing to say no, you have not yet made a commitment. Commitment applies in the same way in the workplace and it has the same salutary effect. Once you commit to a course of action or to accomplishing a goal, you will know exactly what to do when decisions must be made.

COURAGE AND DEVELOPMENTAL LEADERSHIP

Courage is a fundamental aspect of developmental leadership. This is because to do the right thing in a given situation, executives, managers, and supervisors must sometimes swim against the current of organizational orthodoxy. If organizational leaders are going to remain faithful to their principles, they must have the courage to stand up for their beliefs even in the face of adversity. Courage is not a lack of fear. Rather, it is a willingness to do what is right in spite of fear.

To illustrate the concept of courage as it applies to developmental leaders, I often use the example of an individual whose courage in the face of life-or-death adversity personifies the concept. This distinguished leader is a small-town attorney and retired Air Force officer who also served in the United States Marine Corps during World War II. On the outside, he looks like any other American of his generation. But it is on the inside—that place deep in our character where courage resides—that my friend Colonel Bud Day, is different. His is an example of courage and commitment that should inspire all executives, managers, and supervisors who seek to be developmental leaders.

Colonel George "Bud" Day: Courage Personified

Colonel George "Bud" Day is an Air Force Pilot who was a prisoner of war for almost five years during the Vietnam conflict. He was awarded the Medal of Honor for his courageous action in the face of incredible adversity. In 1967, Day was a Major in charge of a squadron of F-100 jets nicknamed the "Misty Squadron." Day and his pilots served as airborne FACs or forward air controllers who flew missions over Communist territory in North Vietnam spotting targets for American bombers.

On one of these missions, Day's jet was hit by ground fire from the enemy, knocking out its hydraulic system and sending it into a steep dive. Day had just enough time to bail out before the jet crashed into the jungles of North Vietnam. However, in the process of ejecting, Day was thrown against the fuselage, breaking his arm, fracturing his knee, and raising a golf ball-sized lump that completely closed one of his eyes. His parachute opened in time, but it brought him down into the waiting arms of the enemy. Upon landing, Day twisted his knee adding yet another painful injury.

Fully aware of his injuries, the enemy guerillas forced Day to hobble for miles through the jungle to their camp. Upon arrival, they immediately began to interrogate him. When Day refused to cooperate, they tortured him. Their methods were brutal and included hanging Day in an excruciatingly painful position and beating him. When this failed to break the courageously stubborn pilot, the enemy soldiers staged a mock execution that, as far as Day knew, was going to be the real thing. They forced him into a kneeling position and placed a pistol against his head. Day heard the sickening click as the pistol was cocked.

Certain he was about to die, Day thought one last time of his wife, Doris, and then said a prayer while awaiting his fate. Just before pulling the trigger, the interrogator turned the pistol away just enough to ensure that the round to would miss Day's head by only a fraction of an inch. It did, but the guns' explosive report damaged Day's ear drum. It took the stunned pilot a moment to realize he was still alive.

Despite this cruel hoax, his painful injuries, and the brutal torture, Day persevered in resisting. He steadfastly refused to give in to his captors. The torture continued for several days until it appeared the beaten and bloodied pilot could not possibly live, much less escape. One night the guards failed to watch their battered prisoner as closely as they should have, and he slipped quietly into the jungle and escaped. It was hours before his captors realized that their prisoner was gone. In the meantime, Day used these hours to put as much distance as possible between himself and his captors.

When Day thought he had gained a sufficient head start on his captors, he began to sleep in jungle thickets during the daylight hours and travel mostly at night. After a couple of days on the run, the battered pilot was sleeping in a jungle thicket trying to preserve his failing strength when he was startled awake by an ear-splitting explosion. An American bomb or missile—no doubt intended for his pursuers—had exploded nearby driving hot shards of burning shrapnel deep into his leg.

Day's growing inventory of injuries and wounds now included a broken arm, twisted knee, swollen eye, lacerations from the shrapnel, and contusions from the beatings. To complicate matters, in the harsh jungle environment his wounds were rapidly becoming infected. In spite of his mounting injuries, Day continued to slowly and painfully hobble in a southerly direction. His goal was to reach friendly territory in South Vietnam and rejoin his squadron. But his festering wounds, fetid jungle environment, and a lack of food and water began to take their toll.

After at least ten days—Day lost count—with with little food or water, the pilot was suffering from dehydration, starvation, and a host of festering wounds. In spite of this, he persevered. With every ounce of strength he could muster, Day continued his trek south toward freedom. Then, one day he heard the sound of helicopters. Knowing they had to be American, Day made his way as fast as he could manage toward the noise, a noise that meant freedom. Unfortunately, in what had to be a heart-wrenching scene, unaware of his presence, the helicopter took off without Day.

On the good side though, Day realized he had made it to the river separating North and South Viet Nam. On the other side of the river, freedom and access to the world's best medical care awaited him. All that stood in his way now was a river, or at least that is what Day thought at the time. Unfortunately, a closer look proved otherwise. As he strained to see beyond the river, Day found that the jungle along the river's edge was crawling with Viet Cong guerillas. So close, yet so far. Day was now only a few miles from freedom, but those last miles would turn out to be the most difficult of them all.

With all the patience and stealth he could muster, Day crawled down to the river's edge and slipped quietly into the river. Taking advantage of a log floating by, Day used the log as cover to float undetected down the river. When he had gone far enough that he could no longer see enemy guerillas, Day crawled ashore on what he thought of as the freedom side of the river—exhausted but full of hope. With new found strength, he quickly began making his way south to freedom.

He never made it. As Day hobbled toward freedom, hope growing with every step, he stumbled right into a Viet Cong ambush. Shots were fired, and Day was hit in the leg and the hand by rounds from an AK-47 rifle. After persevering in evading the enemy for two weeks while enduring dehydration, starvation, and a host of debilitating wounds, Day was recaptured within sight of freedom. The ordeal of escape and evasion were over, but the ordeal of his life had just begun.

Day was returned to the same camp from which he had escaped two weeks earlier. But this time his captors had a better idea of the type of person they were dealing with. Rather than waste time trying to torture him into submission, his captors tossed him unceremoniously into the back of a Russian-made truck and shipped him off to the infamous *Hanoi Hilton;* the prisoner of war camp in the capital of North Viet Nam. It would be years before Day would once again breathe the fresh air of freedom.

When Day arrived at the Hanoi Hilton, he was suffering from malnutrition, dehydration, infected wounds, exhaustion, and loss of blood. In response to physical trauma he had endured, Day's hands were curled tightly into claws that he could not open. When he was carelessly tossed onto the hard, damp concrete floor of his jail cell, Day could neither feed nor dress himself. Thus began a period of systematic torture, privation, and cruelty that would last for five years; a period in which Day's character, courage, and commitment would be tested in ways most people cannot even imagine.

Having thrown Day into a cell, his captors simply left him—thinking they were leaving him to die. But once again they had underestimated the courage, perseverance, and commitment of this American patriot. With the help of his cell mates, Day was eventually able to regain the use of his hands sufficiently to dress and feed himself. In addition, over time his broken bones and wounds began to heal, although not properly. As a result Day would suffer lifelong pain, a never- ending reminder of the harsh treatment of his captors.

As one of the senior officers in his cell block, Day knew it was his responsibility to set an example of resistance for the other prisoners of war (POWs). Day vowed that he would never give in to his communist captors and never quit on his men or his country. He would do whatever was necessary to maintain his honor as an Air Force officer and his dignity as a human being. Day would pay a heavy price for his courageous commitment, but he stuck steadfastly to his vow even in a nightmarish situation that only got worse over time.

Day's determination to persevere extended beyond just his personal resistance. He also worked hard to help his fellow POWs maintain their honor and dignity while resisting their brutal captors. To give them hope in the midst of what seemed to be a never-ending ordeal, Day and a few other officers began conducting religious services, an act strictly forbidden by their communist captors. One day in the middle of a service, Day and his fellow prisoners were interrupted by North Vietnamese guards who burst into their cell with rifles loaded and ready to fire.

The prisoners froze where they stood. Nobody moved. The air was charged with anticipation and dread. The slightest misstep could spark a slaughter. This was the moment of truth. Day knew the guards would have no qualms about shooting American POWs, but he also knew that leadership demanded a strong stand at this critical point in their captivity. Consequently, moving slowly and deliberately Day stood up, faced the guards who were now pointing there rifles at him, and began singing America's national anthem. Moved by Day's courageous act, the other prisoners soon joined in and made it a chorus. At first the communist guards were so taken aback by this courageous act of leadership that they did not know how to react. But their confusion lasted only seconds. After all, they always had their favorite back up plan. Grasping Day and another officer, they led them out of the cell toward the torture chamber.

Day and his fellow POWs were finally released from captivity on March 14, 1973, thereby ending a five-year ordeal that few people could endure without breaking. But through it all, Day courageously persevered. He never gave up and never gave in. As a result, on

March 6, 1976, Day was awarded America's highest award for valor in combat—the Medal of Honor.

Executives, managers, and supervisors trying to become developmental leaders will face situations requiring courage. Standing up for what is right can be hard, and there is often a price to pay. You might suffer the rejection of peers, pressure from superiors, and even threats to your career. When this happens, think about Colonel Bud Day and the courage he showed throughout his ordeal. If he could endure the torture, privation, and cruelty of being a POW at the hands of his brutal captors, you can endure the challenges of being a developmental leader.

CREDIBILITY AND LEADERSHIP

Credibility is what leaders have when employees believe in them and when they are seen by employees as people who are worthy of confidence. Organizational leaders who care about employees, have exemplary character, communicate effectively, have clarity of purpose, are committed to the mission, and display quiet courage will earn credibility in the eyes of employees. In other words, organizational leaders earn and maintain credibility by exemplifying the other seven Cs of developmental leadership explained in this chapter.

COMPETENCE AND DEVELOPMENTAL LEADERSHIP

The final "C" of the Eight Cs of developmental leadership, is competence. Executives, managers, and supervisors who want to be developmental leaders must get good at what they do. They must strive to be the best in the organization at their particular jobs. If you are an engineer, strive to be the best engineer in the company. If you are in sales, strive to be the company's leading sales representative. Regardless of career field, do what is necessary to be competent.

It is always easier to lead others who look up to you as a recognized expert in your field. For example, a batting coach who was an outstanding hitter when he played baseball will find it easier to earn the credibility of the players he instructs. His competence will help him win the respect of his players. This same principle applies to executives, managers, and supervisors who want to be developmental leaders. In addition to learning the skills of developmental leadership, it is important to continually improve your career-specific skills.

GROUP ACTIVITY

Have you ever worked with someone higher than you in an organization who exhibited any or all of the Eight Cs of Developmental Leadership? If so, describe this individual and explain how it was to work with him or her. Have you ever worked with an individual higher in the organization who exhibited none of the Eight Cs of Developmental Leadership? If so, describe this individual and how it was to work with him or her.

Two

CORPORATE CULTURE

***Best Practice Number 2:** Establish a corporate culture that encourages, supports, and rewards peak performance and continual improvement.*

A quiet but persistent barrier to peak performance and continual improvement is often an organization's corporate culture. In order to consistently perform at peak levels, employees must work in an environment that encourages, supports, and rewards excellence. Executives, managers, and supervisors who are not attentive to the issue of corporate culture are not likely to develop peak-performing employees. Often a necessary first step in transforming employees is to transform the corporate culture. This chapter provides the guidance necessary to establish and maintain a culture of excellence that equips, enables, and empowers employees for peak performance and continual improvement.

CORPORATE CULTURE DEFINED

Every organization has a corporate culture—planned or unplanned. An organization's culture is the everyday manifestation of its corporate values and traditions. An organization's corporate culture determines how its personnel: 1) interact with each other; 2) do their work; 3) treat customers, suppliers, and the community at large; 4) solve-problems; 5) react to change; and 6) respond to adversity. What follows are characteristics of organizations with the kind of corporate culture that encourages peak performance and continual improvement.

- Behavior, decisions, and actions of personnel at all levels match the organization's slogans and stated corporate values.

- Performance expectations are clearly communicated and employees are equipped, enabled, and empowered to meet expectations.

- Executives, managers, and supervisors are committed to peak performance and continual improvement. Further, they create a work environment that makes these things possible.

- Executives, managers, and supervisors provide sufficient resources to employees when and where they are needed to support peak performance and continual improvement.

- Education and training are provided to ensure that employees have the knowledge, skills, and attitudes needed to perform at peak levels and improve continually.

- Rewards and recognition are based on performance and the improvement of performance.

ESTABLISHING AND MAINTAINING A CULTURE OF EXCELLENCE

Organizational excellence is a cultural concept. It can be achieved only in organizations that establish and maintain a corporate culture that expects, encourages, supports, and rewards excellence. Winning teams have winning cultures. It is the same with organizations. What follows is a ten-step model organizational leaders can use to establish and maintain a culture of excellence—a culture in which peak performance and continual improvement are the norm. For the sake of systematic presentation, the steps are presented separately. However, in reality some of the steps overlap and can be carried out simultaneously.

Expect Excellence

People typically want to live up to expectations. In any situation, knowing what is expected of them is one of the first things people typically want to know. Consequently, organizational leaders should make a point of letting employees know what is expected of them. Before employees can live up to expectations they have to know: 1) what the expectations are, and 2) that the expectations are worthy of their effort. Consequently, organizational leaders should make sure that all employees understand the organization's corporate culture and its corresponding expectations and that the expectations are worthy of an employee's commitment.   Cultural expectations should be established by the organization's executives and communicated constantly by all organizational leaders.   What follows is a list of expectations one would expect to be emphasized in organizations that are committed to excellence:

- Consistent peak performance

- Continual improvement

- Positive attitudes

- Teamwork

- Perseverance in the face of adversity

- Honesty and integrity

- Dependability

- Cooperativeness

- Initiative

- Resourcefulness

- Punctuality

- Effective communication

- Positive change agency

- Effective conflict management

- Critical thinking

- Self-motivation

This is not an exhaustive list. But it is a list of the types of cultural expectations found in organizations that equip, enable, and empower their employees for peak performance and continual improvement. The actual list for any given organization might differ from this one. Executives in an organization are responsible for developing their own list of cultural expectations. However, before their list is finalized, it should be circulated among organizational leaders at all levels including managers and supervisors. Once feedback has been collected from all of these sources, the list can be finalized for use in completing the next step.

Develop a Corporate Culture Statement for the Organization

All organizations have a corporate culture, whether planned or unplanned. Organizations that fail to pro-actively and purposefully establish their own corporate culture will have one established for them by default. When this culture-by-default phenomenon is allowed to occur, the culture that results is not likely to be one that encourages peak performance and continual improvement. This is why organizational leaders must take the initiative in establishing a peak-performance corporate culture. An important step in establishing a corporate culture is describing it. This can be done be transforming the organization's list of cultural expectations from the previous step into a written corporate culture statement.

Such a statement describes the corporate culture and explains its basic tenets. What follows is an example of a corporate-culture statement:

> *ABC, Inc.'s corporate culture determines how our personnel interact; do their work; treat customers, suppliers, vendors, and the community at large; solve problems; react to change; and respond to adversity. It is the sum of our company's written and unwritten expectations and traditions. ABC, Inc. is committed to maintaining a corporate culture that encourages, supports, and facilitates peak performance and continual improvement. The leadership team at ABC, Inc. believes that organizational excellence, peak performance, and continual improvement are essential to achieving world-class quality and global competitiveness. To this end, the following factors are the building blocks of our company's corporate culture: consistent peak performance from all personnel at all levels, continual improvement of performance, positive attitudes at all times, effective communication, teamwork,*

perseverance in the face of adversity, honesty and integrity, dependability, cooperativeness, initiative, resourcefulness, and punctuality.

This corporate culture statement is brief but comprehensive. It uses language that is simple and easy to understand to establish the company's expectations of all personnel. These expectations, in turn, establish a firm foundation for pursuing organizational excellence, peak performance, and continual improvement.

Communicate the Cultural Expectations

Once the corporate cultural statement has been finalized it must be communicated to employees. It is not sufficient to simply hand employees the statement, although doing so should certainly be part of the communication process. Do not stop with just the statement though. Human communication is an imperfect process. Some people are better listeners than others. Some are better readers. Most need the information they receive to come in a variety of formats. To accurately and clearly communicate cultural expectations to employees, organizational leaders should use a variety of methods such as the following:

- Put the specific cultural expectations from the corporate culture statement in employee job descriptions.

- Distribute the corporate culture statement during unit-level orientations and discuss the expectations contained in it openly and at length with employees.

- Include criteria in performance-appraisal forms that match cultural expectations.

- Role model the cultural expectations.

- Monitor employee behavior on a daily basis to ensure that it matches cultural expectations, and act immediately when it does not.

- Display the organization's corporate culture statement conspicuously throughout the organization's facility.

- Use unit, team, and departmental meetings for discussions that help employees understand how culture expectations translate into behavior and actions on a daily basis.

Make Cultural Expectations Part of the Orientation Process

The organization's cultural expectations should be conveyed in both the new-employee orientation provided by human resources personnel and during unit-level orientations provided by departmental managers, supervisors, and team leaders. An effective approach is for employees to receive a copy of the corporate culture statement during their in-processing orientation and to hear a big-picture explanation of it from human resources personnel. Then the statement should be explained again in more specific terms during unit-level orientations. At the unit level there should be plenty of give and take, questions, discussion, and even illustrative examples.

Organizational leaders must understand that it is important to place the desired corporate culture in front of new personnel before some salty, disgruntled employee pulls them aside and explains "how things are really done." Even in the best organizations, there will always be a few employees who want to undermine management by expressing perspectives that run counter to the desired corporate culture. An effective way to head this off is to deal with it during orientation sessions. Make sure that new employees get the correct view of the desired corporate culture before malcontented employees have a chance to give their perspectives.

Role Model what is expected of Employees

Organizational leaders must be consistent role models of what they expect of employees. In fact, they must be the personification of these expectations. Telling employees to "Do as I say, not as I do" will encourage neither peak performance nor continual improvement. Employees are more likely to follow the examples of leaders than their words. In order for words to have the desired effect, they must be reinforced by a corresponding example. When words are not backed up by actions, their credibility is called into question and the perception of employees will be that organizational leaders are not serious about cultural expectations. If this perspective persists, employees will ask themselves the obvious question: "If organizational leaders are not serious about the cultural expectations, why should we be?"

Mentor Employees on the Basis of Cultural Expectations

As soon as new employees have been assigned to their unit and have completed their unit level orientation, they should be assigned a mentor. This individual should be someone who exemplifies the corporate culture and can help new employees in the following ways: 1) teach and role model the corporate culture, 2) build character, 3) develop job-related skills, 4) demonstrate how to get things done in the organization, 5) demonstrate how to interact with team members, supervisors, managers, executives, customers, and suppliers, and) 6) demonstrate how to behave in unfamiliar settings. The best mentors are those who are willing and able to do the following things for new employees:

- Communicate openly, frankly, tactfully, and frequently

- Serve as a sounding board while listening patiently and attentively

- Provide recognition, encouragement, and support

- Provide a steady flow of accurate up-to-date information about progress, performance, issues, problems, and options

- Consistently role model the organization's cultural expectations

- Help set goals and realistic timetables for achieving them

- Help develop effective strategies for meeting the goals

- Make introductions to useful contacts

- Demonstrate how to deal with problems, face adversity, and conduct oneself in ways that are consistent with the organization's corporate culture

Train Employees on the Basis of Cultural Expectations

Many organizations provide employee training of various types, but few think of cultural expectations when selecting training topics. This is a mistake. Organizational leaders should never assume that employees automatically understand what cultural expectations mean in practical, everyday terms. Why are such things as peak performance, continual improvement, teamwork, positive attitude, perseverance, honesty, integrity, dependability, cooperativeness, initiative, resourcefulness, and punctuality important? What do these things look like when put into practice on a daily basis? How does an employee develop these characteristics? All of these are questions that can be answered by providing employee training that focuses on cultural expectations.

A training program that focuses exclusively on cultural expectations is an effective way to help new employees adopt and internalize the organization's corporate culture. The case study approach is an especially effective way to teach cultural expectations. With this approach, the trainer collects cases that demonstrate the value of various cultural expectations (e.g. teamwork, integrity, dependability, cooperativeness, initiative, punctuality, etc.). Trainers may find applicable cases in their professional literature and/or use actual cases of their own. An effective approach is to mix in some cases that demonstrate what happens in an organization when cultural expectations are not met.

Participants are put into small groups and each group selects a recorder and a reporter. The recorder's job is to summarize the findings and recommendations of the group. The reporter's job is to speak on behalf of the group in explaining its findings to the larger group. Each group receives a copy of the case in question and reads it. The cases should be brief and to the point. The facilitator/trainer asks each group to discuss specific questions and come to agreement within groups concerning their answers. Each group's reporter explains how his or her group answered the questions. Then the facilitator leads the large group in a discussion of the answers provided by the small groups.

For example, assume that what follows is a case selected for use by the trainer: *John is just not dependable. Sometimes he arrives at work on time and sometimes he doesn't. Sometimes he gets his work done on time and sometimes he doesn't. Sometimes the quality of his work is good and sometimes it is unacceptable. You just never know which John is going to show up for work on a given day.* The trainer might ask such questions as:

- Would you want to work with a person like John?

- How might John's up-and-down behavior affect the performance of his team?

- If John does not change, will he ever achieve peak performance?

- What effect could less than peak performance from John's team have on the organization's ability to compete?

- What might happen if John's organization is not able to compete in the marketplace?

With just this one brief case and several carefully scripted questions, the trainer would be able to lead participants through a discussion of dependability and its affect on both performance and employee job security. The same methodology will work well for illustrating the importance of all cultural expectations.

Monitor Employee Performance and Behavior

Developmental leaders know that daily monitoring of the performance, behavior, and actions of all employees is important, but it is especially important with new employees. This is because new employees are still learning how to put cultural expectations into action. It is important to ensure that they learn the right things and to do things the right way. Human behavior can become habitual. If people learn to do something the wrong way and are not corrected, the wrong way can become the habitual way. Habitual behavior is difficult and sometimes impossible to change.

When monitoring employee performance, behavior, and actions developmental leaders never ignore the unacceptable. To do so is to give the unacceptable de facto approval. Once cultural expectations have been communicated to employees, developmental leaders monitor constantly for compliance. In addition, they act immediately to correct performance, behavior, or actions that do not live up to cultural expectations. Monitoring of employee performance, behavior, and actions never ends, but it must be more frequent with new employees who are still learning to comply with cultural expectations.

Reward Behavior that Exemplifies the Cultural Expectations

Developmental leaders know that when dealing with people, it is wise to reward the types of performance, behavior, and actions that are desired. People respond well to rewards (positive reinforcement). The previous strategy emphasized the importance of monitoring constantly and acting immediately to correct unacceptable behavior. This strategy is the other side of that coin—rewarding exemplary behavior. With people you generally get more of what you reward.

Rewards can be formal or informal. Formal rewards include recognition awards, performance bonuses, pay increases, promotions, and other tangible things. Informal rewards can be as simple as a "well-done" or a pat on the back delivered in a public setting. The key to making rewards result in more of the exemplary behavior is to tie them to the cultural expectations. With formal rewards, this means making sure that living up to cultural expectations is an important criterion when making decisions about recognition awards, performance bonuses, pay increases, and promotions. With informal rewards, it means saying more than just "well done" or giving an individual a public pat on the back. It means stating specifically what the employee did to deserve the public recognition.

For example, a supervisor might make the following comment to an employee who has displayed consistent integrity: "Jane, I appreciate the way you are always honest with me. When I ask you a question, I always get an honest answer. If you are wrong, you always admit it without beating around the bush or trying to cover up. Your integrity is an asset to me and the organization." The same leader might make the following comment to an employee who exemplifies dependability: "John, I gave you the XYZ project because I knew I could count on you to get it done right and on time. Knowing I can depend on you is very helpful to me." In both of these cases, the leader gave an employee an informal reward—public recognition—and tied it to a specific cultural expectation. This is the approach that will result in more exemplary behavior from the employee in question. Further, by making the recognition public the leader shows others what they need to do to be recognized.

Evaluate Employee Performance, Behavior, and Actions

Organizational leaders perform a type of evaluation every time they monitor the performance and behavior of employees. Observation is a type of informal evaluation. However, the strategy explained in this section is about conducting formal evaluations or, as they are more commonly known, performance appraisals. The key to using periodic performance appraisals to help employees internalize the organization's corporate culture is to have specific criteria in the appraisal form for all cultural expectations. This may sound like it should go without saying, but a surprisingly common situation is for organizations to expect one thing of employees and evaluate another. This happens when there is a mismatch between what is expected of employees and the criteria included in the performance-appraisal form.

A performance-appraisal that does not include criteria covering what the organization expects of employees will not encourage peak performance or continual improvement. Employees are just like college students—they want to know what is on the test. The human tendency is to put more effort into doing well on the criteria that performance will be measured against. Consequently, if organizations want employees to be punctual, dependable, honest, cooperative, positive, steadfast, or resourceful for example, there must be criteria in the appraisal form for evaluating these characteristics. All cultural expectations should be covered in some way during the performance-appraisal process.

Develop Tailored Improvement Plans for Individual Employees

To make the performance appraisal a more effective tool for facilitating peak performance and continual improvement, organizational leaders can add one more step to the appraisal process. Typically the process concludes when the employee signs the appraisal form acknowledging that he or she has reviewed it. The form is then placed in the employee's file and the process is considered over until the same time next year.

This traditional approach is not sufficient in organizations striving for peak performance and continual improvement.

Organizational leaders can improve the performance-appraisal process by adding an additional step to enhance its value. This additional step involves writing Tailored Improvement Plans or TIPs. A TIP is a brief plan for improvement in areas where the performance appraisal indicates there is a need. The idea is for the executive, manager, or supervisor who conducted the performance appraisal and the employee in question to agree on specific areas in need of improvement and specific steps that will be taken to make the improvements. A TIP is developed as follows:

- All appraisal criteria that receive a rating below a specific level are noted and written down. It is up to the person who does the performance appraisal to establish the level of rating that is acceptable (unless the organization adopts a standard for making this determination). Deciding what level of performance is acceptable requires the application of common sense. It should be rare for an employee to receive the highest possible ratings on appraisal criteria since there is always room for improvement. Since this is the case, there has to be a cut-off score established or every performance criterion will end up in the TIP. Another issue is that in order to promote continual improvement, it may be necessary to use a different cut-off score with different employees. This is one of the reasons the concept is called a "Tailored" Improvement Plan. With new employees, the goal might be to get all of their ratings to an acceptable level during the next rating period as a first step toward excellence. With an experienced employee, the goal might be to move to yet an even higher level of performance.

- All performance criteria that fall below the cut-off score are written down and prioritized. This step is important because not all criteria carry the same priority when it comes to peak performance and continual improvement. Prioritizing the areas in need of improvement will help ensure that improvement efforts are invested optimally. Common sense is important in this step because it might be necessary to select the top three to five areas in need of improvement, depending on whether the employee in question is new or experienced. With new employees there are likely to be more areas in need of improvement than with experienced personnel. Do not create a TIP that contains so many areas of improvement that it overwhelms a new employee. On the other hand, if an experienced employee has an inappropriately long list of areas in need of improvement it may be time to ask if his or her continued employment is wise.

• With the list of areas in need of improvement prioritized and finalized, specific action steps for making the needed improvements are planned and written down. This step is collaborative in that the organizational leader and the employee in question complete it working together. It is important that every action step included in the TIP have the agreement of the employee and the evaluator. Every action step listed for each improvement area should indicate the party responsible for carrying it out—the employee, the evaluator, or both. This means that any enabling actions needed to facilitate the employee's improvement are also included in the TIP so that it is clear who is going to do what. For example, assume that an employee needs to improve his math skills. An action step agreed to by both parties is for the employee to take a Math course at the local community college. Enrolling in the class and completing it is the employee's assignment. But the evaluator also has an assignment in this case. Her assignment is to arrange for the course to be paid for through the company's tuition-reimbursement program.

• With the actions steps completed and the party responsible for each step indicated, the evaluator and the employee collaboratively decide on deadlines for completing each step. It is unwise to agree on a list of actions to be taken and then leave their completion open-ended. Actions steps without deadlines encourage procrastination. TIPS should contain specific actions with specific deadlines for completing them.

- The evaluator and the employee keep a copy of the completed TIP and meet periodically throughout the next rating period to monitor progress, deal with unexpected roadblocks, and make any adjustments that might be necessary in scheduled deadlines. Used as explained herein, the TIP can be an invaluable tool for facilitating employee development and, in turn, peak performance and continual improvement.

Every organization has a corporate culture that determines how things are done. In fact, an organization's corporate culture is sometimes defined as *how things are done when the boss isn't looking.* Organizations that hope to excel should begin by establishing a culture of excellence; a culture that encourages, supports, and facilitates peak performance and continual improvement.

GROUP TRAINING ACTIVITY

Assume that your organization is experiencing widespread employee problems (e.g. high absenteeism, tardiness, poor performance, negative attitudes, and a lack of initiative and resourcefulness). In short, your organization has a counterproductive corporate culture. A cross-functional team has been formed to make recommendations for transforming the corporate culture into one that encourages, supports, and facilitates peak performance, continual improvement, and organizational excellence. Your group is this cross-functional team. Discuss strategies for transforming the corporate culture of your organization. Make a list of specific action steps you recommend for transforming the organization's culture.

Three

UNIT-LEVEL ORIENTATIONS

Best Practice Number 3: *Use unit-level orientations to help employees understand the organization's big picture and where they fit into it.*

People in organizations are like pieces in a complex jigsaw puzzle—there are lots of pieces and every piece has an important role to play in making the puzzle come together. It is important for employees to see the big picture and to know where they fit into it. Employees perform better when they understand their role within the context of the organization's big picture. Ensuring that employees understand the big picture as well as where they fit into it is an effective strategy for helping equip, enable, and empower employees for peak performance and continual improvement. Understanding the big picture helps employees understand what the organization is trying to accomplish. Knowing their role in the big picture helps employees understand how they can make the greatest contribution to the organization's success.

Explaining the big picture as well as where employees fit into it is best done at the unit level and should be an agenda item for unit-level orientations. Most organizations provide orientations for newly hired employees. These orientations are typically handled by the human resources department and cover pay, benefits, and other important issues of concern to newly hired personnel. New employee orientations provided by the human resources department are important—even critical—but for organizations striving for excellence this traditional orientation is not enough. In-processing orientations for new employees should be followed up with more detailed, more specific unit-level orientations.

Many organizations fail to provide structured, systematic unit-level orientations that help employees see the big picture as well as where they fit into it. This is a serious mistake. For helping new employees understand their role in the organization, where they and their unit fit into the big picture, and specifically what is expected of them, unit-level orientations are a must. This chapter explains how organizational leaders can provide unit-level orientations that will give employees a good start on the road to peak performance and continual improvement.

AN ORGANIZATION'S BIG PICTURE

An organization's big picture is a composite of its vision, mission, strategic goals, and current status. Employees who understand an organization's big picture can better understand its purpose (why it exists) as well as its aspirations (what it hopes to accomplish). Employees who understand why an organization exists and what it hopes to accomplish are in a better position to do their part in helping it achieve its mission and realize its aspirations. Putting employees in this advantageous position is the purpose of the unit-level orientation recommended in this chapter.

In trying to help employees see the big picture as well as where they fit into it, organizational leaders will find several tools helpful. These tools are readily available in most organizations, and should be in all. In fact, if they are not available in your organization, developing them should be a high priority. The best tools for showing employees the big picture and where they fit into it are those listed below:

- Strategic plan

- Organizational chart

- Team charter

- Job descriptions

Strategic Plan as a Big Picture Tool

An organization's strategic plan, if properly developed, will answer three critical questions for employees concerning the big picture: Who are we?, Where are we going?, and How are we going to get there? These questions correspond with the three basic components of an organization's strategic plan: mission (Who are we?), vision (Where are we going?), and strategic goals (How are we going to get there?). This is valuable information for employees who need to understand the organization's big picture. Unfortunately, in many organizations this information never leaves the executive suite. The following case illustrates the value of a strategic plan in showing employees the big picture and where they fit into it.

Case: Using the Strategic Plan as a Big Picture Tool

I learned the value of using an organization's strategic plan as a big picture tool early in my career. Three of us had just been hired to work in the engineering department of a company that designed, manufactured, and erected the structural components for large construction projects. Our supervisor, the company's chief engineer, sat us down in a conference room and gave each of us a copy of the company's strategic plan. He directed our attention to the company's vision, mission, and strategic goals.

Beginning with the mission, he said (paraphrased): *Our mission is to design, manufacture, and erect the structural components of large commercial and industrial projects such as parking decks, bridges, sports stadiums, condominiums, shopping malls, warehouses, factories, office buildings, and cooling towers.* The chief engineer then explained what this mission statement meant to us as employees. Because we had been hired to work in the engineering department, we fit into the design element of the mission. Whenever the company received a contract, the engineering department was responsible for designing the structural components of the job, writing the specifications, and producing the engineering drawings. He stressed that the manufacturing and construction departments could not begin their work until we completed ours. He also explained that the quality and timeliness of their work was dependent on how well we did ours.

Right away, we could see that the engineering department did not operate in a vacuum. Rather, it was just one department that had to work cooperatively with the other departments in the company. This turned out to be an important point because we soon learned that everything in the company operated on a carefully orchestrated schedule, and that if one department fell behind schedule it would throw off the schedules of the other departments. As we soon learned, failing to meet scheduled deadlines could be an expensive proposition for our company.

Our company received contracts that had substantial penalties built into them for failing to complete all requirements on time. Late penalties that amounted to thousands of dollars per day could quickly eat up our company's profits. This was new information to all three of us. In college, we had studied design as if it were an entity unto itself. We had no idea how it fit into a larger organization. To see how our work in the engineering department affected the success of the overall organization was an epiphany for me and the other new employees. In fact, all three of us began to shift uncomfortably in our seats as the weight of responsibility settled on us. However, we were pleased to learn the importance of our role, where we fit into the organization, and what would be expected of us.

Moving on to the company's vision statement the chief engineer said (paraphrased): *Our vision is to be the leading pre-stressed concrete company in the Southeastern United States.* He then explained that this meant we had to outperform a long list of competitors, and that most of them had the same vision as ours. He let us know that the company needed our absolute best work every day if it was going to achieve this vision. He made sure we understood that our company's success in the marketplace and, in turn, our job security and potential for advancement depended on our company achieving its vision. Again, this very practical and pertinent information had not been covered in our college studies.

All three of us had held various part-time jobs during college. However, in those jobs we had felt like just another member of the herd. We had no understanding of the big pictures of our employers and nobody seemed interested in sharing this information with us. All we knew was that we showed up at the appointed time and did what we were told. For this we received a paycheck. Unfortunately, this is how it is in many organizations. In too many cases, employees have no understanding of their organization's big picture, where they fit into it, or the role they play in helping their employer succeed. Nor do they understand the symbiotic relationship between employer and employee when it comes to success in the marketplace, job security, and career advancement. This is why a unit-level orientation is so important.

The chief engineer closed out our orientation by reviewing the company's strategic goals. He explained that the goals showed what had to be done in order to achieve the company's vision, again emphasizing the importance of doing so. His final message to us was that we now understood the company's big picture and where we fit into it (project design, engineering drawings, and specifications). We also understood that we were expected to give our absolute best every day to help the organization achieve its strategic goals and, in turn, its vision. This brief explanation of our company's big picture and where we fit into it helped us become productive employees in a relatively short period of time. From the outset we understood our company's big picture and how we could help achieve it. We also understood why it was important to the organization and to us as individuals that we perform at peak levels and continually improve.

Organizational Chart as a Big Picture Tool

Most organizations have an organizational chart that shows lines of authority and how functional units fit together. Organizational charts can be helpful tools for informing employees where their functional unit fits into the overall organization, as well as how it relates to other units. When employees can see where their unit fits into the organization, they can—by extension—see where they fit into it. An additional benefit of the organizational chart is that it gives a concise summary—typically just one page—of the composition of the entire organization. This helps employees see that they are part of a bigger organization which, in turn, can help eliminate the problems often caused in organizations by compartmentalized thinking.

Employees who do not understand where they and their functional unit fit into the overall organization sometimes develop tunnel vision. They come to believe that their unit is the only one in the organization, or at least the only one that matters. Organizations that are striving for excellence cannot allow this to happen. Just as the organization needs individuals to work cooperatively for the good of the team, it needs functional units to work cooperatively for the good of the organization.

This is easier to accomplish when employees can see a chart of all of the various functional units in the organization showing how they fit together.

I once worked in an organization in which the various functional units not only failed to work cooperatively they actually worked against each other, something that is surprisingly common. Each functional unit in this organization was a kingdom unto itself. Egos and office politics took precedence over performance. Not only did employees in the various departments not understand the company's big picture and how they fit into it, they did not care. Not a thought was given to the need for functional units to work cooperatively. Employees did not know or care how their performance affected the performance of the company. They seemed to have no idea that the success of the company had a direct effect on their job security and potential for advancement. When the company eventually failed, its personnel were shocked. They should not have been. The company's vendors and customers certainly weren't. The wonder was that the company lasted as long as it did.

Team Charter as a Big Picture Tool

A team charter is a brief document containing the mission and guiding principles for individual teams within organizations. It is developed by the team leader and team members working cooperatively (see Chapter 9). The team leader develops the team's mission statement. Then, working cooperatively, team members and the team leader develop a list of guiding principles. The mission statement explains the purpose of the team and its place in the organization. The guiding principles explain how team members are to interact with each other as they work together to accomplish the team's mission.

A well-developed team charter can be an excellent tool for helping employees understand where they fit into the organization, especially when used in conjunction with an organizational chart. The organizational chart will show employees where their functional unit fits into the larger organization. The team charter will show employees what their team does, why it exists, and how it contributes to the overall mission of the organization. Using the team charter in conjunction with the organizational chart gives team leaders an opportunity to explain how the overall organization operates and how the various functional units interact in carrying out the overall mission. Understanding the big picture to this extent personalizes for employees the importance of peak performance and continual improvement.

The Job Description as a Big Picture Tool

An employee's job description is not a big picture tool per se. However, it can be used in conjunction with the other tools explained in this chapter for adding to the understanding of employees concerning the big picture and where they fit into it. The job description lets employees know their specific duties and responsibilities. When employees understand the organization's purpose and aspirations, how the various functional units fit together, where their specific units fit in, their unit's responsibilities, and their individual duties and responsibilities, they know everything they need to know about the big picture and their place in it. At this point they should fully understand the value of peak performance and continual improvement to them and to the organization.

USING THE TOOLS IN COMBINATION

An effective way to help employees understand the big picture and where they fit into it is to use a five-step approach that combines all of the tools explained in this chapter. The five steps are as follows:

- Explain the organization's mission, vision, and strategic goals as set forth in its strategic plan.

- Show employees how the organization is structured to carry out its mission using the organizational chart.

- Explain where the employee's functional unit fits into the organization using the organizational chart.

- Explain the mission of the employee's functional unit using the team charter.

- Explain the employee's individual duties and responsibilities using the job description.

Employees who complete this five-step process will be well-informed concerning the organization's big picture and where they fit into it. As a result, they will be better prepared to play an effective role in helping the organization excel. Because they understand the big picture and where they fit into it, properly orientated employees will be able to make the connection between their individual performance and the organization's overall performance. In any situation that might arise requiring a decision, employees who understand the big picture and their role in it will not have to guess as to the best course of action. They will know the course of action that is most likely to help the organization achieve its vision. Bringing employees to this point is the goal of unit-level orientations.

GROUP TRAINING ACTIVITY

Discuss the following question: Have you ever worked in a situation in which you did not understand the big picture and where you fit into it? Ask group members who have had this experience to describe how it affected them individually as well as how it might have affected the overall organization. Discuss this follow-up question: Would being provided the type of unit-level orientation described in this chapter have helped group members perform better?

Four

EXECUTION OF PLANS

Best Practice Number 4: *Demonstrate for employees how to effectively execute plans.*

In organizations striving for excellence, having good plans—both strategic and operational—is important. But executing the plans is critical. This point can be illustrated using a football analogy. Any time two football teams meet, they both have a plan for winning the game. However, only one team will win. Is the winning team always the one with the best plan? Not necessarily. More often, the team that wins is the one that does the best job of executing its plan. A mediocre plan executed well is better than an outstanding plan executed poorly.

The best plan in the world is just a collection of ideas until it is effectively executed. It is one thing to plan, but quite another to execute. Having a plan is important but executing the plan is essential. Organizational excellence, peak performance, and continual improvement require that executives, managers, supervisors, and employees know how to do their respective parts in executing plans.

EFFECTIVE EXECUTION DEFINED

More often than not, where plans break down is in the execution phase. This is why it is important for organizational leaders to become skilled at executing plans themselves and at helping employees develop execution skills. Effective execution of plans means:

> *Systematically initiating, following through on, and completing all tasks necessary to effectively implement a plan. Execution involves applying such strategies as establishing expectations, assigning responsibility, setting deadlines, establishing accountability, allocating resources,*

identifying and overcoming inhibitors, monitoring progress, adapting as necessary, and following through to completion.

There is an old saying that the devil is in the details. This principle certainly applies when executing plans. Whereas planning is about conceptualizing the possible and envisioning the future, executing plans is about rolling up your sleeves and dealing with the practical realities of the here and now. The former involves making theoretical projections while the latter involves dealing with practical realities. Planning is nothing more than an academic exercise unless the plans are going to be effectively executed. Therefore, organizational leaders must learn how to effectively execute plans while also helping employees develop execution skills.

GOOD PLANS—BAD RESULTS

Plans are developed in the air-conditioned comfort of offices and conference rooms under conditions that can be controlled, but they are executed in settings where roadblocks often pop up unexpectedly, conditions are difficult or impossible to control, and competitors are doing their best to prevent the organization's success. This point can be illustrated by returning to the earlier football analogy.

For every football game, each coaching staff develops a game plan designed to give its team the victory. The game plans are developed in the comfort of the coach's offices under conditions that can be controlled. It is not difficult to study game films and draw Xs and Os on a marker board. However, the real game is played on a field where conditions cannot be controlled or even predicted with one-hundred percent accuracy and the Xs and Os are real people.

For example, it might rain unpredictably—a fact that could undermine the game plan of a running team. The team's best player might sprain an ankle on the opening kickoff. Another important player might come down with an illness that keeps him out of the game. The list of unexpected roadblocks that can pop up is almost infinite. Add to this that the other team has a plan of its own, and part of that plan is to undermine your team's plan.

Consequently, it is important for organizational leaders to understand that: 1) planning and execution are two vastly different activities, and 2) plans do not just executive themselves. Organizational leaders who understand these two points and act accordingly are more likely to enjoy the fruits of well-executed plans. Those who are striving to equip, enable, and empower employees for peak performance and continual improvement must help them develop execution skills that are appropriate for their level of involvement in executing plans. Effective execution of plans requires the best efforts of organizational leaders and employees.

A fact that often complicates the effective execution of plans is that organizations can be their own worst enemies in this area. Football teams hurt themselves by fumbling the ball, missing blocks, throwing pass interceptions, and missing tackles. Organizations have their equivalents of fumbles, missed blocks, pass interceptions, and missed tackles, and these things can undermine the execution of plans just as effectively as the best efforts of competitors. Consequently, it is important for organizational leaders and employees to learn how to be "sure-handed" when carrying out a plan or any portion of a plan for which they are responsible.

Another factor that can undermine the effective execution of plans is what I call the *dirty-hands syndrome*. This syndrome can be seen in people who are reluctant to step outside the safe and comfortable intellectualism of planning, and get their hands dirty sorting through the often messy details of execution. Such people are like the architect who is comfortable sitting in an air-conditioned office designing a building, but is uncomfortable donning a hard hat and visiting the job site to check on the messy details of construction.

Planning involves considering the possible, envisioning the ideal, and looking to the future. It is an appealing intellectual activity full of promise and hope. Execution, on the other hand, involves digging into the details, dealing with reality, and focusing on the here and now. It is a practical, roll-up-your-sleeves type of activity that is tempered by the everyday realities of the workplace.

EFFECTIVELY EXECUTING A PLAN

Before beginning the actual execution of a plan, whether strategic or operational, it is a good idea to conduct what I call a *roadblock analysis*. The roadblock analysis involves assessing factors that might inhibit the effective execution of the plan. For example, assume you plan to drive your family to Orlando for a vacation at Disneyworld. A roadblock analysis would involve the family sitting down and discussing what could go wrong on the way so that the adults can be prepared. Your list of roadblocks might include car trouble, botched hotel reservations, rain, detours, and so forth. If the adults who plan the trip are wise, they will build contingency plans into the larger vacation plan to accommodate these potential roadblocks or, at least, to mitigate their effects.

Conducting a roadblock analysis for an organization or any subunit in an organization consists of convening a meeting of the personnel who will have to carry out the plan and asking them the following questions:

- What factors might inhibit our efforts to implement this plan fully and on time?

- Do we have the resources to implement this plan fully and on time?

- Do we have the expertise to implement this plan fully and on time?

- Are there existing habits, attitudes, procedures, or informal ways of doing things that might inhibit the effective implementation of this plan?

- Are there threats from outside the organization that might inhibit the effective implementation of this plan?

Once the roadblock analysis has been completed, the following strategies can be helpful for overcoming or mitigating any obstacles identified and for executing the plan: 1) develop assignment sheets, and 2) gain momentum and reinforce it.

Develop Assignment Sheets

Plans contain goals. Your organization has resources it will dedicate to accomplishing these goals. For example, when an organization develops a plan it devotes resources in the form of money, people, processes, and technologies to executing the plan. But just devoting resources is not enough to ensure an effective execution. There is still a missing ingredient. What is needed is a tool for transforming the goals listed in the plan into action items so that resources such as money, people, processes, and technologies can be focused on carrying out the action items and, in turn, accomplishing the goals. Each specific action item should be assigned to a responsible individual and given a deadline. Wise organizational leaders know to assign both intermediate and final deadlines for each action item. An effective tool for accomplishing this is the *assignment sheet*.

How the assignment sheet works is best illustrated by an example. Assume you are the CEO of a successful organization that has an opportunity to grow. One of the goals in your organization's strategic plan is: *Construct a new corporate facility on a 50-acre tract of land outside of town.* You have identified a contractor who can do the work. This contractor has all the resources needed to construct the facility (e.g., raw materials, people, technologies, processes, etc.). However, there is still one thing missing—something without which the contractor cannot construct the facility. The missing ingredient is a comprehensive set of construction plans.

The contractor understands the goal of constructing a new corporate facility, but he needs the goal to be translated into more specific operational terms. The tool for doing this is a comprehensive set of construction plans containing the architectural and engineering drawings, specifications, and bill of materials. The plans give the contractor the specific, detailed information he needs to construct the facility and, thereby, achieve the goal.

Like the contractor in this analogy, people who will be assigned responsibility for executing parts of an organization's plan need a set of "construction drawings" to translate their responsibilities into operational terms. When it comes to executing organizational plans, it is not real drawings that are needed, of course, but a tool that has the detail and specificity of construction drawings. This tool is the assignment sheet.

Assignment sheets contain all of the specific activities that must be completed in order to achieve a certain goal in the plan, the person or group responsible for completing the activities, and projected completion dates—intermediate and final—for each activity. Assignment sheets show all stakeholders what tasks must be accomplished, who is responsible for completing each task, and when each task must be completed. This is an important step.

In order for a plan to be effectively executed, someone has to be responsible for every action item required. Organizational leaders should never make the mistake of thinking that once a plan is developed people will just automatically accept responsibility for executing it. "I thought someone else was going to do that" is one of the most common excuses heard in the aftermath of a failed plan. When everyone is responsible, no one is responsible. Specificity is critical to the effective execution of plans.

Gain Momentum and Reinforce It

Executing a plan is like rolling a ball up a hill. It is difficult at first, but if you can keep pushing until the ball reaches the crest gravity will take over and it's all down hill from that point on. When executing plans, "gravity" is provided by the momentum that accompanies success. This is an example of the maxim that says *success breeds success*. The need to gain momentum is why it is important to begin the execution of plans by picking any low hanging fruit that is available. In other words, identify those execution assignments that can be quickly and easily accomplished, and complete them first. Success early in the process will build momentum for additional success by quieting the naysayers and winning the commitment of personnel who are open to the change but are not sure it will work.

Once the assignment sheets for a plan have been developed and are being worked on, execution of the plan will begin to pick up momentum. If the organization can maintain this momentum, the ball being pushed up the hill will make it over the crest and begin the easier downhill-phase of the journey. Organizational leaders can use the following strategies to gain and maintain momentum when executing plans:

- *Model positive execution behaviors.* While employees are working on their assignments, it is important that they see organizational leaders working on theirs. Employees will take their cues from those above them in the organization. If they see executives, managers, and supervisors putting in the time and effort needed to carry out execution assignments, they will be more inclined to commit to carrying out theirs. Organizational leaders must understand that the execution of a plan can quickly breakdown if they are perceived as failing to do their part.

- *Talk about execution.* Any time employees who have assignments are gathered together, organizational leaders should talk about the progress being made in completing assignments. This will make it obvious to all who have specific assignments that executing the plan is a high priority. By talking about the execution process, organizational leaders keep all stakeholders informed and those with assignments focused on completing their tasks. Organizational leaders with overall responsibility for a given assignment sheet or any portion of one should apply this strategy on a regular basis.

- *Monitor progress.* Assignment sheets make it easy for leaders in the organization to monitor the progress of a plan's execution on a daily basis—an important task. This strategy can be combined with an earlier strategy—talk about execution. Employees with specific assignments should be asked to keep copies of their assignment sheets close at hand. Organizational leaders should talk to every employee with tasks on their assignment sheet(s) everyday and not just to ask about progress, but to see actual evidence of progress. Executives, managers, and supervisors must understand that even the most dedicated employees will encounter problems in carrying out their assignments. By monitoring progress daily, organizational leaders can help those with assignments overcome problems before they interrupt the progress of the execution.

- *Celebrate progress.* One of the best ways to maintain momentum when executing plans is to reinforce progress by celebrating it. This can be done in a number of ways. One of the easiest, quickest, and most effective is for organizational leaders at all levels to give public recognition to employees every time they complete a significant intermediate step on their assignment sheets. Written notes of congratulations from executives, reports in company newsletters, recognition given during small group meetings, periodic written progress reports that recognize the good work of employees who complete assignments, and organization-wide luncheons in which people are recognized are just a few of the many ways progress can be reinforced. The method is actually less important than the fact that recognition is given and that it is given publically.

Good planning but poor execution is a common problem in organizations. There are many reasons why good plans often produce bad results. However, there is only one way that good plans will produce good results. This will happen only if organizational leaders put as much effort into executing plans as they do into developing them. The strategies presented in this chapter will help executives, managers, and supervisors who want to be developmental leaders become effective at executing plans and at equipping, enabling, and empowering employees to play their part in the process.

GROUP TRAINING ACTIVITY

Assume you have been put in charge of your organization's annual Christmas Party. Work together as a group to develop a plan for the party. Then prepare to execute the plan by: 1) conducting a roadblock analysis, and 2) developing assignment sheets.

Five

WORK ETHIC AND THE ENTITLEMENT MENTALITY

Best Practice Number 5: *Exemplify all of the attributes of a positive work ethic and help employees develop these attributes.*

Whatever happened to the work ethic? I am frequently asked this question by leaders in organizations. Employers I work with as a corporate trainer and consultant often tell me that something has changed in the attitudes of people toward work. Employers tell me that things they used to be able to take for granted about employees can no longer be assumed. For example, they can no longer assume that new employees will understand the need to show up for work on time, work hard, and contribute to the organization's success. Things that employers could once take for granted now seem like alien concepts to employees who often seem to have an *entitlement mentality.*

WORK ETHIC AND ENTITLEMENT MENTALITY DEFINED

A positive work ethic is a belief that it is intrinsically good to work hard and work smart, and that doing so is the best way to succeed. People with a positive work ethic take pride in their work and believe that a commitment to doing the best possible job, regardless of the nature of the job, is a virtue. Organizations that operate in a competitive environment need their employees to have a positive work ethic. It is the only way they can compete against organizations in developing nations where the typical employee is a PHD—an individual who is poor, hungry, and driven.

An entitlement mentality is the opposite of a positive work ethic. People with an entitlement mentality think they are owed the perquisites of success without the need to earn them and the benefits of hard work without having to do any. Organizations with entitled employees cannot possibly compete against their counterparts in emerging nations where the workforce is still poor, hungry, and driven.

A business executive who is a long-time friend and client summed up his views for me on the entitlement mentality as follows: (in paraphrase): *Why should I have to explain to well-paid employees that they have to come to work on time and actually work when they get here? It's as if being a contributing member of a team has never entered their minds. I do not understand employees who think they are entitled to raises, promotions, bonuses, and perquisites they have not earned.* The frustration of employers who are dealing with entitled employees is certainly understandable. Those that must outperform competitors from emerging industrialized nations need employees who will give them peak performance and continual improvement.

Baby boomers were born after World War II and grew up during a time of unprecedented growth and prosperity in America. As a result, the baby boomers were one of the most prosperous generations in the history of this country. But boomers were not just given their prosperity. Rather, those who were willing to work long, hard, and smart found that opportunities to build financial security and material wealth were boundless and unprecedented.

The baby boomer generation responded to its new-found prosperity by being generous in providing the benefits of material wealth for their children. As a result, many children of baby boomers grew up wanting for nothing. In fact, in many cases they were given everything they needed in life except the two things they needed most—responsibility and accountability. As a result, many of the children of baby boomers developed an entitlement mentality that affects their performance in the workplace.

THE WORK ETHIC AND THE ENTITLEMENT MENTALITY

In his book, *Blue Monday: The Loss of the Work Ethic in America*, Robert Eisenberger makes the point that: "A primary reason the United States became a great economic power was the industriousness of its people. Most Americans believed that hard work and profits provided a righteous and worthwhile life. The American vision involved not only economic betterment but also a willingness to work toward that more prosperous future."(1)

Evidence that the traditional "industriousness" of Americans is on the wane is inescapable. For example, a major coal company in Eastern Kentucky—citing a declining work ethic among workers in Eastern Kentucky—petitioned the state mining board to be allowed to hire Hispanic miners. (2) The company was forced to submit its petition because Kentucky statutes required miners to be fluent in English for safety purposes. In its petition the coal company referred to the changing attitudes of the indigenous population toward work, attendance, and drug use. The company claimed that the declining work ethic among East Kentucky workers was affecting productivity.(3)

A positive work ethic and the entitlement mentality are diametrically opposed concepts. In fact, the entitlement mentality is the antithesis of a positive work ethic. People with a positive work ethic believe that work is intrinsically good and that it should be approached with diligence. People with this outlook view work as the best way for them to attain financial security, professional success, personal satisfaction, and material wealth. They also tend to believe that hard work contributes to the betterment of society and makes their employers more competitive.

People with an entitlement mentality view the world through a different set of lens. Like people with a positive work ethic, they want to achieve financial security, professional success, personal satisfaction, and material wealth. But they differ from their positive counterparts in two essential ways. First, entitled employees do not think they should have to work hard to achieve success and all that goes with it. Through a complex set of causal factors that are described later in this chapter, they think they are entitled to the perquisites of success. Second, they have little or no concern for the best interests of employers or society. One of the defining characteristics of employees with an entitlement mentality is the belief that "It's all about me."

PEOPLE WHO WANT A JOB BUT DO NOT WANT TO WORK

As a college professor for more than 35 years, I have observed first-hand the changing attitudes of young people toward work. Assignments that were considered just routine by an earlier generation of business students seem like insurmountable obstacles to many members of the current generation. As a corporate consultant during this same period, I have listened as hundreds of organizational leaders complained about the declining work ethic among their employees.

Over the past three decades, changes in the work ethic have accelerated and the corresponding complaints from employers have become more frequent. For example, in reviewing the notes I keep of my meetings with my consulting clients a comment often made to me—especially over the last ten years—can be paraphrased as follows: *The employees I hire these days have no work ethic.*

A physician and friend put the problem of the declining work ethic in perspective for me one day while he updated the prescription for my contact lenses. As he busied himself pointing to eye charts, I asked about the quality of the job applicants he sees in his office. I could tell immediately that my question struck a nerve. This physician said, "The problem with the applicants I interview is that they want a job, but don't want to work." (4)

Have we spawned a generation of young people who are so self-indulgence that they no longer value work? Have we raised a generation of young people who view work as something to be tolerated, and then only to the extent that it satisfies their need for material comfort? Have we allowed a generation of young people to believe that the American dream is about winning the lottery instead of succeeding through hard work? My interaction with employers suggests that many of them think the answer to these questions is an unqualified "yes."

Other researchers in the field have come to the same conclusion. For example, R. B. Hill in his article, "Historical context of the work ethic," explains that it has become increasingly difficult for organizations to find employees who have those qualities associated with the traditional work ethic; qualities such as honesty, diligence, integrity, dependability, self-discipline, industriousness, initiative, and pride in a job well done.(5) Research such as that conducted by Hill and others verifies empirically what employers already know from daily experience: the entitlement mentality has become a serious problem in the workplace.

Characteristics of Employees with an Entitlement Mentality

In an article for *Career Development Quarterly,* Amy McCortney writes this about people with an entitlement mentality: "…earlier events in the twentieth century—such as increased education, baby boomers raised in affluence, industrial and technological progress, mass marketing, and a good economy—contributed to the development of a nation of people who believe in being better off economically than their parents' generation and who regard the good life as a kind of birthright."(6) Hoping to be better off than your parents is a good thing, but thinking you are entitled to be is not.

Employees with an entitlement mentality typically exhibit several characteristics including the following:

- Me-centered attitude

- Need for instant gratification

- Short attention span

- Expectation of being taken care of by others

- Aversion to constructive criticism

These characteristics are widely associated with employees who have an entitlement mentality. A comment I hear over and over from employers is that entitled employees have no concept of working for something bigger than them, something such as a team, department, or organization. Instead, they think it's all about them.

Americans who lived through the Great Depression are sometimes described in the same way as people in emerging industrialized nations: as being PHDs (people who are poor, hungry, and driven). This poor, hungry, and driven mentality reinforced the American work ethic and helped make this country the most productive nation in history following World War II. Unfortunately, over time America's PHD mentality began to erode and be replaced by an entitlement mentality. Americans are no longer poor, hungry, or driven when it comes to their attitudes toward work. Instead, many feel entitled. Transforming entitled employees into peak performing producers is one of the most formidable developmental challenges facing organizational leaders.

RESPONDING TO THE ENTITLEMENT MENTALITY

There is a glimmer of hope in the midst of this gloomy scenario about the entitlement mentality. As frustrating as they can be to employers, entitled employees can be transformed into peak performing producers, but not without a concerted effort. Further, employers cannot rely on parents, schools, or colleges to take the initiative in assisting in the transformation. Organizations are pretty much on their own when it comes to transforming entitled employees. Organizational leaders are going to have to take responsibility for facilitating the transformation themselves and approach it as a do-it-yourself-project.

The transformational process must begin with an understanding of the causes of the entitlement mentality, which are as follows:

- Overindulgent parents

- Misguided school systems

- Entertainment media

- Government "entitlement" programs

OVERINDULGENT PARENTS

Many parents of entitled employees are people who grew up in lesser socio-economic circumstances than they now enjoy. These parents worked long and hard to build better lives for themselves and their families. Having done so, they vowed that their children would not have to endure the same tribulations they had suffered. As a result, these well-meaning parents became overindulgent. They unwittingly *protected* their children from the very trials, challenges, disappointments, and consequences that would have prepared them for life as responsible adults. Too often, overindulgent parents gave their children toys instead of time and latitude instead of responsibility.

This concept of *protecting* children from the normal trials and problems of growing up as well as the attendant responsibility, accountability, and consequences associated with them is what gave rise to the term "helicopter parents." Helicopter parents are mothers and fathers who hover over their children throughout their formative years, rushing to the rescue any time their bad behavior or poor choices result in negative consequences. When their children get at odds with authority figures, helicopter parents tend to respond with such comments as: "My son would never do such a thing" or "Why are you being so hard on my daughter—she is just a child?"

Whereas the parents of previous generations tended to side with authority figures—principals, teachers, coaches, and police officers—the parents of entitled employees tended to side with their children. This was often done reflexively without even taking the time to learn the facts of the situation in question. Further, they typically continued to side with their children no matter what the facts revealed about the situation in question. Some of the errors often made by helicopter parents are: 1) shielding their children from the consequences of their behavior; 2) reinforcing false expectations in their children; and 3) giving their children too much latitude and too little responsibility. Ironically, these types of errors tend to reinforce the behaviors that get their children into trouble in the first place.

"Protecting" Children from the Consequences of their Behavior

As a child, I made my share of poor choices as did many of the employers who complain to me about entitled employees. For example, after getting a BB gun as a gift for my eighth birthday, I decided to have some target practice. The targets I chose were the windows of an old shack my friends and I often played in—a shack we thought of as ours. It wasn't. As it turned out, the old shack belonged to a man I will call Mr. Smith. Mr. Smith lived in a house across the street from the old shack, an excellent vantage point from which to watch as I methodically shot out all of its windows.

Just as I finished shattering the last window, Mr. Smith walked up with the town constable in tow. When my parents were called to join me and Mr. Smith in the constable's office, they could have shielded me from what was to follow by simply paying for the windows. However, this was a different era and my parents were not of the helicopter variety.

Rather than indignantly claim that their son would never do such a thing or simply pay Mr. Smith what was owed, my parents told the constable and Mr. Smith that I would assume full responsibility for my actions. Then they worked out an arrangement by which I would pay off my debt by spending afternoons and weekends for the next three months mowing, trimming, and cleaning yards for Mr. Smith, a man who, as it turned out, owned a lot of old shacks.

Watching my friends play in the afternoon and on weekends, I chafed under the yoke of what I saw as an unreasonably harsh sentence. However, since none of the adults involved were inclined to leniency, I worked until the entire debt was paid off. In the process, I learned a valuable lesson about responsibility, accountability, and suffering the consequences of my actions. Fortunately for me, I learned this lesson in a situation that required nothing more of me than time and hard work.

Fast forward to the present and consider how the helicopter parents of an entitled employee might handle the same situation. The parents would be more likely to argue that the old shack wasn't worth much anyway and that boys will be boys. They might also argue that their son could not possibly spend his weekends doing manual labor. On one hand, such chores would be demeaning and on the other hand they would interfere with his soccer matches and summer camp. These helicopter parents would be more likely to simply pay for the windows themselves or, better yet, file a lawsuit against the owner claiming his old shack is an eye sore and a hazard to innocent little boys. The child in this scenario would learn a lesson, just as I did. Unfortunately, it would be the wrong lesson.

Even in the best of circumstances, a person's life will have its share of disappointments. People lose loved ones, don't get a promotion they deserve, develop health problems, lose a job, have a major setback in the stock market, or experience any number of other disappointments. Problems such as these are inevitable; such is the nature of life. Further, as they grow into their teen and young adult years, children can get themselves into situations that are beyond the scope of their parent's ability to intervene. In order to learn to deal intelligently and maturely with problems, children must first learn that actions have consequences and they, not their parents, will have to deal with those consequences.

Young people learn how to deal with the big problems of adulthood by dealing with the small problems of childhood. Consequently, when overindulgent parents protect their children from the relatively minor consequences of youthful indiscretions, they unwittingly leave them unprepared to deal with the larger problems of adulthood and the consequences of those problems. This lack of preparation and inability to handle responsibility then shows up in the workplace.

When helicopter parents automatically take the side of their children in disputes with authority figures, they send the wrong message and teach the wrong lesson. Over the course of my career in higher education, I have been confronted hundreds of times by angry, protective parents whose sons or daughters have run afoul of the college's rules. Remember, these were parents whose children were college-age adults. Maturity, of course, is another matter. These parents had been intervening on behalf of their children all of their lives and saw no reason to stop when they went to college.

I occasionally teach a graduate course for people who want to be school administrators. Many of the students in this class are experienced teachers. This particular class includes a lesson on establishing positive working relationships with parents. Every time we come to this lesson, practicing teachers in the class tell horror stories about parents coming to the *rescue* when their children are caught breaking the rules. Teachers have told me of instances in which they were asked by parents to look the other way in situations where students had wantonly lied, cheated, and stolen. Worse yet, teachers who refuse to overlook the bad behavior often see the tables turned on them by parents who try to portray them as tyrants who are just picking on their poor innocent children.

Teachers in this graduate course have related stories about how parents repeatedly miss out on what they call "teachable moments"—opportunities to teach their children about responsibility and accountability while the consequences of their behavior are still relatively minor. The more experienced teachers tell stories of children, misguidedly protected by their parents, whose bad behavior increased over the years until, eventually, it led to heartbreaking problems in their teen and early adult years. Invariably, these were problems the helicopter parents could not sweep under the rug or make go away.

Is it any wonder that people who are protected from the consequences of their behavior while children grow up expecting to be protected in the same way as adults? Individuals such as these enter the workforce ill-equipped to deal with the everyday realities of a competitive workplace; a place where pressure, consequences, and difficulty abound. The protectiveness of well meaning but misguided parents is a major factor in the aversion to responsibility and accountability that is a characteristic of entitled employees.

Reinforcing Inflated Expectations

A formerly entitled employee who had transformed himself told me of his surprise when, during his first job interview after college, he learned that the company offering him a job would not be providing him a company car and other perquisites. He went on to explain that his dad, a professional in the same field, had a company car, so he just assumed that he would get one too. When he asked his dad about it, this young man was shocked to learn that his dad had worked in the profession for more than fifteen years before rating a company car. Having inflated expectations is a characteristic common among entitled employees.

Many entitled employees grew up being told *"You can be anything you want to be."* They heard this message so often from so many different authority figures that, in their minds, it came to represent a statement of entitlement rather than a philosophical ideal meant to encourage. Think of the old Disney song that says: "When you wish upon a star your dreams come true." The message in this song was intended to be an inspiring ideal that would motivate young people to set their sights high. Over time it evolved into an expectation that entitled people felt they had a right to.

Worse yet, entitled people began to literally accept the part of the message that says "When you wish…" as if wishing is all it takes to make a dream come true. This misconception, in turn, contributed to the development of an entitlement mentality in people who came to believe they should actually have anything they wished for irrespective of merit or effort. Employers now find themselves dealing with this attitude of entitlement more and more.

In the United States, people may certainly aspire to become anything—all Americans have that right. And, of course, many Americans, by dint of hard work, wise choices, and perseverance have translated opportunity into inspiring success stories. But having the right to pursue a goal is a far cry from having a guarantee of achieving it or being entitled to achieve it. Achieving goals requires commitment, determination, diligence, hard work, talent, and perseverance. In other words, achieving goals requires a positive work ethic. There are just too many factors that can prevent the philosophical ideal of achieving success from becoming a practical reality. Unfortunately, this bubble-bursting disclaimer was not shared with people who grew up to be entitled employees.

It is certainly understandable and even advisable that parents encourage young people to have high expectations and set lofty goals. After all, part of a parent's responsibility is to encourage children to aim high. In addition, America is the land of opportunity. Some of our most cherished, appealing folklore revolves around the rags-to-riches stories of famous Americans. For example, young people in the United States have historically learned that anyone born in this country can grow up to become President of the United States. Products of small-town America such as Abraham Lincoln, Jimmy Carter, Bill Clinton, and Ronald Reagan are often cited as examples of this Horatio Alger phenomenon.

Once again, though, the message that you-can-become-president represents more of a cherished ideal than a statement of fact. Since our nation's inception in 1776, hundreds of people have wanted to be President of the United States, but fewer than 50 have actually achieved this lofty goal. Americans are rightfully proud of the fact that anyone born in this country can aspire to be president. However, parents of entitled children often overlook the fact that anyone who aspires to be President is well advised to have a Plan B. While helicopter parents should be commended for encouraging their children to aim high, they must also bear the responsibility for failing to make them aware of the practical realities of life and work.

During more than 35 plus years in higher education, I have dealt with many young people who harbored inflated expectations—expectations reinforced by their parents. For example, every year thousands of college athletes hope to become professionals, but relatively few ever make it. Thousands of young people hope to become singers, dancers, and actors, but few ever make it. Unfortunately, of those who fail to achieve their aspirations—aspirations that for many are both inflated and unrealistic—few have developed a realistic Plan B. In fact, the college students I interact with on a daily basis do not like to even consider the possibility that they might need a Plan B.

The unrealistic expectations of entitled people manifest themselves not just in the selection of career fields such as professional sports and entertainment. Even those who select more realistic career fields often have unrealistic expectations about such things as starting salaries, benefits, perquisites, working hours, how long it will take to climb the career ladder, and the very nature of work itself. A common complaint among my colleagues in higher education is that their students expect to receive a passing grade if they do nothing more than show up for class. Forget that they complete none of the assigned work and fail all of the tests. Just showing up is supposed to be good enough to earn them a "C." This is just one more manifestation of the entitlement mentality.

Too many middle and upper-middle income parents have been lax about informing their children of the facts concerning how long and hard they had to work to achieve their current economic status. As a result, their children unrealistically expect to achieve in their 20s what their parents worked hard to achieve by their 40s and 50s. They expect to begin their careers at the same economic level as their parents without having to experience what their parents went through to get there. Parents contribute to the unrealistic expectations of their children by reinforcing society's you-can-be-anything-you-want-to-be message without informing them of what it will take to achieve their dreams. Then these young people with unrealistic and inflated expectations enter the workforce and organizational leaders find themselves trying to overcome 18 or more years of helicopter parenting.

Giving Too Much but Requiring Too Little

One of the most widely shared traits of the parents of entitled children is overindulgence, at least in the material sense. Parents of the entitled—many of whom grew up having to share everything with siblings if they had anything to share—have given their children their own televisions, computers, cell phones, clothing, cars, and various types of handheld communication devices. The bumper sticker that reads "He who dies with the most toys wins" is emblematic of the attitudes that overindulgence has spawned.

Many parents who had to run errands, mow yards, and do chores to earn enough money to rent a tuxedo or buy a dress for their high school's junior/senior prom now give their children thousands of dollars to pay for limousine service, extravagant prom parties, and condominiums for prom weekend. Parents who never even went on a senior trip while in high school now pick up the tab as a matter of course to send their children to Disneyworld, New York, Europe, or the Caribbean islands for their senior trip. Is it any wonder then that young people with these types of experiences find it difficult to adjust to entry-level salaries and unyielding responsibilities when they begin their careers?

This phenomenon of having it better at home is one of the principle drivers behind the "boomerang movement." This movement consists of young people in their 20s and early 30s who tire of the everyday realities of life—realities such as buying groceries, paying for utilities, doing their own laundry, and fixing their own meals—and return to the material comfort and logistical support of their parent's home. Whereas previous generations valued the opportunity to leave their parent's nest and make a life of their own, boomerangers place more value on material comfort and being taken care of.

In addition to giving their children so much in the material sense, helicopter parents are often overindulgent in giving them unconditional praise and unprecedented latitude. Parents of the entitled have tended to tell their children "good job" even when they have done poorly. They have tended to tell them how special they are even when their behavior, choices, or efforts have been anything but special. In addition, many parents have given their children much more latitude than they, themselves, had as children and teenagers.

Children of baby boomers who were allowed to whatever they pleased while mom and dad picked up the tab, may be the norm rather than the exception. Helicopter parents have given their children material advantages, but have failed to give them responsibility and accountability, two things that are essential to the maturation process and are part of the foundation of a positive work ethic.

While helicopter parents were typically given responsibility by their parents, they have tended to give their children latitude; the freedom to do what they want without the inherent restrictions of responsibility, accountability, and consequences. The result of this unprecedented latitude has been to undermine the maturation process. Maturity is not just about age; it's also about responsibility and accountability. An individual does not become mature until he is able to accept responsibility for his actions and until he is willing to be held accountable for his choices.

Young people mature by learning to accept responsibility. A willingness to seek and accept responsibility is a mark of maturity, but it's more than just that. It is also one of the defining characteristics of successful people and productive employees. Consequently, every time helicopter parents give their children latitude without balancing it with responsibility, they rob them of opportunities to mature in ways that would serve them well as adults and make them more productive employees. The result has been that when young people enter the workplace, too many of them view responsibility and accountability as alien concepts and, hence, have an entitlement mentality rather than a positive work ethic.

Case: *What Can Happen When Parents Give Too Much but Require Too Little*

The story of the old man and the squirrel is analogous to how helicopter parents have raised their children. After losing his wife and seeing his children grow up and move away, the old man was alone in the world. Consequently, he grew attached to a little squirrel that lived in a huge pecan tree in his back yard. The old man liked nothing better than to sit in a rocking chair on his back porch and watch the little squirrel scamper down the trunk of the tree to fetch ripe pecans that had dropped to the ground.

But something disturbed the old man about the little squirrel. Remembering his own years of privation during the Great Depression, he was troubled by how hard the little squirrel had to work to break open the tough-shelled pecans. Just like it had been for him during the Great Depression, getting a meal was hard work for the squirrel. Remembering those days of hardship and privation were unsettling to the old man.

One day he decided that his little friend should not have to work so hard for his meals. To lighten the squirrel's burden, the old man began to purchase shelled pecans and spread them around under the tree. His gift was received with delight by the little squirrel which pounced on the shelled pecans with relish, eating it's fill without having to work at all. Seeing the squirrel's pleasure, the old man was filled with joy. He loved the little squirrel in the same way that people can love a dog or cat. As pets can do, the little squirrel gave the old man companionship and provided a welcome diversion from his loneliness.

This scenario repeated itself everyday for several months with the little squirrel growing fatter by the day. Then, after some time had passed the old man noticed that the squirrel came down the tree to eat less frequently, and that when he did climb down he moved slowly. The old man also noticed that the little squirrel that had once grown so fat now appeared to be losing weight in spite of the fact that the ground under the pecan tree was littered with shelled pecans. One morning a few weeks later, while spreading a handful of shelled pecans around the base of the tree, the old man came upon the little squirrel lying in the grass. It was dead.

With tears coursing down his wrinkled cheeks, the old man put the little squirrel in a box and drove to the local veterinarian's office. There he learned that the squirrel had slowly starved to death because, over time, his teeth had grown so long that he could no longer eat. It seems that a squirrel needs to gnaw on the tough shells of nuts in order to continually grind down its ever-growing teeth. By feeding his little friend shelled pecans, the well-meaning but misguided old man robbed it of a basic necessity for survival. This was a hard lesson for the old man to have to learn. He had meant well and wanted only what was best for his friend. After all, he loved the little squirrel. Unfortunately, he loved it to death.

Helicopter parents may not be guilty of loving their children to death, but like the old man in this story they are robbing them of an essential life skill and in so doing are impeding their ability to succeed. When parents fail to require their children to carry out age-appropriate responsibilities and when they fail to hold them accountable they handicap them. Giving young people material gifts without any corresponding obligations, allowing them latitude without any attendant responsibilities, and protecting them from the consequences of their actions are all analogous to feeding shelled pecans to little squirrels.

MISGUIDED EDUCATION SYSTEM

Entitled employees in the 18 to 40 year old age group grew up in an era when public schools in America underwent a major philosophical shift in their approach to preparing young people for life as responsible, contributing, productive citizens. When previous generations attended school, it was thought that setting high standards, having high expectations, and teaching self-discipline constituted the best way to prepare young people for life as productive citizens. This all changed for the children of baby boomers.

During the formative years of the children of baby boomers—the Entitlement Generation—the focus of public education in many school districts shifted from high standards to inclusiveness. Educators in these school systems still hoped to turn out responsible, contributing, productive citizens, but they came to believe that developing self-esteem and being inclusive were the best strategies for achieving this goal. It should be noted here that this major philosophical shift was more a product of the heart than the mind since there is no credible evidence supporting its viability. It should also be noted that in trying to artificially develop self-esteem in students, educators were trying to *give* what can only be *earned.* Self-esteem is not a gift that can be given to an individual. Rather, it is like a masonry wall—it must be built slowly and surely one brick at a time.

Florida State Senator, Don Gaetz, when serving as Superintendent of Schools for Okaloosa County, Florida put the issue in perspective when he said: "Self-esteem is not a gift from government. Self-esteem is what you earn when you achieve something that's hard to achieve, but you achieve it on your own..." 7 His point is critical. Self-esteem is not a gift—it cannot be given. It must be developed over time; each step in the process being a hard-won achievement by the individual in question.

The philosophical switch from high standards to inclusiveness and from self-discipline to self-esteem led to a number of misguided choices on the part of educators. The misguided choices most closely related to the entitlement mentality are: 1) emphasizing self-esteem to the exclusion of self-discipline, and 2) emphasizing inclusiveness to the exclusion of performance. The net result of these two practices has been to transform schools into artificial environments that are at odds with the realities of the workplace and that, as a result, fail to develop students into mature adults who will become productive citizens and effective leaders.

Case: Self-Esteem Instead of Self-Discipline

After a distinguished career in the Air Force, a man I will call Jack was finally realizing his long-time dream of being a high school teacher. During his military career, Jack's favorite assignments had been instructor billets. He had a special knack for helping young people develop, learn, and mature, an undertaking that gave him great satisfaction. Consequently, one day when we talked he should have been on top of the world enjoying his new life as a high school teacher. Unfortunately, he wasn't. In fact, after just two years in the classroom, Jack was frustrated, disillusioned, and contemplating a career change.

Jack explained that things had changed radically since his days in school, and he stressed that he was not talking about technology. Such things as deportment, respect for teachers, and academic performance no longer seemed important. Further, he was distressed about a woeful lack of support from parents. Instead, the bottom-line goal for teachers now seemed to be the self-esteem of students. According to Jack, one of the worst sins a teacher can commit in today's classroom is to hurt a student's feelings. He explained that he was expected to tell students they were doing well when they obviously weren't, to avoid the word "failure" at all costs, and to be understanding even when students had clearly not tried on an assignment—assuming they had done the assignment at all.

Jack's story is just one representative example of others I have heard from veteran teachers over the past decade, teachers who still think education should be about setting high standards and helping students meet them. Many teachers—dedicated professionals like Jack— expressed deep reservations about the misguided practices of the self-esteem philosophy. Like Senator Gaetz, they know that self-esteem must be earned. It cannot be given.

Misguided Practices of the Self-Esteem Philosophy

The shift in emphasis from self-discipline to self-esteem resulted in classroom practices that have left young people not only unprepared for what they would face in a competitive workplace, but completely out of step with the real world outside the classroom. The most harmful of these practices—those that did the most to create an entitlement mentality—are explained in the paragraphs that follow.

Praising Inappropriately

A common practice among teachers who are proponents of the self-esteem philosophy is giving students unconditional praise. The idea is to build up the students' self-esteem, an act that will, supposedly, cause them to produce better work. This is a temptingly attractive theory for people who think with their hearts instead of their minds. Attractive though it may be to self-esteem advocates, the truth is that unconditional praise doesn't work. In fact, as an educational strategy not only has it failed, it has backfired. Just ask executives, managers, and supervisors who evaluate the performance of entitled employees; employees who have learned to expect unconditional praise rather than constructive criticism.

There are a number of problems with the concept of unconditional praise, the most important of which is that it does not work. Young people, regardless of their academic talent, have an inherent sense of how well they have performed on school assignments, the athletic field, and in other school-related endeavors. They know whether or not they have put forth sufficient effort to deserve the praise they receive and they know the truth about how their performance compares with that of other students. Further, no matter how often teachers and parents tell them not to compare themselves with others, they still do it.

Praising young people whose performance does not warrant it runs counter to the merit-based realities of the world in which they will live and the organizations in which they will work. Leaders in organizations that compete in a global environment are not going to praise poor performance just to make employees feel good. The hard truth is that false praise does not really build self-esteem anyway. It just contributes to the development of an entitlement mentality. Young people who are praised undeservedly on a regular basis come to think they are entitled to praise irrespective of merit.

Failing to Correct Student Work

The way teaching is supposed to proceed is in at least four well-defined steps: *preparation, presentation, application,* and *evaluation.* Think about a class you took in high school or college. In the old days, the teacher would: 1) *prepare* a lesson and require students to prepare themselves for the lesson by reading the appropriate chapter in the textbook; 2) *present* the lesson to students by lecturing, explaining, and demonstrating how to work several problems; 3) require *application* of the material in the lesson by assigning a number of problems for classroom work or homework; and 4) *evaluate* how well students learned by grading/correcting their homework and giving them tests.

This traditional approach to teaching and learning offers several benefits for students, one of which is that it reflects what happens in the workplace when a supervisor gives an employee a work assignment. Unfortunately, many teachers who advocate the self-esteem philosophy are averse to the evaluation component of the teaching-and-learning process. As a result, they are inappropriately lax in correcting student work. They also praise when they should give constructive criticism. In the more extreme cases, they do not correct student work at all. Teachers who advocate this approach claim that evaluation practices such as correcting and grading will only hurt students' feelings, dampen their creativity, and, in turn, damage their self-esteem.

In reality, all the self-esteem philosophy accomplishes is giving young people an aversion to constructive criticism. This, in turn, leaves them unprepared for those times at work when customers or supervisors will most assuredly evaluate their work, and sometimes with little regard for their feelings. When people are not given constructive criticism as children, they will not know how to accept it as adults in the workplace. This is unfortunate because the problems they will face as adults in the workplace are likely to be worse than any hurt feelings they might have experienced in the classroom as the result of honest corrective feedback. Entitled people who begin careers unprepared to have their performance evaluated have been cheated out of an important success skill: the ability to continually improve by accepting constructive criticism and acting on it in a positive manner.

Inclusion Instead of Performance

One of the most misguided aspects of the self-esteem philosophy is its focus on the concept of inclusion rather than performance. Inclusion is one of those concepts that tugs at the heart strings of well-meaning people who want everyone to succeed. After all, who wouldn't be pleased if everybody could succeed? Consequently, in the name of inclusion, many schools adopted some misguided practices that tend to undermine the performance of young people when they eventually graduate and enter the workforce. The worst of these in terms of contributing to an entitlement mentality are:

- Eliminating so called *exclusive* practices such as naming a class valedictorian, assigning class rankings, and publicizing the honor roll.

- Eliminating such practices as naming the most-valuable-player on sports and academic teams, or selecting one student in the senior class as most likely to succeed.

- Allowing all who sign up to make the team (sports or academic).

- Giving all participants a trophy regardless of which team wins or loses.

- Requiring that all members of the team get to play in every game regardless of their talent, effort in practice, attitude, or other considerations of merit.

Education, like competing globally, is an inherently exclusive enterprise or, at least, it is supposed to be. The hard truth is that in education, as at work, some succeed while others fail, some excel while others just get by, and some stand out from the crowd while others blend into it. How education turns out for a given individual depends on a host of factors including native intelligence, motivation, desire, effort, and perseverance as well as other factors such as the quality of schools, curriculums, teachers, and parental involvement.

When practiced as a naturally exclusive enterprise—albeit one in which well-trained professionals do everything they can to encourage and promote success—rather than an artificially inclusive enterprise, education reflects the realities of life in general and the workplace specifically. As such, it helps young people develop a positive work ethic, prepares them for responsible lives, and equips them for productive, successful careers. An approach to education that accurately reflects the realities of the workplace as well as life in general is more likely to turn out graduates who can become productive employees and effective leaders.

Practicing education as the naturally exclusive enterprise it is in no way excuses educators from their responsibility to do everything in their power to help every student succeed. Rather, it means that educators should stop telling students they are succeeding when they aren't. It means that instead of using inclusive platitudes to excuse underachievement, educators should give students honest assessments of their performance and continue to work with them until they can achieve their highest potential after factoring in native intelligence, motivation, effort, perseverance, and all of the other factors that affect success. What is required for success in school should be what is required for success on the job and in life: thrift, diligence, self-reliance, self-discipline, responsibility, accountability, deferred gratification, and hard work; in other words, a positive work ethic.

Results of the "Inclusion Syndrome"

Per-pupil funding for public schools in the United States is double that of Japan and other industrialized nations such as Korea, China, Indonesia, and Malaysia. Yet American students perennially lag behind students from these nations in the critical areas of Math and Science. Every year, American students rank at or near the bottom in Math and Science when compared with their counterparts from other industrialized nations.

These facts are well-documented and have received their share of attention in the national news media. Media attention, in turn, is partially responsible for the newly awakened interest in standardized testing that has swept the country in recent years. However, it is not the academic performance of entitled employees that is of primary concern in this chapter. Rather, it is their attitudes toward academic performance, work, and life. This is what educators cannot seem to understand. Improving the performance of American students in the basics will not be achieved by simply requiring standardized testing. I have no quarrel with testing, but American students do not fail to perform because they have not been sufficiently tested. They fail to perform because they have not been sufficiently challenged. American students will not perform better in the basic disciplines until schools once again focus on self-discipline and performance rather than self-esteem and inclusion.

While comparisons of the test scores of American students with those from various other countries are disturbing, a comparison of student attitudes toward those test scores is even more disturbing. Students from Japan, for example, tend to express both disappointment and embarrassment that their test scores are not higher, in spite of the fact that their scores always rank near the top. Students from the United States, on the other hand, say they feel good about themselves in spite of their low test scores.

In other words, students from the United States not only do not feel badly about their comparatively low test scores, they don't see any reason why they should. Rather, they think they are entitled to feel good irrespective of performance. A brief caveat is in order here. Granted that students should not be made to feel they are bad people if they do badly on a test, but they should, at least, feel badly about their performance; badly enough to want to improve it.

ENTERTAINMENT INDUSTRY

The appearance, attitudes, and language of today's young people are tied closely to the entertainment industry. Members of the 18 to 40 year-old age cohort grew up watching television, playing computer games, and surfing the Internet. In fact, for many, the television and computer served as surrogate parents during their formative years or, at least, frequent babysitters. The various forms of entertainment media—television, movies, videos, DVDs, Internet, handheld communication devices with infinite built-in applications, and computer games—have been pervasively influential in forming the values and attitudes of young people toward life in general and work specifically.

Volumes have been written about the detrimental effects of television on the development of young people. For example, television has been tied to the huge increase in reported cases of such learning disabilities as Attention Deficit Syndrome; a syndrome that has been further aggravated by personal computer technology. Further, although some researchers acknowledge the positive effects of a few well-known children's programs aired for those under the age of six, the negative aspects of many television programs far outweigh the positives aspects of these few.

The problems with television, personal computers, and other entertainment technologies as they relate to the development and maturation of young people have been exacerbated by the fact that, as a rule, helicopter parents have not controlled what their children watch, the games they play, or the web sites they visit. Many entitled employees were *latch-key* children during their formative years; children who came home from school before their parents got home from work. Consequently, they carried keys to their houses—hence the name latch-key children—and let themselves in after school. Parents of latch-key children often have no idea of what their young sons and daughters are watching on television, playing on the computer, or seeing on the Internet during the unsupervised hours after school.

From the time they got home from school until the arrival of their parents, the most common activity of many entitled employees during their formative years was watching television, playing computer games, or surfing the Internet. Although the computer, cell phones, and other devices have now edged television out of its position as the pre-dominant electronic companion of young people, the effects are still the same—only worse. While television exposes children to negative images, language, and themes, the computer allows them to actually participate rather than just watch, and it gives them access to much more in the negative sense than the television can.

Rather than belaboring this point, suffice it to say that if you want to know where the entitled employees got their self-expressive mode of dress and self-possessed attitudes, just review the television programs, computer games, and Internet sites that are popular with young people. For most adults, this will be an instructive experience. With that said, I will focus herein on just one aspect of the entertainment industry that contributes significantly to the entitlement mentality: advertising. Advertising that is aimed at young people is a form of entertainment and it is intended to be.

Advertising and the Entitlement Mentality

During the formative years of the children of baby boomers, advertisers perfected the strategy of going around parents and marketing directly to young people. There were at least two reasons for the adoption of this strategy. First, the children of baby boomers, more than any previous generation, had access to disposable cash. In fact, even in their pre-teen years, the children of baby boomers represented a consumer block with enormous buying power; a fact understood by advertisers. When these children reached their teen years, their economic clout only increased. The children of baby boomers either had cash or had ready access to it through their helicopter parents.

Second, advertisers found that one of the best ways to create demand for the products they represented was to create peer pressure among young people. Young people are especially susceptible to peer-pressure. If their friends are buying a gadget, toy, or an item of clothing, they feel like they must have it too. No young person wants to be the only one in his or her group who does not have the latest trendy item. Consequently, children will pester their parents to buy the *must-have* products they see advertised and that others are buying. By making their ads the medium for telling young people what they "had to" purchase in order to be accepted as part of the in-crowd, advertisers became an influential force in the development of today's entitled employees.

Once they learned how to drive demand, advertisers began to tell young people in ways both subtle and direct *it's all about you;* an easy enough message to sell to young people who are hardwired to believe it in the first place. Having received this same message from parents and educators, young people came to believe it. Of course, once you come to believe that you are the center of the universe, developing an entitlement mentality is just a logical next step.

Try the following experiment. For just one week, watch the commercials aired in conjunction with television programs targeted at young audiences. Make note of the advertising themes or slogans used in the commercials you watch. I researched advertising slogans that have been used over the past decade and found that the bulk of them were designed to reinforce an attitude of self-centeredness. Here are some of the themes of ads and commercials that were aimed at young people over the past decade:

- Have it YOUR way

- I want it all!

- You deserve nothing but the best

- Express yourself

- You choose—it's your life

- An Army of One (A recruiting slogan the Army has to drop in 2006 after several years of getting what it asked for—self-centered recruits who thought it was all about them)

- Expect everything!

The list could go on, but there is no need. The *it's-all-about-you* theme does not change. The overarching strategy of advertisers during the formative years of today's entitled employee has been to go beyond just making young people want their products to making them feel entitled to them. Of course, as is always the case with the entitled, someone else is expected to pay. With young people who have helicopter parents, that someone is their parents. With entitled employees, it is the organizations that employ them.

PROBLEMS CAUSED AT WORK BY THE ENTITLEMENT MENTALITY

The entitlement mentality is the antithesis of a positive work ethic. Consequently, it can be a major inhibitor in organizations striving for excellence through peak performance and continual improvement. Employees with an entitlement mentality can cause a number of problems that undermine an organization's performance. The worst of these are as follows:

- **Poor teamwork.** The essence of teamwork can be summarized in one brief phrase: "It's all about us." People with an entitlement mentality have no appreciation of the concept of "us." Rather, their outlook can be summarized as, "It's all about me." Employees who think it's all about them contribute nothing to teamwork. On the contrary, they undermine it.

- **Poor motivation.** Employees who are motivated—whether internally or externally—do their best to earn their pay and other forms of rewards and recognition. Employees with an entitlement mentality, on the other hand, think pay, rewards, and recognition are owed to them. Hence, they have no desire or need to strive to earn them.

- **Poor customer service.** Employees with an entitlement mentality typically deliver poor customer service. When it's all about you, there is no need to try to satisfy customers. In fact, to employees with an entitlement mentality customers are just unwanted intrusions into their daily routine.

- **Aversion to responsibility and accountability.** Employees with an entitlement mentality grew up without being given responsibility. Further, whenever they ran afoul of authority, parents intervened to relieve them of the consequences that are the product of accountability. Consequently, the first time they have faced real responsibility and accountability is when they got a job. Many find the concepts of responsibility and accountability daunting. As a result they are averse to them. One of the ways this aversion manifests itself is in pointing the finger of blame at others any time something goes wrong. One of the fundamental principles of the entitled employee is, "It's not my fault."

- **Aversion to constructive criticism.** In order to help employees continually improve, leaders in organizations give them constructive criticism. Unfortunately, employees with an entitlement mentality have an aversion to constructive criticism because they have seldom been criticized. Rather, they have grown up in an environment that emphasized how special they are and that avoided criticism so to not damage their self-esteem. Entitled employees tend to view constructive criticism as just plain criticism and often respond to it by asking "Why are you always picking on me?"

- **Short attention span and need for instant gratification.** Entitled employees grew up in an environment that almost guaranteed them a short attention span and a need for instant gratification. A steady diet of music videos, television, and computer games reinforced the short attention span. Living in a world of "instant everything" (cell phones, Internet, microwave ovens, etc.) ensured that they never had to wait for anything. Consequently, entitled employees never learned how to focus on a long-term, difficult activity and see it through to completion. This lack of perseverance causes serious problems in the workplace since most projects require staying focused for an extended period of time and delaying gratification until the completion of the projects.

- **Unrealistic expectations.** Entitled employees typically want right now what their more experienced colleagues and superiors worked years and even decades to achieve. Because they have been given so much for so long, they come to the workplace with unrealistic expectations. They often want to go from their entry level positions to the top rung of the career ladder overnight without having to touch any of the rungs in between. Their expectations of earnings, promotions, and perquisites are often unrealistic and completely detached from the realities of the workplace.

TRANSFORMING ENTITLED EMPLOYEES: A TEN-STEP MODEL

As was mentioned earlier, transforming entitled employees into peak performing producers requires a concerted effort and patience, but it can be done. What follows is a ten-step model that is a compilation of the various techniques I have used in working as a business consultant and that I have seen used by developmental leaders in client organizations. A major benefit of this model is that not only will it help transform entitled employees it will reinforce the work ethic of employees who are already peak performers. The model is similar to the one used earlier to establish a peak-performance corporate culture in organizations but modified and tailored specifically for use in overcoming the entitlement mentality in employees. The steps in the model are as follows:

- Expect
- Communicate
- Orient
- Role model
- Mentor
- Train
- Monitor

- Reinforce

- Appraise

- Assess

Setting High Expectations for Employees

Performance begins with expectations. Entitled employees may have never faced a situation in which there are high expectations that are non-negotiable. Consequently, leaders in organizations must begin the transformational process by deciding what the work ethic and performance expectations of employees are and, then, writing them down. An excellent way to capture work-ethic expectations is in a work-ethic statement. Such statements work best when they are adopted for the entire organization rather than just an individual department or some other subunit. Here is an example of a work-ethic statement:

> *Maintaining a positive work ethic is a high priority in our organization. In order to be competitive in today's global environment, our organization must have personnel who are willing to work hard, work smart, and when necessary, work long. We succeed only by outperforming the competition on a consistent basis. In order to do this our personnel must achieve peak performance on a consistent basis and improve continually. High priority work-ethic characteristics in our organization are: diligence, self-reliance, self-discipline, responsibility, accountability, and hard work.*

A work-ethic statement such as this one that is adopted organization-wide will establish high expectations for employees.

Communicate Expectations to Employees

Once the work-ethic statement has been adopted, it must be communicated to employees. This is the responsibility of organizational leaders in all departments and functional units. All employees should receive a copy of the work-ethic statement as part of their unit-level orientation and have it explained to them by the unit leader. In addition to distributing and explaining the work-ethic statement, organizations should convey their performance-related expectations in job descriptions and performance appraisal instruments.

If such characteristics as diligence, self-reliance, self-discipline, responsibility, accountability, and hard work are part of the work-ethic statement, they should also be reflected in the job descriptions of employees. If they appear in employee job descriptions, there should be corresponding criteria for them in performance-appraisal instruments. When employees see what is expected of them in the work-ethic statement, their job descriptions, and the organization's performance-appraisal instruments, they will get the message that the expectations are real and should be taken seriously.

Orient Employees to the Work-Ethic Expectations

Using unit-level orientations to get new employees off to a good start was the subject of an earlier chapter. It is reviewed briefly here since it is the third step in the model for transforming entitled employees. As was explained in the previous step, during unit-level orientations unit leaders distribute the work-ethic statement to new employees and explain it. Employees should be allowed to comment on the expectations and ask questions about them. For organizational leaders, this is an excellent opportunity to tactfully welcome members of the entitlement generation to the *real world*.

Role Model the Work-Ethic Expectations for Employees

The most important rule of leadership is to set a positive example. This rule is especially important when trying to transform entitled employees. Leaders in organizations must be exemplary role models of what they expect of employees. Entitled employees will be even quicker than others to use the leader's poor example as an excuse for ignoring expectations. Leaders who expect diligence, self-reliance, self-discipline, responsibility, accountability, and hard work from employees must show them what these things look like in practical terms by their examples.

Mentor Employees in Accordance with the Work-Ethic Expectations

It is important to expect diligence, self-reliance, self-discipline, responsibility, accountability, and hard work from employees, but it is not enough. Organizational leaders must understand that entitled employees may not know what these things look like in practical terms. They may not know what it means to be diligent and self-reliant, for example. For this reason, a mentor should be assigned to new employees. A good time to do this is at the end of the unit-level orientation. The mentor should be an experienced team member who is an exemplary role model of the organization's work-ethic expectations and corporate culture. The mentor will work with new employees for a specified period of time or until she determines that they understand the organization's performance expectations and have internalized them.

Train Employees in Accordance with the Work-Ethic Expectations

When trying to transform entitled employees into peak-performing producers it important to provide more than just job-specific training. As important as job-specific training is, it tends to be technical and, thus, does not get at the issue or work-ethic expectations. This is why organizational leaders should provide training on such concepts as diligence, self-reliance, self-discipline, responsibility, accountability, and hard work for employees in addition to job-specific training. There is a great deal of training material available on these and other work-ethic concepts that organizations can use for helping employees adopt the desired work-ethic characteristics.

Monitor in Accordance with the Work-Ethic Expectations

Monitoring on a daily basis is an important part of transforming entitled employees. Whatever is expected of employees should be monitored. Ignoring actions and behaviors that are at odds with performance expectations is a mistake. Entitled employees tend to interpret what is ignored as being acceptable. The minute leaders observe unacceptable behavior from entitled employees, they should act. Human behavior can become habitual. Consequently, it is important for leaders in organizations to correct unacceptable behavior immediately before it becomes habitual.

Reinforce the Work-Ethic Expectations

Just as leaders must act immediately to correct inappropriate behaviors from entitled employees, they must also reinforce appropriate behaviors. Public praise is an effective form of reinforcement. What makes it effective is its public aspect. When employees are recognized in front of their peers, the value of the recognition is multiplied. To make public praise even more effective, tie it to a specific act or behavior. Go beyond telling the employee he has done well—tell him specifically what he has done well. This will reinforce the appropriate behavior for the employee in question and for those who witness the recognition.

Evaluate in Accordance with the Work-Ethic Expectations

It is a mistake to expect one thing from employees and evaluate another. Consequently, organizational leaders should make sure that there are criteria in performance-appraisal instruments that match the work-ethic expectations. One way to do this is to have one criterion for each expectation listed in the work-ethic statement. Another is to have one broad criterion covering all work-ethic expectations. Either way is acceptable. What is not acceptable is to leave work-ethic expectations off of performance-appraisal instruments.

Assess the State of the Work Ethic throughout the Organization

Periodically assessing the state of the work ethic is a good idea. Typically conducting an organization-wide assessment every five years is sufficient unless there are obvious reasons for doing it more frequently. An effective way to conduct an organization-wide assessment is to turn the work-ethic expectations into a survey instrument that is distributed to all personnel in the organization and completed without attribution. Using on-line survey software will make the assessment easier to distribute, collect, compile, and analyze.

Work-ethic expectations are converted into survey questions by writing them in statement form and asking personnel to rate the statement according to a scale provided. For example, the following scale works well:

- 0 = Completely false

- 2 = Somewhat false

- 4 = Somewhat true

- 6 = Completely true

The work-ethic expectations are turned into statements that can be rated according to this scale or any other that leaders in organizations might adopt. What follows are examples of work-ethic expectations that have been turned into survey statements:

- All personnel in our organization are diligent in their work.

- All personnel in our organization are self-reliant in their approach to work.

- All personnel in our organization are self-disciplined in getting their work done.

- All personnel in our organization seek responsibility.

- All personnel in our organization hold themselves accountable for the quality of their work.

- All personnel in our organization are willing to work as hard as necessary to get the job done.

The organization-wide mean score for each statement is computed—something the survey software will do automatically. With the results compiled, leaders in the organization can analyze them and determine where problems exist. Problems identified can then be worked on.

Most new hires in organizations will come from the 18 to 40 year-old population cohort. This is the age group whose members are most likely to have an entitlement mentality. Of course there are many in this age group who do not have an entitlement mentality and there are those in other age groups who do. Regardless of their age, entitled employees represent a major challenge for leaders in organizations that are trying to help employees achieve peak performance and continual improvement. But this is a challenge that can be mastered. The ten-step model presented herein is a good place to start.

GROUP TRAINING ACTIVITY

Assume that your group is an ad hoc committee that has been formed to advise higher management on how to establish a positive work ethic as a major element of the organization's corporate culture. Assume further that the work ethic problems observed by executives, managers, and supervisors are not limited to new employees or those that fall into the 18 to 40 age cohort. Develop a draft plan for enhancing the work ethic organization-wide that can be submitted to higher management.

NOTES

1. Robert Eisenberger. *Blue Monday: The Loss of the Work Ethic in America.* Retrieved from http://www.amazon.com/Bule-Monday-Loss-Ethic-America/dp/1557781338 on December 8, 2008.

2. Lee Mueller. "Coal Firm Wants to Hire Hispanics: Cites Declining Work Ethic of E. KY. Miners," *The Lexington Herald-Leader.* Retrieved from http://www.redorbit.com/modules/news/tools.php?tool=print&id=382822 on March 24, 2009.

3. Ibid.

4. Conversation with Dr. Michael Fregger in February 2007 in his office (quote used with permission).

5. R. B. Hill. "Historical context of the work ethic." Retrieved from www.coe.edu/~rhill/workethic/hist/htm on December 13, 2006.

6. Amy McCortney. "Revisting the work ethic in America." Career Development Quarterly. Retrieved from http://findarticles.com/p/articles/mi_m0JAX/is_2_52/ai_112090762 on December 19, 2008.

7. CHOICE Institutes Brochure. Okaloosa Public Schools, September 2006.

Six

MOTIVATION

Best Practice Number 6: *Become proficient at motivating employees and helping them become self-motivated.*

Good leaders are good motivators. They have to be. Motivating employees is an important leadership skill. People can be incredibly persistent and creative at accomplishing things they really want to achieve, a fact that makes motivation all the more important. A highly-motivated individual can be an unstoppable force. Even in the face of major roadblocks and severe adversity, highly-motivated employees will typically find a way to get the job done. For this reason, motivating employees to achieve peak performance and continual improvement in pursuing the organization's goals is a worthy endeavor for organizational leaders.

In organizations, the short-term goal of motivation is to encourage employees to achieve peak performance and continual improvement. This is external motivation. The long-term goal of motivation is to help employees become self-motivated. When employees become self-motivated, striving for peak performance and continual improvement becomes normal behavior. Self-motivated employees require little supervision and will work just as well when they are not being observed by organizational leaders as when they are being observed.

MOTIVATION DEFINED

When it is said that an individual is motivated, it means that she feels driven to do something. This drive can be internal, external, or a combination of both. The ideal state is for motivation to be internal. When leaders in organizations speak of motivation, they are speaking of the drive to perform at peak levels, continually improve, and strive for excellence. A highly-motivated employee is one who will consistently strive to excel and for whom peak performance is the norm. Such an individual will strive for excellence, not just when supervised but also when unsupervised. Developing self-motivated employees must always be a goal of executives, managers, and supervisors who want to be developmental leaders.

Often an organization's performance-appraisal form will contain a criterion that asks how well employees work without supervision. This is an important criterion because organizations need employees who will do their best, not just when they are being observed, but also when they are not. Employees who need close and constant attention can take up so much of a leader's time and energy that there is little left over for other responsibilities. When this happens, organizational leaders are no longer leading, guiding, and assisting, they are babysitting. Babysitting of employees is a counterproductive enterprise that contributes nothing to achieving peak performance or continual improvement.

MOTIVATIONAL CONTEXT

When learning specific motivational techniques, it helps to view them in a context that allows for systematic observation. Abraham Maslow established a workable context for motivational techniques with his well-known *hierarchy of human needs*. Maslow posited that people are motivated by basic human needs that can be categorized according to level, from the lowest level to the highest. An important point to understand about motivating employees is that there are two sides to the formula. One side involves proactively doing things that motivate people. The other involves eliminating factors that are de-motivators.

When reading the motivational techniques explained in this chapter, remember that there are times when the best way to motivate employees is to remove de-motivators. De-motivators are factors that rob employees of their drive to perform at peak levels. All motivational techniques presented in this chapter are explained within the context of Maslow's hierarchy of needs. The levels of human need set forth by Maslow from lowest to highest are as follows: (1)

- Physiological needs

- Safety and security needs

- Social needs

- Esteem needs

- Self-actualization needs

Maslow posited that people will focus on their lowest unmet needs. Although his work concerning human needs applies to life in the broader sense, it can be applied specifically to the workplace. Maslow's five levels of human needs provide a context for systematically learning techniques for externally motivating employees. Employees who are externally motivated to achieve peak performance and continual improvement will experience the rewards that come to those who excel. Once they experience the rewards that result from their externally-motivated performance, they will be more likely to become self-motivated.

PHYSIOLOGICAL NEEDS AND MOTIVATION

The physiological needs of a human being—sometimes referred to as the basic survival needs—include air, water, food, clothing, and shelter. In Maslow's hierarchy, these represent the lowest level of human needs. Unless these basic needs are satisfied, people will focus on little else. For example, in the days before a natural disaster such as a hurricane, tornado, or earthquake, people in organizations are focused on normal work-related concerns such as meeting deadlines, job security, earning promotions, salary increases, benefits, taking vacations, relationships with their colleagues, getting the recognition they deserve for their work, and so on. However, when their basic survival needs are threatened by a natural disaster, work-related concerns suddenly go by the wayside. The focus of people in the aftermath of a natural disaster becomes basic survival needs, and what motivates them is anything that will contribute to meeting those needs.

At first glance it might seem that basic survival needs have nothing to do with an individual's motivation at work. However, a closer look reveals direct ties between an individual's job and the quality of the air, water, food, clothing, and shelter available to that individual. In fact, having a job is how most people generate the income to provide these basic needs for themselves and their families. This fact can be used to help motivate employees in organizations. Employees who understand Maslow's hierarchy of needs and the place basic survival needs hold in the hierarchy are more likely to appreciate having a job.

Organizational leaders must understand that the key to using basic survival needs to motivate employees is helping them make the connection between their job and these needs. Many people take life's basic needs for granted. As long as they have a good job, they give little or no consideration to such concerns as air, water, food, clothing, and shelter. But people who have experienced the debilitating effects of long-term unemployment have a different perspective. They know first-hand how losing a job can change their circumstances as well as their focus.

During the great recession that began in 2007, many people who had been corporate executives one day found themselves in the unemployment line the next. People who had never known want suddenly found themselves worried about securing the most basic of necessities. This connection between employment and life's basic needs can be used to motivate employees if it is used right. Using basic survival needs to motivate is simply a matter of helping employees see the connection between basic needs and their jobs. Employees who understand the connection are less likely to take the needs or the job for granted.

Talking about the connection between basic human needs and employment during team meetings and in one-on-one conversations can enhance the value of having a job in the eyes of employees. Further, it can eliminate the tendency of people to take life's basic needs for granted. An effective and non-threatening way to initiate conversations about the connection between work and basic human needs is to use unemployment stories from the local newspaper.

The key to helping employees make the connection without feeling threatened by it is tact. Think of tact as driving in the nail without breaking the board. The point of this motivational technique is to helps employee see their jobs as being worthy of working hard to keep. Of course, this technique works better during difficult economic times than during times of prosperity, but if used effectively and with tact it can be helpful at any time.

SAFETY AND SECURITY NEEDS AND MOTIVATION

The next level of human needs in Maslow's hierarchy is safety and security. Safety and security needs include safety from physical harm and security from crime, health problems, and financial adversity. For most people, these needs relate directly to their employment. By working, people are able to earn the income necessary to provide a measure of safety and security for themselves and their families. The better the job and the higher the income, the more the individual can invest in safety and security. A home in a safe neighborhood, a security system, financial investments, quality healthcare, and various types of insurance are all things people use to ensure safety and security for themselves and their families. Of course, all of these things cost money.

Most people must work to earn the income necessary to provide a measure of safety and security for themselves and their families. Consequently, for working people job security is a major concern. No job—no security. This fact allows leaders in organizations to use job security as another tool for motivating their personnel. The key to using safety and security needs to motivate employees is helping them understand the role their individual performance can play in securing their own job security.

In order to provide jobs for people, private-sector organizations must be able to compete in their markets and win the competition on a consistent basis. For some, the competition is local. For others it might be regional, national, or global. Regardless of the nature of the competition, all private-sector organizations face the daily challenge of having to outperform the competition in order to survive.

Public-sector organizations also have to face the daily challenge of competition, but in a different form. The competition for public-sector organizations is to provide the highest-quality services possible while requiring the lowest possible tax support. Public-sector organizations compete against their own internal benchmarks as well as other public-sector organizations that might perform better by comparison. The same can be said for non-profit organizations. The key here is to understand that all organizations—private, public, and non-profit—face competition in some form.

Whether they work in a private-sector firm, a public-sector agency, or a non-profit organization, employees can contribute much to their own job security, a fact that can be used to motivate them. People place a high value on job security because their job is the principal vehicle for satisfying their other security needs. This is why organizational leaders must make sure that employees understand how their individual performance affects the overall performance of the organization. The connection employees need to understand is this: 1) the better they perform, the better the organization performs; 2) the better the organization performs the more competitive it will be; and 3) the more competitive the organization the more job security it can offer its employees.

Executives, managers, and supervisors sometimes make the mistake of assuming that the connection between employee performance and job security is intuitively understood by their personnel. This is a bad assumption. Not only do organizations have employees who do not understand the connection between performance and job security, these uninformed employees are surprisingly common. However, once employees understand the connection between performance and job security, they typically find its significance motivating. Consequently, explaining the connection between employee performance and job security can be an excellent motivational technique.

Case: Motivating by Connecting the Dots for Employees

A supervisor I know in a mid-sized technology company often uses the connection between job security and employee performance to motivate his team members. He is known for frequently reminding his personnel that every day of the week there are people in competing firms in China, Japan, Korea and other countries trying to take their company's customers away. He tells his team members that these foreign competitors strive to get their employees to work harder and work smarter so they can outperform them and their company. He tells his team members that if foreign firms take their company's customers away, they will also take their jobs away.

This supervisor tells his team members that they can lose their jobs to foreign competition on any given day, but that this does not have to happen—not ever. All they have to do to keep foreign competitors from taking their jobs is outperform them. He encourages his team members to give their best every minute of every day and to get better all the time. Finally, he reassures his team members by telling them that if they work harder and smarter than their counterparts in competing firms, they have nothing to fear.

SOCIAL NEEDS AND MOTIVATION

Organizational leaders should remember that people are social beings. It is part of the nature of most people to need relationships with others. The social needs of people include their need for family, friends, and a sense of belonging—a sense of being part of a group. An individual's job can have a lot to do with meeting these needs. On the other hand, it can also fail to help meet these needs and become forty hours a week of high stress and drudgery. Many of the relationships in people's lives are tied to their jobs. In addition to providing for relationships, a job can also help meet an individual's need for a sense of belonging.

Positive relationships with team members, colleagues, supervisors, and managers are important to people at work because these relationships help meet the individual's social needs. People who have negative relationships with people at work often experience low morale and high stress. Positive relationships at work can help motivate employees to perform at peak levels. Conversely, negative relationships can rob employees of the motivation to perform well. Organizational leaders who understand the importance of positive relationships can use building relationships at work as a motivating strategy.

For organizational leaders, relationship building has three components: 1) establishing positive working relationships with employees, 2) facilitating positive working relationships among employees, and 3) repairing damaged or broken relationships. Executives, managers, and supervisors can establish positive working relationships with their personnel by: 1) communicating often and well, 2) being good listeners, 3) being honest and trustworthy, 4) encouraging employee input and feedback, 5) being fair and equitable, 6) treating employees with respect, 7) being a positive and consistent example of what is expected of employees, 8) sharing the same burdens and circumstances employees face, 9) recognizing employees for doing a good job, 10) caring about employees as well as the work to be done, 11) being advocates for employees with higher management, and 12) forthrightly admitting it when wrong and apologizing.

In addition to building positive relationships with employees, organizational leaders must be attentive to facilitating the establishment and maintenance of positive relationships among employees. This can involve both teamwork and conflict management. Both of these topics are covered in detail elsewhere in this book. That coverage will not be repeated here. At this point, it is important only to understand that positive peer relationships at work motivate while negative peer relationships de-motivate. Creating opportunities for employees to get to know each other as people and interceding to help resolve conflicts will help motivate them and minimize the de-motivating effects of conflict.

Other relationship-oriented techniques that can be used to motivate employees relate to the concept of *affiliation.* Some people are achievement-oriented while others are affiliation-oriented. Affiliation-oriented people are motivated by being part of a team or some other defined group. They are motivated by the esteem they feel from their peers for helping the team perform better. Another name for affiliation-oriented people is team players. Every employee can and should learn to be a good team player, but affiliation-oriented people are natural team players—they do not have to learn the concept.

Organizational leaders can recognize affiliation-oriented employees by watching for people who show signs of needing to be part of something—needing to belong. The needs of some people to belong to a group can be used to motivate them by applying the following techniques:

- Provide opportunities for social interaction with team mates and peers (e.g. after-hours social events).

- Ask affiliation-oriented employees to help others in the team improve in specific areas of weakness.

- Ask affiliation-oriented employees to keep their fingers on the pulse of the team's morale and share any problems they sense with the team leader.

A word of caution is in order here. Affiliation-oriented employees will sometimes choose team harmony over team performance. Consequently, organizational leaders should make a point of talking with these types of employees one-on-one and reminding them that going along to get along will rarely improve team performance and that a happy team is not necessarily a productive team.

ESTEEM NEEDS AND MOTIVATION

People have an inherent need for self-esteem as well as for the esteem of others. Esteem relates to the self-respect, worth, and dignity people feel. People with positive self-esteem feel good about themselves. They have self-respect and self-worth. Typically, people who lack self-esteem also lack self-respect and self-worth. A lack of self-esteem can result in feelings of inadequacy, and such feelings can be powerful de-motivators. Consequently, as with most motivational techniques, when using esteem needs to motivate employees to peak performance it is important to also remove de-motivators.

In helping people at work build self-esteem and win the esteem of their peers, a variety of techniques are available including: 1) achievement, 2) competition, 3) potential for promotions, 4) incentives, and 5) legacy. All of the techniques that are explained in the following paragraphs can help employees build self-esteem and win the esteem of peers.

Using Achievement Activities to Motivate

Achievement can result in a feeling of accomplishment. Accomplishing tasks that are both important and difficult helps build self-esteem. Most people have an inherent need to achieve, although some do not. Because there are people who are not motivated by achievement, the first step in applying the techniques explained in this section is to identify those team members who are achievement-oriented.

Such people are usually easy to recognize. They tend to be task and goal-oriented. They are typically independent-thinkers who need continual reinforcement and who focus intently on evaluations of their performance. Achievement-oriented employees like to collect physical evidence of their achievements such as certificates, trophies, plaques, and other recognition memorabilia. The message in this for leaders in organizations is that recognition is important to achievement-oriented people. Understanding this, organizational leaders can use the following techniques to motivate achievement-oriented employees:

- Share the goals of the organization, department, or team with achievement-oriented employees and tell them specifically what they can do to help accomplish the goals.

- Put achievement-oriented employees in charge of specific high-priority projects they can call their own. Let them know what needs to be done and give them a deadline. Then step back and give them room to work. Do not micromanage achievement-oriented employees.

- Recognize achievement-oriented employees both formally and informally. Informal recognition need be nothing more than a public pat on the back from time to time. Formal recognition may be public rewards such as certificates, plaques, trophies, or other memorabilia appropriate to the achievement. The important aspect of this technique is the public aspect. Achievement-oriented employees need to be recognized publically. Public recognition in the presence of their peers and others whose opinions they value is part of what achievement-oriented employees seek.

A word of caution is in order when using achievement to motivate. Achievement-oriented employees who appear to be self-serving and more interested in personal glory than the organization's best interests can damage employee morale. Affiliation-oriented employees are especially sensitive to self-serving behavior in other employees. To get the most from achievement-oriented employees without damaging team harmony, organizational leaders should confront the issue directly.

Talking with achievement and affiliation-oriented employees one-on-one and explaining the contributions each can make to team performance will help. Explaining how achievement and affiliation-oriented team members are needed as well as how they can complement each other will help get the best from both groups. Reminding achievement-oriented employees to thank those who helped and supported them whenever they are recognized will help maintain team harmony. It also helps to maintain a balance between achievement and affiliation-oriented team members to the extent possible.

Using Competition to Motivate

Most people like to win personally and to be affiliated with a winning team. Winning builds self-esteem. Watch children as they play games. They like to outperform other children who challenge them. A child's competitive spirit is nurtured through play and often through participation in organized sports. Organizational leaders can use the natural competitive spirit most people have to motivate employees, but caution is the order of the day when using competition as a motivational technique. In order to have the desired effect, competition on the job must be thoroughly planned, closely monitored, and carefully controlled.

Competition that is not properly planned, monitored, and controlled can go awry and result in a win-at-any-cost attitude. When this happens, employees can lose sight of the real goal of improved performance. If winning at any cost becomes the goal instead of improved performance, undermining the work of other employees becomes a legitimate strategy. Out-of-control competition can lead to cheating and hard feelings among team members. If this is allowed to happen, the competition will do more harm than good.

The following tips can help leaders in organizations ensure that competition is properly controlled and that it contributes to improved performance:

- Involve the employees who will compete in planning the competition, and explain to them that improved performance is the goal. Be frank in letting employees know that behavior that undermines the team's performance is unacceptable and will only hurt them and everyone else on the team.

- To the extent possible, plan the competition so that it is between teams rather than individuals. Competition between individuals can quickly become personal and counterproductive.

- Make sure the competition is as fair as it can possibly be by dividing resources equally or proportionally among the teams that will compete.

- Be specific in selecting the basis of the competition—what is actually to be improved. Several areas that lend themselves to positive competition are quality, waste rates, sales volume, production rates, absentee rates, and safety records.

- Establish benchmarks and make sure everyone involved understands how performance improvements will be measured against these benchmarks.

Case: Competition Can Get Out of Hand

The following case illustrates how competition intended to improve performance can go awry and actually undermine it. A manufacturing company had two shifts, a day shift and a night shift. Both shifts used the same machines and equipment and produced the same parts for the automotive industry. At the end of its shift, the day crew was responsible for performing routine maintenance on all machines and getting them ready for the night shift. The night shift, in turn, was to reciprocate in kind. The basis of the competition was to see which shift could produce the most parts in a month while simultaneously maintaining or improving quality and waste rates.

The competition went well for the first month with the day shift edging out the night shift in a tight race that saw both shifts improve their productivity, quality, and waste rates. Then in the second month when it looked like the day shift was going to win again, things began to happen—bad things. Day shift machinists began to complain that the night shift was not performing the routine maintenance and set up tasks they were responsible for. This forced the day crew to waste valuable production time setting up the machines before they could begin work. Predictably, the day shift retaliated in kind. Soon both shifts were complaining that routine maintenance was being neglected and that end-of-shift set up was no longer being done.

By the time management figured out what was happening, the situation had deteriorated to the point of sabotage. Members of both shifts were actually sabotaging the work of their competitors. Before long quality problems and waste rates were at record high levels and productivity was lower than it had been before the competition. In addition to these performance problems, employee morale hit an all-time low and supervisors spent more time refereeing than supervising.

An investigation into the situation later revealed that winning the competition had become more important than the original goal of improving performance. Once this win-at-any-cost attitude set in, the way the scenario unfolded was predictable. The best way to beat the competition is to outperform them, but if this is not working another way is to undermine them. When the night shift thought it was about to lose the competition two months in a row, desperation set in and some of its members began to take drastic action. Once the night shift's cheating was recognized by the day shift, a payback mentality set in and the cheating spiraled out of control.

This case is not intended to argue against using competition to motivate. Rather, it is provided to remind leaders in organizations to take human nature into account when using competition. Once the competition has been planned but before getting started, conduct a *roadblock analysis.* This is done by brainstorming with other leaders and employees about what roadblocks or unintended consequences might arise that could derail the competition and undermine performance. Once all potential roadblocks have been identified, go back to the planning phase and find ways to eliminate, mitigate, or control them.

Using the Potential for Promotions to Motivate

Employees typically want to climb the career ladder. Ambitious, self-motivated employees hope that over the course of their careers they will be promoted to increasingly higher levels and higher paying jobs. When this happens, it builds self-esteem and helps earn the esteem of colleagues. Consequently, opportunities for promotions can motivate employees who are career-minded. However, like most motivation strategies promotions can have either a positive or negative effect depending on how they are handled. The two basic approaches to promotions are: 1) promoting from within, and 2) hiring from outside. Of the two, promoting from within is the approach most likely to be a motivator, provided the promotion process is effective.

The following rules of thumb will help ensure that the organization's process for filling higher level positions by promoting from within is an effective motivation strategy:

- *Never promote solely on the basis of seniority.* An employee with many years of experience might not necessarily be the best qualified person for a given position. Seniority is a legitimate factor to consider when making promotions, but it should not be the only factor. It is better to use seniority as a tie breaker when the other factors considered are equal. If a senior employee is promoted over a less senior but more qualified employee, morale will suffer and the promotion process will be a de-motivator.

- *Do not promote on the basis of popularity.* Personal popularity is no guarantee of effectiveness in a new and higher level position. It is not uncommon for a team member to be popular for reasons that have nothing to do with performance. Even if an individual is well-liked, she will still have to be able to do the new job and do it well. If the popular employee is not able to perform the new job effectively, she will not be popular long, and the credibility of the promotion process will suffer.

- *Do not promote on the basis of friendship.* Friendship should never be the reason behind an employee promotion. Promotions that are viewed by other team members as being influenced by friendship are doomed from the outset. Further, allowing friendship to influence promotions will not only serve to de-motivate employees, it will undermine the promotion process.

To ensure that the possibility of being promoted is a motivator, organizational leaders must tie promotions to performance. Employees must know that if they consistently meet or exceed performance expectations, they have a realistic chance of being promoted. If they believe the process is tainted by seniority, popularity, or friendship, the promotion process will be a de-motivator.

Using Incentives to Motivate

One of the most common topics of conversation among people at work is wages and salaries. There is more than economics to an individual's paycheck. There is also the issue of esteem. Generally speaking, the more people earn the more they are esteemed by their peers and the greater their self-esteem. One can debate the advisability of tying esteem to income, but there is no question that people do it.

One way for employees to increase their income is by earning incentive pay. For those motivated by money, incentive pay can be doubly motivating. First, there is the obvious motivation of receiving the extra money. But this is not the only motivational benefit of properly managed incentive programs. Such programs also give employees opportunities for achievement. Just the fact that employees receive incentives over and beyond their normal pay—irrespective of the actual amount—can be a motivator because doing so represents an achievement. This is one of the reasons that achievement-oriented employees typically respond well to incentives.

In order to gain the motivational benefits of incentives, organizational leaders must plan and manage incentive programs carefully. Poorly planned and managed incentives can quickly become de-motivators. The following strategies can help ensure the effectiveness of incentive programs:

- *Define the objectives.* The overall purpose of an incentive program is to motivate employees to perform at peak levels. This should be understood by leaders and all employees who might earn the incentives. But just stating this overall purpose is not enough. Organizational leaders must take the next step and define specifically what is to be accomplished. Does the organization hope to improve productivity? Quality? Safety? Customer satisfaction? All of these? In addition to making employees aware of the overall purpose of the incentive program, it is also important to make them aware of the specific objectives.

- *Set a positive example.* By offering incentives, leaders in organizations establish high expectations for employee performance. This means that certain types of performance-enhancing behaviors are expected of employees. It is not enough to just offer incentive money for those who demonstrate the expected behaviors and produce the desired results. Organizational leaders must also make a point of exemplifying the expected behaviors. Remember that one of the most fundamental principles of leadership is setting a positive example. Organizational leaders can do this by exemplifying the behaviors they expect of employees. This is sometimes referred to as walking the walk instead of just talking the talk.

- *Award incentives to teams whenever possible.* Awarding incentives to teams can be more effective than awarding them to individuals. An exception to this rule of thumb is sales. Often sales personnel operate like independent contractors. However, in most cases people work in teams. In teams people depend on each other to get the job done. Because of this interdependence, other team members who have contributed to improved performance might resent just one member receiving the incentives. If this happens the incentive program can backfire and do more harm than good.

- *Make incentives meaningful.* For an incentive program to be effective, the incentives offered must be meaningful to potential recipients. Giving employees rewards they do not value will not produce the desired results. An effective way for ensuring that incentives are meaningful to employees is to involve them in developing the list of incentives that will be made available. The employees who are to be motivated know better than anyone else what types of incentives will motivate them and what types will not. In other words, if you want to know what types of incentives will motivate employees, ask them.

- *Establish specific criteria.* If the purpose of the incentives is to improve various aspects of performance—productivity, quality, customer service, safety—there must be specific criteria for measuring improvements. On what basis will incentives be awarded? Specific criteria should be developed to define the levels of performance that are to be rewarded. For example, assume that one of the areas of improvement is customer satisfaction and the satisfaction rate is currently 78 percent. The overall goal in this area is 100 percent customer satisfaction. However, organizational leaders might decide to award incentive bonuses every time the customer service rate improves by a certain amount—say five percent. It is important for employees to know specifically how performance improvements will be measured. This means establishing benchmarks against which improvement will be measured and establishing intermediate and overall improvement targets.

- *Communicate, communicate, communicate.* Employees must be completely informed about the incentive program if the incentives are going to have the desired motivational effect. Employees should know the purpose of the incentive program, its specific objectives, the improvement criteria, when incentives will be awarded and how often, changes that are made to the program, and anything else that will help maintain the program's effectiveness and credibility. With incentive programs, there should be no surprises.

Case: An Effective Incentive Program

A case from the textile industry illustrates how effective a properly planned and managed incentive program can be. A textile plant that manufactured tee shirts was having productivity problems. The quality of its product was excellent, but it was taking too much time per garment to produce its products. In order to compete with off-shore companies, this firm needed to maintain a specified volume of work for each of its production cells on every shift while holding the scrap rate to less than two percent. In the beginning, the company was not meeting the minimum production volume or scrap-rate goals.

The leadership of this company decided to use incentives to improve productivity. The overall purpose of the incentive program was to improve productivity while maintaining quality. Specific performance criteria were: 1) increase the number of tee shirts produced in a shift by each production cell by 25 percent, and 2) maintain a scrap rate of less than two percent. For every five percent of improved production, a production team (cell) would receive an incentive bonus that would be divided among its members—provided, of course, that the scrap rate was less than two percent. The incentive dollars earned would be paid weekly as an addition to employee paychecks.

When the employees in each work cell understood how much extra income they could earn by meeting the new performance criteria, their attitudes toward work improved noticeably. Prior to establishment of the incentive program, employees in each work cell earned the same amount of money no matter how many tee shirts they produced in a given shift. The producers and the slackers were paid the same amount without consideration of their performance. Predictably, employee breaks were frequent and long, there was much idle conversation in the work cells, and using company time to attend to personal business by telephone was common.

However, once the incentive program was established on a team basis, the income of team members was determined in large part by the performance of other team members. Establishing a benchmark production quota and offering incentive pay to those teams that exceeded the quota cast the work of each cell in a new light. Suddenly, team members expected each other to arrive at work on time, start work immediately, minimize breaks, and strive to maximize performance.

In the past employees had simply looked the other way when team mates who were perfectly well took paid sick-leave days, but after the incentive program was established peer pressure to be at work became intense. Word soon got out that anyone who took a day of sick leave had better really be sick, and it was employees spreading this message, not managers. This particular plant went from being one of the parent corporation's worst performers to being its best performer. The year after the incentive program was established the plant won the corporation's "top performer" award.

Using the Legacy Question to Motivate

Employees tend to go through stages in their careers. In each stage they are likely to focus on different concerns. For example, when young people first begin their careers, money is their primary work-related concern. This is the income phase of their career. Young people in this phase are concerned primarily with income because they are at the bottom of the pay scale and are just learning what it means to be on their own without the financial support of mom and dad. People who have just begun their careers often suffer from sticker shock when they learn how much it costs to buy or rent a home and pay for gas, water, sewer, electricity, and groceries. This is why they tend to focus so intently on income and why they are typically good candidates for being motivated by monetary incentives.

Once people at work reach the point in their lives where they are earning enough to pay the bills, they begin to focus on whether or not they like their jobs. This is the personal-satisfaction phase of their career. People in this phase want their job to provide them with a sense of personal satisfaction and enjoyment. Of course all jobs have their good days and bad, but people in this stage want to like their jobs, at least generally speaking, after balancing the good days with the bad. In this phase the issue is not money but the extent to which employees enjoy their jobs. For example, there are people who make plenty of money but hate their jobs. On the other hand, there are people who love their jobs in spite of meager earnings.

In the final phase of their careers, people who are relatively satisfied with their income and generally like their jobs begin to focus on the legacy question. The legacy question grows out of a need people have to know that their work matters—that their work is important, has meaning, and allows the individual to make a difference. For most people, knowing that their work is important builds self-esteem. Knowing that others think their work is important adds to the esteem. When they believe that their work matters, people are more likely to believe that they matter. Philosophers and theologians will argue that people have value irrespective of their work—and they certainly do. However, there is no denying that people tend to tie their self-worth to the relative worth of their jobs. People with this perspective consider their life's work a major part of their legacy.

This human desire to matter and to leave a worthy legacy can be used to motivate employees who are in the legacy phase of their careers. Legacy-minded people will work harder and smarter when they believe their work matters. Consequently, organizational leaders can motivate legacy-minded employees by helping them see the importance of their work and the contributions they make. The story of the three laborers illustrates how important it is that people understand the value of their work.

Case: Seeing the Value in your Work.

Three laborers had been hired to dig irrigation ditches for a farmer. A man walking by saw them working and was curious, so he stopped and asked the first laborer, "What are you doing?" The laborer—obviously was not enjoying his work—stopped digging, scowled and said, "Just digging a ditch." The man thanked him and approached the next laborer. He asked this worker the same question: "What are you doing." The laborer stopped digging, wiped his brow with a handkerchief, and said with a shrug, "Just trying to make a living." The man thanked him and walked over to the next laborer.

"What are you doing?" The laborer stopped digging, smiled broadly, and with great enthusiasm said: "Mister, I'll tell you what I'm doing. I am creating a masterpiece! See this field. Right now it's just dirt and dust. But close your eyes and open your mind as I describe what it is going to be. When I finish digging these irrigation ditches, the farmer who owns this land will plant seeds and use these ditches to water them. Then, in a matter of just a few weeks, this forty-acre tract of bare earth will be transformed into a Garden of Eden. There will be row upon row of fresh fruit and vegetables of every description. Hundreds of people will have delicious, nutritional food on their tables, and all because of these ditches I am digging. Most people look at this shovel and see a tool for a laborer, and at this field and see just dirt. But I view this shovel as my brush and this field as my canvas."

Because he saw the value in his work, the third laborer worked harder than the other two and was more pleased with the results of his work. He knew he was leaving a legacy that would outlast his life. Organizational leaders who can help their employees gain the perspective of this laborer will take a giant step forward in equipping, enabling, and empowering them for peak performance and continual improvement.

SELF-ACTUALIZATION NEEDS AND MOTIVATION

Self-actualization refers to the human need to achieve one's full potential. In order to achieve self-actualization, people must first satisfactorily meet all of their other needs: basic survival, safety/security, social, and esteem. In reality, few people ever achieve self-actualization. However, with self-actualization the pursuit may be more important than the accomplishment, at least from the perspective of motivation. The U.S. Army was appealing to the human need for self-actualization when its recruiting slogan was: "Be all that you can be."

The key to using self-actualization to motivate is the concept of potential. Leaders in organizations can use the concept of potential to motivate people who want to climb the career ladder as well as those who want to expand their career horizons. Expansion refers to learning new career skills or even a new job through cross-training. The key is to tie both concepts—advancement and expansion—to performance. Those who consistently perform at peak levels must be the ones who advance the fastest in the organization and the ones who are given opportunities to expand their horizons by learning new job skills.

The fact that advancement and expansion should be tied to performance would seem to go without saying, and it should. However, there are organizations that tie advancement and expansion to nothing more than seniority. Further, there are too many cases in which advancement and expansion decisions are influenced by such factors as friendship, who knows whom, and favoritism. Self-actualization needs can be used to motivate only if the potential for advancement or expansion is tied directly to performance. An actual case illustrates this point.

Case: No Self-Actualization in this Organization

John was an advancement-oriented individual. He was a high performer and a good learner. John was always trying to expand his job skills so that he would be a greater asset to his employer and, as a result, climb the career ladder faster. As an engineer, the next step up the ladder for John was project Engineer. In his company, project engineers coordinated specific projects and project teams consisting of other engineers, drafting technicians, and support personnel. To improve his chances of advancing to the level of project engineer, John took a college class in project management. In this class he learned organizing, scheduling, budgeting, staffing, teambuilding, leadership, progress monitoring, and other skills important to project engineers.

As an engineer, John had served on teams led by project engineers who had no project management skills. They had more seniority than John and were good engineers, but could not match his ability to manage projects. It was difficult for John to serve on a project team that was poorly led and badly managed, but this happened all the time. Out of frustration, John began to quietly help the project engineers who led the teams he served on. John did not want to be presumptuous or overstep his authority, so he was quiet and tactful in offering assistance where it was obviously needed. As a result, he became a sought-after team member. Before long word of his prowess spread and all of the project engineers in the company wanted John on their team.

Within a year, a position for a project engineer opened up in John's company. John applied and, because of his widely-acknowledged expertise, was sure he had a good chance of getting the promotion. Consequently, he was shocked when not only was he refused the promotion, but it went to an individual who was widely recognized as the most disorganized engineer in the company. This individual could not even organize his own work, much less that of a project team. Then, to add insult to injury, John was asked to serve on this individual's project teams to help him strengthen his project management skills.

Over the course of a couple of years, this situation repeated itself two more times before John decided he had had enough. Each time John missed out on a promotion to project engineer the decision was attributed to the fact that the person chosen had more seniority. Swallowing his anger, John decided to approach the situation wisely. He worked up a resume and began looking for another job. Before long a competitor hired him. During his exit interview, the company's chief engineer was shocked to learn that losing John—by now a widely-acknowledged asset for the company—was a self-inflicted wound. John did not want to leave, but it had become clear that he would never reach his full potential unless he did. Had this company tied its promotions to performance, it could have retained an outstanding engineer and project manager. As it was, John went to work for a competitor and was soon using his skills to help his new employer outperform his former company.

DEVELOPING PERSONAL MOTIVATION PLANS

There is no one-size-fits-all strategy for motivating people at work. Because motivation is based on meeting individual needs—needs that vary from person to person—developmental leaders are prepared to personalize their motivational strategies. What will motivate a given individual depends on where that individual is in Maslow's Hierarchy of Needs as well as other factors specific to the individual. This is why developmental leaders take the time to get to know their team members. They know where their team members fit into Maslow's Hierarchy and they are aware of other motivation-related factors affecting individuals.

Many developmental leaders develop Personal Motivation Plans (PMPs). A PMP is a brief plan for motivating an individual that takes into account that individual's specific human needs. If the individual in question is achievement-oriented, her PMP will be based on meeting those kinds of needs. If the individual is concerned about his legacy, the strategies in the PMP would be based on meeting legacy needs. The key is to personalize the strategies in the PMP to the individual in question.

A prerequisite to motivating people at work is to develop an understanding of human needs. People are motivated by actions that meet their specific and individual needs. Although the specific needs of individuals differ, there are generic needs that are felt by most people. Abraham Maslow summarized and categorized these generic human needs in his Hierarchy of Needs. Organizational leaders who learn to tie the needs Maslow identified to motivational strategies can become effective at motivating people to perform at peak levels.

GROUP ACTIVITY

Assume that you have just been promoted to the position of department manager. Your department has people in it who are at various stages of their careers. Three of your team members are in need of motivation. One of these team members is a new employee who is just starting her career, one is a long-serving employee who will be eligible to retire in five years, and one is in mid-career and seems to be an achievement-oriented person who is not achieving much. Develop a personal motivation plan for each of these employees. What strategies does the group recommend for each employee?

ENDNOTE

1. Kendra Cherry. "Hierarchy of Needs: The Five Levels of Maslow's Hierarchy of Needs." Retrieved from http://psychology.about.com on February 4, 2011.

Seven

INTEGRITY AND ETHICS

Best Practices Number 7: *Maintain the highest standards of integrity and ethics and help employees emulate this example.*

One of the key building blocks of peak performance is trust. A lack of integrity among leaders in organizations can undermine the trust that is essential to positive relationships with employees—relationships that are essential to peak performance and continual improvement. Without winning the trust of employees, leaders in organizations cannot effectively lead, inspire, or motivate them. Without the trust of their peers employees cannot win acceptance as part of their work team. Without the trust of customers and suppliers, organizations cannot remain competitive. Providing an ethical environment in which trust can flourish is of paramount importance when striving to achieve peak performance and continual improvement.

ETHICAL BEHAVIOR: EASIER TO BELIEVE IN THAN ACHIEVE

Several factors can make working with integrity difficult for people at all levels in an organization. One of the most pervasive of these factors is misguided self-interest. As a concept, misguided self-interest is like a two-sided coin. Side A relates to the potential for personal gain, gain that can be driven by positive factors but that can also be driven by greed, ego, unbridled ambition, or expedience. If the potential for personal gain is sufficiently high, some people will put aside their reservations and make decisions they know are unethical. In these cases, the miscreants either try to rationalize their unethical behavior or simply proceed down the wrong path and hope they will not get caught.

The instinct for survival—Side B of the human-interest coin—can also lead to unethical behavior. This happens when people are under intense pressure to make a certain decision. Because they feel threatened, they respond by making unethical decisions to protect their jobs, careers, egos, or something else of value to them. In these cases, the people in question know they are behaving unethically but feel they have no choice.

Another factor that can lead to unethical behavior in organizations is the human tendency to want immediate tangible results or rewards. Deferred gratification is often a difficult concept for people who grew up in the age of credit cards, cell phones, fast food, overnight delivery, the Internet, microwave ovens, and various other on-demand options. This is unfortunate because the tangible benefits of integrity are often realized only in the long run. Setting aside the personal satisfaction of knowing you have done the right thing, the benefits of integrity are seldom immediate. The long-term payoff can be difficult to accept for people who are accustomed to getting what they want without having to wait.

The intangible rewards of working with integrity such as a clear conscience or personal satisfaction are immediate, but the tangible rewards such as recognition, promotions, salary increases, and bonuses often are not. This is the nature of the workplace. People who are impatient for tangible rewards occasionally try to hurry things along by taking unethical shortcuts. This approach will sometimes produce the desired results in the short run, but in the long run it can cause problems for the individuals in question as well as the organization.

When leaders in organizations pressure employees to take unethical shortcuts or just look the other way when they do, they are setting themselves, the employees, and the organization up for a day of reckoning that will eventually come. When unethical behavior is discovered, as it typically is, the damage is seldom limited to the individuals who are directly involved. Rather, all stakeholders in the organizations—the many—are likely to suffer as a result of the unethical practices of the few. In fact, it is not uncommon for the public to impute the unethical practices of a relatively few people in an organization to everyone in the organization.

Case: Unethical Behavior Tars Everyone in the Organization

I once provided a series of seminars for a sheriff's department in the aftermath of an ethics scandal that resulted in disgrace and prison time for the sheriff and several of his top personnel. Most of the sheriff's deputies knew nothing about the misconduct that brought the sheriff down and were not involved in it. However, for months afterward they were subjected to constant ridicule, animosity, and even scorn by the public they were sworn to serve. Deputies told stories of people trying to refuse speeding tickets claiming the deputies were probably just going to "pocket" the money themselves. They also told of numerous other instances of behavior that was not just disrespectful but bordered on criminal resistance. These were deputies whose behavior was unquestionably ethical and who were just trying to perform their sworn duties. But because of the unethical behavior of a few, the entire sheriff's department was painted with the same broad brush by the public. This is precisely what can happen when a few people in an organization make unethical choices.

DEFINITION OF INTEGRITY

Integrity requires living and working according to an unchanging set of core values. People with integrity adopt a set of core values that guide their behavior, decisions, and actions in all aspects of their lives. The actions of individuals with integrity are consistent with their beliefs. Unlike so many people, those with integrity do not say one thing but do another. Integrity, or a lack of it, manifests itself in the choices people make and the actions they take on a daily basis. People with integrity are committed to doing the right thing and speaking the truth in all situations, even when doing so does not benefit them personally, is painful, or might result in negative consequences for them.

ATTITUDES TOWARD CHEATING

Cheating has become commonplace in American society, but has it become so commonplace that it is now considered acceptable? Does society condone cheating? Do organizations actually condone or even encourage cheating? According to David Callahan, America has developed a "cheating culture."(1) Callahan cites numerous examples to support his contention that cheating in America has become an institutionalized practice that is widely accepted with a wink and a nod in spite of rules to the contrary.

Callahan cites such examples of endemic cheating in American society as: 1) psychiatrists who are willing—for a fee—to falsely diagnose young people as learning disabled they will be allowed more time when taking the SAT or ACT tests for college admission; 2) researchers at prestigious universities who allow themselves to be enticed by major pharmaceutical companies into downplaying the negative side effects of new drugs while overstating the benefits ; 3) people who falsely claim to have experience and credentials they do not actually possess when applying for jobs; 4) people who keep the receipt for the total cost of a business meal so they can claim the entire cost on their expense account even though their colleagues paid their portions of the bill; 5) people who use technology to pirate software and music from the Internet; 6) newspaper reporters who fabricate quotes and makes up stories; and 7) corporate executives who cheat in business-related golf matches (in a survey 82 percent admit to cheating).(2)

Callahan's concern is not just that people cheat, but that cheating seems to be so widely accepted. He gives the following reasons for society's widespread acceptance of cheating:

- *Increased pressure to perform.* As a result of globalization, the daily pressure to perform at a competitive level has become so intense that questions of right and wrong give way to acts desperation and expedience.

- *High stakes.* In high-stakes business deals, the size of the potential pay-off can be so large that the potential gain simply overpowers any ethical considerations. Correspondingly, the cost of failure can be so high that people simply ignore ethical considerations.

- *Poor enforcement.* The temptation to cheat increases in proportion to any decrease in the ability or willingness of authorities to effectively enforce regulations and laws. A major factor in unethical decisions is the belief of offenders that they will not get caught.

- *Poor examples.* Normally honest people who observe corporate executives or elected officials who appear to prosper by cheating can find themselves thinking, "If these big-shots do it and get away with it, why shouldn't I?" The unethical behavior of seemingly successful people can have a negative trickle-down effect on others who would like to improve their lot in life.(3)

THE END OF THE STORY HAS NOT YET BEEN WRITTEN

I am occasionally contacted by people who read my books or attend my seminars who find themselves caught up in an ethical dilemma and are at a loss concerning what to do. In many cases, the individuals in question are upset because others in their organization appear to be prospering from their unethical behavior. A comment I often hear is this: "It's not fair. I obey the rules and do what is right, but the cheaters always seem to win."

This type of situation is understandably frustrating for ethical people. Further, the situation becomes even worse when it appears that someone in a position of authority condones or even encourages the unethical behavior. My response to these inquiries is always the same. I tell the individuals who contact me to remember two things: 1) the end of the story has not yet been written—those who appear to be benefitting from their unethical behavior at the moment have a day of reckoning coming in the future, and 2) the executive, manager, or supervisor who condones or encourages the unethical behavior of employees today will be the first person to turn on them when their transgressions become public. Then I tell my ethical but frustrated callers the following story—a story that illustrates a hard fact about the lack of integrity: when people behave unethically the truth eventually comes out and, when it does, the negative consequences almost always outweigh the earlier supposed benefits.

Case: The Price of Unethical Behavior

John and Joe grew up together, graduated from high school in the same class, attended the same university, majored in the same field, made the same grades, and graduated from college on the same day. On the surface the two friends looked like carbon copies of each other. Their resumes and transcripts were interchangeable. However, as it turned out, John and Joe were two very different people.

After graduating from college, John and Joe went to work at different companies in the same town. They began their careers at the same level, but within a short time it became clear that John was outpacing his friend on the climb up the career ladder. John was being promoted faster than Joe and, based on the material evidence, making a lot more money too. At first Joe attributed John's evident success to superior performance on the job. He had seen what John could do when he committed himself to achieving a goal. John could be like a pit bull in his single-minded determination.

Then, one day while the two friends were having lunch, John brought up the subject of Joe's comparatively slow career advancement. The lunch discussion turned out to be a real eye opener for Joe. He learned that John was more talented at self-promotion, office politics, backstabbing, cutting corners, and shading the truth than he was at actually doing his job. It was these things and not his talent and hard work that were catapulting John past his contemporaries. When Joe questioned the ethics of his behavior, John just laughed and told Joe he was naïve. John's defense was: "Everybody does it, I just do it better."

After this revealing discussion, the two friends drifted apart. However, as Joe continued to slowly but surely advance in his career, he kept tabs on his old friend's meteoric progress. By the time Joe was a mid-level manager in his company, John had achieved his ultimate career goal. He was president and chief executive officer of his company. As a corporate executive, John became a major contributor to their alma mater and soon had the ear of local politicians. The gap between their circumstances became so pronounced that Joe began to doubt the veracity of his value system. Perhaps John was right. Maybe integrity was nothing more than an excuse for "losers."

As John's material success and public recognition continued to grow, Joe's self-doubt increased. Maybe he was a naïve loser who didn't understand how the business world really worked. While Joe was struggling with this crisis of conscience, he opened his newspaper one morning and found himself staring at a photograph of an obviously distraught John. His old friend was being escorted to a waiting police car in handcuffs. The accompanying story summarized a long list of criminal charges alleged against John that included fraud, income tax evasion, bribery, and money laundering.

When all was said and done with John's case, it turned out that his propensity for cutting corners, telling half-truths, and persistently putting self-interest above all other considerations had escalated over time from unethical to illegal behavior. Ironically, the same characteristics, behaviors, and choices that propelled John to the top in record time became what eventually led to his ignominious downfall. Not always, but often this is the case with unethical people. In the aftermath of their disgrace, all the "Johns" of the world typically say the same thing: "I didn't think I would get caught."

If this was a fiction story rather than one based on facts, there would be an epilogue with the good news that after John's well-publicized departure Joe was hired as the company's new CEO to clean up the mess his former friend had made. There would be poetic justice in such an ending, but that's not what really happened. In reality, Joe continued his slow but steady climb up the career ladder. Eventually, he did make it to the top in his profession and did become a CEO. It took him longer to get to the top than John, but when he got there he stayed. Further, during his climb to the top—because of his integrity—Joe was able to sleep well at night on that most comfortable of pillows—a clear conscience.

CHARACTERISTICS OF PEOPLE WITH INTEGRITY

People with integrity are guided by an internal moral compass rather than the ever-fluctuating whims of peer expectations or other outside pressures. People with integrity behave the same way when among friends as they do when among strangers. Their behavior is the same when they are out of town as it is when they are at home. The refreshing consistency of people with integrity comes from their unchanging internal values. There are several characteristics that people with integrity have in common. People with integrity are:

- *Genuine.* They engage in neither pretense nor hypocrisy. They are who they are. They refuse to be guided by peer pressure, and they refuse to go along to get along. People with integrity have a strong sense of who they are and do not try to be anything or anyone else.

- *Values-guided.* The core values of people with integrity are so much a part of them that the person and the values are inseparable. All aspects of their lives are guided by their internal moral compass, the points of which are their core values. Because of their values, people with integrity admit it when they make mistakes or are responsible for the errors of others. In addition, they behave as if they are always being observed by the ever-present eye of their conscience—which, of course, they are.

- *Consistent in their behavior.* Because their behavior is guided by a set of core values, people with integrity are consistent and predictable in their behavior. They are the same person out of town that they are at home. They can be depended on to keep their word and to do what is right rather than what is expedient. When they make promises, they keep them.

- *Fair.* People with integrity make decisions based on what is best for their organizations or for the greater good rather than self interest. Whereas less ethical people will use high-minded rationalizations to justify making self-serving decisions, people with integrity simply do what is right and fair. They do not make decisions on the basis of friendship, quid pro quo relationships, or other factors that are inherently unfair.

- *Concerned more with substance than image.* Integrity is about substance not image. One of the disadvantages of television is that the medium has conditioned people to focus too intently on image. For example, it is believed by many political scientists that Abraham Lincoln—a great president but homely in appearance—could not be elected in today's media-driven age of image-fixation. There is nothing wrong with being concerned about professional image—everyone who works should be. Presenting a positive professional image is important for those who want to inspire and motivate others to higher levels of performance. But to focus on image to the exclusion of substance is a mistake. An empty box is still empty no matter how well decorated it might be on the outside.

- *Selfless.* One of the hallmarks of people with integrity is selflessness. One cannot be self-centered and self-serving and also have integrity. The concepts are mutually-exclusive. People who are ultimately the best leaders are good stewards of the resources entrusted to them—human, financial, and physical. Selflessness means thinking of others and the organization before thinking of self. Selfless people care about the greater good first—an approach that requires integrity.

INTEGRITY IS CRITICAL TO PEAK PERFORMANCE

Leaders without followers are not really leaders at all, regardless of their position in the organization. Any person who hopes to lead employees in achieving peak performance and continual improvement must have their trust. This is why integrity is so important to those who aspire to be developmental leaders. A leader can lead only if people will follow, and people will follow only if they believe in, trust, and respect the leader.

The credibility of those who want to lead is based on several factors—none more important than integrity. Without integrity, a leader will be without followers. If its leaders have no followers, an organization is in trouble. This makes integrity critical to peak performance and continual improvement. Some other reasons why integrity is so important to organizations are as follows:

- *Integrity builds trust.* Most work in organizations is done in teams. Consequently, effective teamwork is important. In order for people in teams to work together in ways that ensure peak performance, they must trust each other. People in organizations want to work with team members they can trust. In addition, they want to be led by executives, managers, and supervisors they trust. Employees are more likely to strive for peak performance and continual improvement in an environment of trust. On the other hand, employees will only reluctantly and half-heartedly go along with those they do not trust. Organizational leaders who are not trusted by employees receive *reluctant compliance* from them rather than whole-hearted commitment. People who are trusted are more likely to get action from their co-workers, colleagues, teammates, and direct reports. People who are not trusted typically get only half-hearted commitments—in other words, they get reluctant compliance. Half-hearted commitment and reluctant compliance are the antithesis of the attitude necessary for peak performance and continual improvement.

- *Integrity leads to influence.* In order to gain a whole-hearted commitment from employees, leaders must have influence with them. This is why it is so important for leaders in organizations to understand that employees will not be influenced by those they do not trust. Executives, managers, and supervisors who fail to win the trust of employees will not have the influence needed to achieve buy-in, commitment, and a willingness to persevere when the job becomes difficult.

- *Integrity establishes high standards.* People with integrity consistently set an example of doing the right thing as opposed to what is expedient or self-serving. They say "Do as I do" rather than "Do as I say." By their positive examples, organizational leaders with integrity set high standards for employees. In turn, employees with integrity set high standards for their teammates. This is important because high standards are an essential ingredient in achieving peak performance and continual improvement.

- *Integrity puts substance behind the image.* Many people who want to be leaders spend a great deal of time, money, and effort trying to look like leaders. They dress for success, spend hours in the gym, and enroll themselves in image-building seminars. Once when I was speaking at a national conference in Chicago, the program included a seminar presented by an image consultant on how men my age could compensate for thinning hair. His message was that baldness is an image killer. My immediate thought was, "Tell that to Michael Jordan." At the time, a completely bald—or at least shaved—Michael

Jordan was the highest paid player in the NBA and had just led his team to another national championship. He is now in the basketball hall of fame. While image is important for leaders, image without substance will eventually lead to failure. For example, people who lack integrity will eventually reveal the fact through their actions no matter how hard they work on their image. For those who want to lead others to peak performance and continual improvement, integrity must come first and image second. The good news is that, in the long run, once a reputation for integrity has been established, projecting a positive professional image becomes easier. Substance is the best image enhancer there is.

- *Integrity builds credibility.* Credibility is what people have when others believe in and respect them. It is a critical characteristic for those who hope to lead others to peak performance and continual improvement. In order to establish credibility, there must first be trust. People will neither believe in nor respect someone they do not trust. To establish credibility, organizational leaders should first strive to establish trust.(4)

ETHICS AND INTEGRITY

Ethical behavior is the practical application of integrity. It follows from this that ethical behavior means doing the right thing within the context of a value system. In order to behave ethically, people must have integrity—they must live and work according to a set of values that guide their behavior, decisions, and day-to-day interaction with other people. To encourage ethical behavior at all levels, organizations should adopt a set of corporate values and communicate them to all personnel.

In a nation as diverse as the United States, there is no universally accepted set of values. For example, the values of young people often differ from those of older people. The values of urban people often differ from those of rural people. Easterners can differ from Westerners and Northerners from Southerners. Consequently, organizations are well-advised to adopt a set of corporate values to provide an ethical framework for their personnel no matter their individual backgrounds or worldviews.

People in organizations often face situations that force them to weigh their self interests against the needs of the organization, balance personal responsibilities to family against work responsibilities, and deal with pressure to engage in questionable activities such as cutting corners in the name of short-term profitability. Making decisions that have high ethical content can put people through a difficult process known as *soul searching*. This process involves weighing what one truly believes is right against the pressure felt to make a certain decision while also considering the potential consequences of the eventual decision.

Making unpopular decisions is one of the most difficult challenges leaders in organizations face, and they face this kind of dilemma frequently. To make a decision that is right as opposed to popular, leaders must have the moral courage and resolve to persevere against the inevitable pressure they will feel from a variety of sources (e.g. the marketplace, bottom line, superiors, colleagues, subordinates, and even family members). But the most difficult foe of the person who wants to do the right thing instead of what is popular or expedient is misguided self-interest. Most human beings are driven, at least in part, by self-interest. Organizational leaders must understand that every time they make an unpopular decision, they put their self-interest at risk.

People who disagree with a leader's decision can be persistently determined in finding ways to retaliate, ways that are both overt and covert. Even when they know the leader in question made the right decision for the organization, some people will still want to retaliate if the decision runs counter to their self-interest. People can be surprisingly narrow-minded when it comes to protecting their perceived self-interests. Consequently, leaders in organizations should never be so naïve as to expect those who are opposed to their decisions to just sit back and accept them.

If the unhappy person is a superior, doing the right thing might result in various types of retaliation such bad performance appraisals or being passed over for a promotion. If the unhappy person is a colleague, an individual's ethical stand might cause her to be isolated from the group—shunned personally and professionally. If the unhappy people are subordinates, doing the right thing might result in an attitude of reluctant compliance or even covert disobedience.

In all of these cases, it is important to remember that the negatives one sometimes suffers for doing the right thing are usually temporary, whereas the positives are permanent. It might take a while for the positive results to be realized and even longer for dissenters to come around, but doing the right thing has a way of winning in the long run. In the long run, doing the right thing is not just good ethics it's good business.

It is not uncommon for people to pay a price for doing the right thing—at least in the short term. At the very least, the threat is always there. This is why executives, managers, and supervisors who are trying to lead others to peak performance and continual improvement sometimes feel as if they are caught between a rock and a hard place. If they choose Option A because they think it is the right thing to do when others want them to choose Option B, they risk feeling the lash of resentment and perhaps even retaliation from discontented stakeholders. On the other hand, if they go along to get along and choose Option B only to have it fail, they will be blamed by the very same people who pressured them to choose Option B in the first place.

This kind of Catch-22 dilemma can prevent people who might otherwise become good organizational leaders from ever achieving that status. The perceived benefits of unethical shortcuts are often immediate while those of integrity can be delayed, a hard fact that some people simply cannot handle. However, those who hope to lead others to peak performance and continual improvement must be able to handle this Catch-22 dilemma.

If the pressure on a leader to decide one way or the other came only from self-interested teammates, integrity would be a less difficult a concept. However, even while receiving pressure from various sources to choose a given option, leaders in organizations cannot escape the ever-looming consequences of their decisions. Leaders who know what is right but succumb to pressure to do what is wrong do not have the luxury of saying "I told you so" when the long-term results of their decisions turn out badly. This is a dilemma often faced by executives, managers, and supervisors who hope to lead others to peak performance and continual improvement. Positive results are the best defense of the ethical leader.

Those, who for reasons of self-interest, pressure leaders to choose Option "A" will be first in line to criticize when the long-term results of Option A do not turn out well. This is a practical reason why organizational leaders should decide what is right and do it. In many cases, organizational leaders are going to be criticized regardless of what decision they make. Consequently, they may as well be criticized for doing the right thing. Newspapers and professional journals are replete with stories that chronicle the startling downfalls of organizational leaders who gave into pressure and made unethical decisions that appeared beneficial in the short run, but had devastating effects in the long run.

The double jeopardy sometimes faced by leaders in organizations when they make decisions might seem unfair, and it probably is. But, then, this is just one of the many reasons that the number of people who are effective in leading others to peak performance and continual improvement is always limited. Few people understand the unfairness of life better than those who are successful enough to become top-level decision-makers in organizations. When the decisions of leaders turn out to be right, people are quick to tone down the self-interested criticism they aimed at them for making what they—the critics—thought was the wrong decision. But when leaders are wrong, circumstances, justifications, and logic rarely matter to their detractors. This is the origin of the old saying: *It's lonely at the top.* A life of integrity can occasionally be a lonely life for executives, managers, and supervisors.

ETHICAL ASPECT OF DECISION MAKING

Knowing the right thing to do is not usually the problem when making decisions that have high ethical content. Organizational leaders typically know the right thing to do in a given situation. More often than not what complicates their decision-making are extenuating circumstances that cloud their judgment. In other words, executives, managers, and supervisors typically know the right thing to do, but for a variety of reasons may want to do something else.

However, there are times when people in organizations really will not know what is right in a given situation. In some cases, the internal struggle is the result of their desire to rationalize a decision they know is unethical but want to make any way for reasons of self-interest. However, there are times when even the most ethical people will be stumped—they simply will not know what to do in a given situation. Organizational leaders caught in this kind of perplexing situation can clear away the fog by asking themselves the following question:

> *How would I feel about my decision in this matter if all the details were printed on the front page of my local newspaper to be read by family, friends, colleagues, and teammates?*

Asking this question will help clear away any mental or emotional fog created by extenuating circumstances and get leaders focused on the right course of action. This question cannot guarantee that organizational leaders will follow through and make the right decision, but it can ensure that they know what the right decision is.

How to Handle Extenuating Circumstances When Making Decisions

Where leaders in organizations sometimes go astray from an ethical perspective is in doing bad things for good reasons—reasons that are well-intended and even admirable. For example, I once had to deal with a situation in which a popular and effective employee was claiming overtime-hours to generate the extra money needed to pay his parent's mortgage payment so they would not lose their house. The problem stemmed from the fact that he wasn't really working overtime. This outstanding employee was close to his parents and could not stand the thought of them being evicted from the family home. His fraudulent overtime was driven not by dishonesty, but desperation.

The inescapable fact was that this employee was committing fraud. In fact, his actions went beyond being unethical—they were illegal. However, there were extenuating circumstances that had to be considered. These circumstances included his popularity as an employee, his effectiveness at his job, and, of course, his parent's predicament.

I could have simply confronted him with the facts and taken appropriate disciplinary action. Had I chosen this option I would have been right, at least from the legal perspective. But I would have been wrong from a human perspective and, in turn, from the perspective of employee morale and performance. Firing the employee in question or taking immediate disciplinary action would have been the by-the-book response, but this approach would have just solved one problem while creating another.

For example, taking disciplinary action without considering the extenuating circumstances of his parents' heart-wrenching circumstances could have damaged morale in our organization and undermined my credibility with those I was responsible for leading. Clearly I had to find a solution that stopped the employee's unethical behavior but also accommodated the extenuating circumstances. I certainly would not have wanted all of the circumstances surrounding a less worthy decision to be printed on the front page of my hometown newspaper. It was this situation that taught me a valuable lesson early in my career about making decisions that have high ethical content. The lesson I learned was this: decide what is right and do it regardless of extenuating circumstances, and then find responsible, helpful ways to deal with the extenuating circumstances.

I confronted the employee with the evidence of his unethical behavior and told him it had to stop immediately. I also told him that the pay he had received fraudulently would have to be returned to our organization on the installment plan, and that a written reprimand would be placed in his personnel file. This was in response to the principle that says, "Decide what is right and do it regardless of extenuating circumstances." Then I asked his permission to undertake a fund-raising effort to solicit funds for helping pay his parent's overdue mortgage payments. This was in response to the principle that says, "Find responsible, helpful ways to deal with the extenuating circumstances."

The employee agreed to both components of the solution and everything worked out well for all involved. When the personnel in our organization heard about their colleague's financial problem, they were enormously generous in responding. Before long we had collected more than enough money to bring his parent's mortgage payments up to date. This was the mind of solution leaders in organizations want—the kind they would be proud to read about on the front page of their hometown newspaper—and the kind that contributes to peak performance and continual improvement.

A FINAL WORD ABOUT INTEGRITY

No human being is likely to ever achieve perfect integrity. It is important to understand this fact or the magnitude of the challenge might become overwhelming. But, on the other hand, neither can those who want to lead afford to let *nobody's perfect* become an excuse for ethical failures. While it is true that people are not likely to achieve perfect integrity, it is equally true that the more persistently they try, the closer they will come. When leaders find themselves struggling with ethical questions, and the pressure of the moment causes them to look for ways to rationalize making the wrong decision, they should remember this unalterable truth: *There is no right way to do a wrong thing.*

GROUP TRAINING ACTIVITIES

1. As the department manager, Mark has to select one of two employees for promotion into a job that has opened up in his department. Wanda is not as qualified for the position as Susan, but Mark likes Wanda. In fact, he would really like to get to know her better in a social setting. Mark doesn't like Susan. She is better qualified than Wanda, but she is all business. She refuses to joke around with Mark and others in the department. Mark thinks Wanda would be better for the morale of the department. Which person should Mark recommend for the promotion and why?

2. Jill sometimes wishes she had never been promoted to supervisor in her company, ABC Inc. Her boss, Marvin Drake, demands peak performance from supervisors such as Jill who lead the various departments in the organization, and he does not care what they

have to do to achieve it. Jill is married to a manager in another company that is competing with ABC for an important government contract. Drake is pressuring Jill to pry information out of her husband that will help ABC, Inc. submit a more competitive bid for the contract. He has hinted to Jill that if ABC wins this contract, she might receive a major promotion and salary increase. On the other hand, if ABC loses the bid the company will probably have to lay off employees including some supervisors. Jill could be the first of the supervisors to get a pink slip. All things considered, Jill finds herself in a real dilemma. What should she do?

ENDNOTES

1. Callahan, D., *The Cheating Culture* (Harcourt, Inc., Orlando, Florida: 2004), viii.

2. Ibid, 8-12.

3. Ibid, 20-24.

4. Maxwell, J. C. *Developing the Leader Within You* (Thomas Nelson, Inc., Nashville, Tennessee: 1993), 38-44.

Eight

COMMUNICATION

Best Practice Number 8: *Become an effective communicator and help employees develop good communication skills.*

Effective communication is essential for organizational leaders who want to equip, enable, and empower employees for peak performance and continual improvement. Communication skills help organizational leaders: 1) win the commitment of employees to excellence; 2) understand what employees are thinking, feeling, and experiencing; 3) sell their ideas to other stakeholders; 4) promote teamwork, cooperation, and collaboration; 5) enhance interpersonal relationships with stakeholders; 6) ensure that their team members understand the organization's big picture and where they fit into it; 7) understand performance expectations; and 8) prevent and resolve conflict.

Good communication is critical to the success of organizations. In fact, if an organization is viewed as a machine, communication is the oil that keeps it running smoothly. Of all the skills needed by organizational leaders, effective communication may be the most important. It is at the very least one of the most important. This chapter explains how to develop the communication skills needed to equip, enable, and empower employees for peak performance and continual improvement.

HOW TO DEVELOP COMMUNICATION SKILLS

Communication is a human process. Like all things human, it is imperfect. Doing it well takes work. This is because the quality of communication is affected by so many different factors (*e.g.* speaking ability; hearing ability; language barriers; differing perceptions and meanings based on age, gender, race, nationality, and culture; attitudes; nonverbal cues; and the level of trust between senders and receivers to name just a few). Because of these and other factors, communicating effectively can be difficult. Regardless of the difficulty, good communication is a skill that must be learned by executives, managers, and supervisors who want to be developmental leaders.

Communication skills can be learned, a fortunate fact for organizational leaders. With sufficient training and practice, most people—regardless of their innate abilities—can learn to communicate well. Developmental leaders need to be good communicators. Consequently, leaders in organizations must learn to communicate well. A leader with poor communication skills is like a carpenter without a hammer.

Case: A Poor Listener Learns an Important Lesson

An individual I will call Jane learned the importance of effective communication while just a freshman in college. Having missed the orientation meeting for an on-line class, Jane asked a friend who did attend to fill her in on what she had missed. The friend obliged, but Jane was distracted by other pressing issues and did not listen well. As a result, there was a major gap in their communication. The friend told Jane she was supposed to read ten chapters in the textbook and answer all of the essay questions at the end of the chapters. The answers to the essay questions were to be typed and submitted for a grade. Jane wrote this down but having done so she tuned out and stopped listening.

As a result of her poor listening, Jane assumed that her friend meant the ten chapters and essay questions were due on the last day of the semester. They were actually due on the date of the mid-term exam. Following the mid-term exam, students who passed would be given their remaining assignments for the course. Poor communication caused Jane to come to the mid-term exam with only half of her required work completed.

Jane compounded the poor communication by failing to go on-line and read the information provided from time to time by her professor. This on-line course was just an elective for Jane and she had little interest in it. Assuming that reading the ten chapters and writing the essays was the sum total of the work required for the course, Jane painted herself into a corner. Rather than tuning out and assuming she had heard her friend correctly, Jane should have made sure by asking a few clarifying questions. Failing to do so resulted in Jane flunking a course she could have easily passed. She flunked the course, but learned an important lesson about communication. From that point on, Jane never again tuned out when she needed to listen carefully. Instead, she developed a habit of listening attentively and asking clarifying questions to verify what she thought she heard.

COMMUNICATION: A DEFINITION

Organizational leaders should never confuse *telling* with *communicating*. Unfortunately, others often do. When a problem develops they are likely to protest, "I don't understand why this didn't get done. I told him what to do." Some people will also confuse *hearing* with *listening*. When problems arise, they are likely to say, "That isn't what I told you to do. I know you heard me. You were standing right next to me!"

In these cases, the individuals in question have confused telling and hearing with communicating. What one person says is not necessarily what another person hears, and what the other person hears is not necessarily what the speaker intended to say. The missing ingredient in these cases is comprehension. Communication may involve telling, but it is not *just* telling. It may involve hearing, but it is not *just* hearing. Because of this, I define communication as follows:

Communication is the transfer of information that is received and fully understood from one source to another.

A message can be sent by one person and received by another, but until the message is fully understood communication has not occurred. This applies to spoken, written, and nonverbal communication.

COMMUNICATION: THE PROCESS

The process of communication has several components: *sender, receiver, method, medium*, and the *message* itself. The sender is the originator or source of the message. The receiver is the person or group for whom the message is intended. The message is the information that is to be conveyed, understood, and acted on. The medium is the vehicle used to convey the message (e.g. telephone, email, social networking software, etc.) The method is the type of communication chosen for encoding the message.

There are three basic categories of communication methods: *verbal,* *nonverbal,* and *written.* Verbal communication includes face-to-face conversation, telephone conversation, speeches, public announcements, press conferences, and other means of conveying the spoken word. Nonverbal communication includes gestures, facial expressions, voice tone, body poses, gestures, and proximity. Written communication includes letters, memorandums, billboards, bulletin boards, manuals, books, and all of the various electronic means of conveying the written word.

Technological developments have significantly increased the ability to convey information, although not necessarily to communicate. These developments include word processing, satellites, telephones, cellular telephones and an ever-growing variety of other hand-held devices, answering machines, facsimile machines, pocket-sized dictation machines, email, social networking, and the Internet. Organizational leaders should make a point of becoming skilled at using various technological aids to enhance communication.

EFFECTIVE COMMUNICATION

When the information conveyed from one source to another is received and understood, communication has occurred. However, understanding alone does not guarantee effective communication. *Effective communication* occurs when the information received and understood is accepted and acted on in the desired manner. For example, a supervisor might ask her team members to work 30 minutes extra every day for the next week to ensure that an important project is completed on schedule. All of the team members verify that they heard the message and understand it.

Then, without informing the supervisor, two team members decide they are not going to stay late. They have other priorities. This is an example of ineffective communication. The two errant employees heard and understood the message, but they did not accept it. Since they did not accept the message, they did not act on it in the desired manner. Rather, they ignored it. The supervisor in this case communicated, but not effectively.

Effective communication is a higher level of communication because it requires not just understanding but acceptance by the receiver. The acceptance aspect of effective communication requires influence, persuasion, and monitoring. Since acceptance of the message is essential to effective communication, organizational leaders need to know how to win acceptance of the messages they communicate.

The first step for ensuring acceptance of messages is to gain credibility with receivers. Organizational leaders who have credibility with employees will find it easier to have influence. The more influential leaders are, the more likely it is that their messages will be accepted and acted on. When credibility and influence are lacking, receivers tend to question or even doubt the veracity of the messages they receive. They may not voice their doubts, but they will make them known by their hesitance to accept the messages and their corresponding reluctance in responding to them.

Persuasion can be an important factor in gaining acceptance of messages. To enhance their persuasiveness with employees, organizational leaders should get into the habit of explaining: 1) the *why* behind their messages, 2) the benefits of accepting their messages and acting on them in the desired manner, and 3) the consequences of failing to accept messages and act on them in an appropriate manner. This is why a dictatorial approach to communication that says "do what I say and don't ask questions" does not work well. In crisis situations where there is no time to explain, acceptance of messages can still be won provided the sender has gained credibility with the receiver(s). This is another reason why credibility is essential to effective communication—leaders will not always have time to explain. However, when there is time to do so, explaining the reasons behind messages as well as the benefits and consequences relating to messages will help gain acceptance of them.

Finally, monitoring is an effective way to ensure acceptance of messages and the corresponding desired action. For example, in the earlier example in which two employees decided they had better things to do than work 30 minutes late, the miscreants would probably have acted differently if their supervisor had monitored them. Instead this supervisor asked her team members to work late then left them on their own. This was both poor communication and poor leadership.

INHIBITORS OF EFFECTIVE COMMUNICATION

There are several factors that can inhibit effective communication that organizational leaders should be familiar with and understand how to overcome. These inhibitors include the following:

- *Differences in meaning.* Differences in meaning are inevitable in communication, because people have different backgrounds and levels of education. In a country as diverse as the United States, people in organizations are likely to mirror that diversity (e.g. difference races, cultures, and nationalities). Because of this diversity, the words, gestures, and facial expressions used by people in organizations can have altogether different meanings. Even people from countries that share a common language find that words can have different meanings. For example, in the United States when someone says they will "ring you up," they are usually talking about checking you out at the cash register. The same thing said in Great Britain means calling someone on the telephone. To overcome this kind of inhibitor, leaders in organizations must invest the time necessary to get to know employees and learn what they mean by what they say.

- *Insufficient trust.* Few factors can inhibit effective communication more surely than insufficient trust. If receivers do not trust senders, they are not likely to trust their messages either. If they do not trust a message they are not likely to accept it and act on it in the desired manner. Instead, they will question the motives of the sender. They will concentrate on reading between the lines and looking for a "hidden agenda." In fact, they might focus so intently on determining what is being said between the lines or what is not being said that they miss the real message. Organizational leaders must understand this and, as a result, strive to build trust with employees.

- *Information overload.* Because of advances in communication technology and the rapid and continual proliferation of information, people in organizations often find themselves with more information than they can process effectively. This is known as information overload, and it can easily cause a breakdown in communication. Leaders in organizations can guard against information overload by screening, organizing, summarizing, and simplifying the information conveyed to employees. For example, leaders should never take the reports they receive from the next higher level of management and just hand them over to their team members. Rather, they should extract or at least highlight any information that is pertinent so that their personnel do not have to waste time reading information they do not need.

- *Interference.* Interference is any external distraction that inhibits effective communication. It might be something as simple as background noise caused by people talking or as complex as atmospheric interference with satellite reception. Regardless of its nature, interference can distort or even completely block the message. Leaders in organizations should be attentive to the environment when trying to communicate with employees. I once had to move an entire audience of 100 people when giving a speech in a resort on the Gulf of Mexico. The beautiful emerald waters of the Gulf were not the problem. Rather, a contractor was doing renovations on the floor directly above and one of his workers was using a jack hammer. Sometimes to ensure effective communication it is necessary to change the setting.

- *Condescending tones.* Problems created by condescension result from the tone rather than the content of the message. People do not like to be talked down to. If employees sense that they are being talked down to they might respond by mentally tuning out. Worse yet, they might resent the condescension enough that they retaliate by not accepting the message and, in turn, not acting on it.

- *Listening problems.* Listening problems are one of the most serious inhibitors of effective communication. They can result from the sender not listening to the receiver and vise versa. To be good communicators, people must be good listeners. This topic is important enough to warrant a section of its own later in this chapter.

- *Premature judgments.* Premature judgments by the sender or the receiver can inhibit effective communication. This inhibitor contributes to and exacerbates listening problems because as soon as people make a premature judgment they stop listening. One cannot make premature judgments and maintain an open mind, and an open mind is essential to effective communication. Therefore, it is important to listen non-judgmentally and avoid making premature judgments when receiving a message.

- *Inaccurate assumptions.* Perceptions are influenced by assumptions. Consequently, inaccurate assumptions can lead to inaccurate perceptions. Here is an example. John has been taking an inordinate amount of time off from work lately. His supervisor assumes that John is goldbricking. As a result, whenever John makes a suggestion in a team meeting, the supervisor ignores him. In reality the supervisor is wrong. He is making an inaccurate assumption. John is actually a highly-motivated, highly-skilled employee. His excessive time off is the result of a problem he is having at home and is too embarrassed to discuss. Because of an inaccurate assumption, John's supervisor is missing out on the suggestions of a highly-motivated, highly-skilled employee. In addition, his misperception points to a need for trust building. Perhaps if John trusted his supervisor more, he would be less embarrassed to discuss this personal problem with him.

- *Technological glitches.* Software bugs, computer viruses, dead batteries, power outages, and software compatibility are just a few of the technological glitches that can interfere with communication. The more dependent we become on technology for conveying messages, the more often these glitches will interfere with and inhibit effective communication.

HOW LISTENING IMPROVES COMMUNICATION

Hearing is a physiological process, but listening is not. A person with highly sensitive hearing can be a poor listener. Conversely, a person with impaired hearing can be an excellent listener. Hearing is the physiological process of receiving sound waves, but listening is about perception. Because of this, I define listening as follows:

Listening is receiving a message, correctly decoding it, and accurately perceiving what is meant by it.

Inhibitors of Listening

Listening can break down if the receiver hears but does not accurately perceive the message. Several inhibitors can cause this to happen. These inhibitors of listening include:

- Lack of concentration

- Preconceived notions

- Thinking ahead

- Interruptions

- Tuning out

To perceive a message accurately, it is necessary to concentrate on what is being said, and how it is being said—verbally and non-verbally. Non-verbal communication is explained in the next section. This section focuses on listening to verbal messages. Concentration requires that extraneous distractions be eliminated or mentally shut out. When people concentrate, they clear their minds of everything but the message being conveyed and focus on the sender.

Preconceived notions also inhibit listening because they can cause people to make premature judgments. Making premature judgments shuts down listening. Leaders in organizations should practice being patient and listening attentively. People who prematurely jump ahead to where they think the conversation is going may get there only to find that the speaker was going somewhere else. Thinking ahead is typically a response to being impatient or in a hurry. Leaders in organization should remember that it takes less time to hear someone out than it does to start over after jumping ahead in the wrong direction.

Interruptions inhibit effective listening and frustrate the speaker. Consequently, it is doubly bad to interrupt someone who is speaking to you. If clarification is needed during a conversation, make a mental note of it and wait for the speaker to reach a stopping point. Mental notes are preferable to written notes. The act of writing can distract the speaker or cause the listener to miss the point. If it is necessary to make written notes, keep them short.

Tuning out inhibits effective listening. Some people become skilled at using body language to make it appear they are listening when in fact their mind is miles away. Leaders in organizations should avoid the temptation to engage in such ploys. An astute speaker may ask the listener to repeat what was said. At any point during a conversation, the listener should be able to paraphrase and repeat back to the speaker what has been said.

Strategies for Ensuring Effective Listening

Organizational leaders can improve their listening by applying the following strategies:

- *Use the five-minute rule*

- *Remove all distractions*

- *Put the speaker at ease*

- *Look directly at the speaker*

- *Concentrate on what is being said*

- *Watch for non-verbal cues*

- *Make note of the speaker's tone*

- *Be patient and wait*

- *Ask clarifying questions*

- *Paraphrase and repeat what the speaker has said*

- *Control emotions*

The Five-Minute Rule

I developed the *five-minute rule* in self defense. Many years ago as a brand new manager, I wanted to maintain an open-door policy for my personnel and an open ear for their problems, concerns, complaints, and recommendations. Having come up through the ranks, I knew first-hand how it was to work for a manager who was not accessible. I was determined to be just the opposite. On the other hand, listening to the problems, concerns, complaints, and recommendations of employees can be time-consuming. Like all managers, I had other duties that needed my attention. Before long my open-door policy had me spending all of my time listening to the input of my personnel. I was making an "A" in listening, but an "F" in attending to my other duties.

My open-door policy was popular with employees and did produce some positive results beyond just the morale boost it gave my team members. On the other hand, I often found myself working until midnight in order to take care of my other duties. Clearly, I had to find a way to retain my open-door policy without allowing employee problems to monopolize all of my time. The answer that eventually came to me and one I recommend to all leaders in organizations was what I call my five-minute rule.

The five-minute rule works like this. Organizational leaders let their personnel know that—within reason—they can have five minutes on a drop-in basis any time they have a complaint, recommendation, or any other type of input to offer. However, their time for these drop-in visits will be limited to five-minutes. Lest the reader think this policy is too restrictive, five minutes is actually plenty of time provided the speaker has thoroughly considered what she wants to say. Preparation is the key. Spending time listening to an employee who rambles on because of poor preparation is time poorly used. Besides, wise managers want their personnel to learn how to prepare brief, succinct, but comprehensive explanations that get right to the point without wasting time. This is a skill that will serve them and the organization well.

The allotted five minutes are not to be used for thinking out load or brainstorming. There is a time and place for these things, but it is not during the five-minute sessions. During the allotted time the employee is expected to explain his problem and offer a recommended solution. Further, recommending poorly conceived solutions is a major faux pas. Proposing a thousand dollar solution to a hundred dollar problem is not acceptable. Employees who ask for five minutes are expected to have already conducted a cost/benefit analysis for the solution they propose or recommendation they make.

The cost/benefit analysis might amount to nothing more than a careful thinking through of the recommendation in question, but even this will help employees realize that some solutions are better than others. There is a cost associated with everything. Consequently, employees who make recommendations should: 1) be aware of the costs associated with their recommendation, and 2) make sure the potential benefits of the recommendation outweigh the costs. The cost-benefit-analysis requirement can prevent time from being wasted considering unrealistic solutions.

Not all issues in organizations can be properly dealt with in five minutes. Issues that are too complex to fit into the five-minute format should be handled in the normal manner (i.e. the employee should make an appointment and ask for as much time as will be needed). The five-minute rule is a strategy for facilitating the open-door policy and making it a valuable communication tool. It is not intended as a replacement for traditional problem-solving methods such as brainstorming, focus groups, team meetings, or quality circles.

Other Listening Improvement Strategies

To gain the most from five-minute sessions with employees, leaders in organizations should apply the other listening-improvement strategies explained earlier in this chapter. The strategy of removing distractions and giving full attention to the speaker is important. Anyone who has ever tried to talk with someone who was distracted by other concerns will understand why. Removing distractions typically involves such things as turning off your cell phone, putting a temporary hold on land-line calls, allowing no other visitors to drop in, and getting away from the paperwork on your desk.

The best way I have found to get away from the clutter without having to clean off your desk every time someone drops in is to have two chairs in your office located somewhere away from your desk. I have two that sit at a small table I keep free of office clutter at all times. Do not try to sit at your desk and listen to employees. Trying to concentrate on what the employee is saying while the paperwork on your desk beckons takes more self-discipline than most people have.

Before asking the speaker to begin, put her at ease—particularly if you sense nervousness or discomfort. Asking about something unrelated to the job such as children, grandchildren, ball games, or hobbies will usually do the trick. Then, once the speaker begins, look directly at her and concentrate on what is being said. Do not waste a moment of the employee's time by being inattentive. Listen not just with your ears, but also with your eyes. In other words, watch for non-verbal cues and listen for voice tone. This strategy is explained in the next section of this chapter.

Do not interrupt or try to push the employee along. Rather, be patient and wait. When there are long pauses in the employee's explanation it can mean that she is trying to decide: 1) how to say what is really on her mind, or 2) if she is really going to say what is on her mind. If you interrupt or try to prompt a hesitant speaker, you risk missing out on the real reason she asked for five minutes in the first place—especially if what the employee has to say is sensitive. Give hesitant employees a positive, affirming facial expression. Then be patient and wait.

Once the employee has stated her case, ask any clarifying questions that might be necessary to gain a more complete and accurate understanding of what she said. Once you think you have a complete and accurate understanding, paraphrase what the employee said and repeat it back to her. Paraphrasing can be beneficial in two ways. First, it shows the employee that you listened. Second, if you have misperceived part of the message it allows the employee to correct the misperception. This latter benefit is important because it will prevent a situation in which you waste time pursuing the wrong problem.

The final strategy—control emotions—is critical. A good rule of thumb for leaders in organizations to remember is this: When dealing with employees, if you lose your temper you lose period. One of the differences between being a leader and an employee in an organization is that there are higher expectations for leaders. When people in organizations step up from the ranks to leadership positions, it is not just their pay that increases. It is also their responsibilities and behavioral expectations.

Leaders in organizations who lose their tempers when employees bring them unwelcome information—in other words those who shoot the messenger—soon find themselves without messengers. This is one of the worst things that can happen to leaders in organizations because the more unwelcome the message the more they need to hear it. They may not want to hear it, but they need to hear it and the sooner the better. Bad news that goes unattended has a way of turning into even worse news.

NONVERBAL COMMUNICATION

Nonverbal messages represent one of the least understood but most powerful modes of communication. Nonverbal messages can reveal more than verbal messages for those who are attentive enough to observe them. Nonverbal communication is sometimes called body language, an only partially accurate characterization. Non-verbal communication does include body language, but body language is only part of nonverbal communication. There are actually three components to the concept: body factors, voice factors, and proximity factors.

Body Factors

An individual's posture, facial expressions, gestures, and dress, in other words his body language, can convey a variety of messages. Even such extras as makeup or the lack of it, well-groomed or messy hair, and clean or scruffy shoes can convey a message. Organizational leaders should be attentive to these body factors and how they add to or detract from verbal messages. Nonverbal cues should agree with, support, and enhance verbal messages.

One of the keys to understanding nonverbal cues lies in the concept of consistency. In a conversation with another individual, are the spoken messages and the corresponding nonverbal messages consistent with each other? They should be. In a conversation, if nonverbal messages do not seem to match the verbal message, something is probably wrong and it is a good idea to find out what it is. An effective way to deal with inconsistency between verbal and nonverbal messages is to tactfully but frankly confront it. A simple statement such as, "Mike your words say that you came to work on time this morning, but your body language seems to disagree." Such a statement can help leaders get to the truth.

Voice Factors

Voice factors are also important elements of nonverbal communication. In addition to listening to employees' words, it is important to listen for voice factors such as volume, tone, pitch, and rate of speech. These factors can reveal feelings of anger, fear, impatience, uncertainty, interest, acceptance, confidence, and so on. As with body factors it is important to look for consistency when comparing words and voice factors. It is also advisable to look for groups of nonverbal cues. A single cue taken out of context has little meaning. But as one of a group of cues, it can be significant.

For example, if you look through an office window and see a person pounding her fist on the desk, it would be tempting to interpret this as a gesture of anger. But is it really? What kind of look does she have on her face? Is her facial expression consistent with desk-pounding anger or could she just be trying to open a drawer that is stuck? On the other hand, if you saw her pounding the desk with a frown on her face and heard her yelling in an agitated tone, your assumption of anger might be well-based. Of course, she might be angry because her desk drawer is stuck, but nevertheless she would still be angry.

Proximity Factors

Proximity factors range from the relative positions of people in conversations to how an individual's office is arranged, the color of the walls, and the types of decorations displayed. A supervisor who sits next to an employee during a conversation conveys a different message than one separated from the employee by a desk. Coming out from behind a desk and sitting next to an employee conveys the message that, "There are no barriers between us. I want to hear what you have to say." Remaining behind the desk sends a message of distance and standoffishness. Of course there are times when this is precisely the message leaders in organizations want to convey, but the point is that you should be aware of the nonverbal messages that can be sent by proximity so that you send the intended messages.

A leader who makes her office a comfortable place to visit is sending a message that invites communication. A leader who maintains a cold, impersonal office sends the opposite message. To send the nonverbal message that employees are welcome to stop by and take advantage of the five-minute rule, consider applying the following strategies:

- Have comfortable chairs available for visitors

- Arrange chairs so you can sit beside visitors rather than behind your desk

- Choose soft, soothing colors rather than harsh, stark, overly bright, or busy colors

- If possible, have refreshments such as water, coffee, tea, and soda available for visitors

Many people like to turn their offices into to shrines to their achievements. In offices that are shrines, trophies, plaques, photos taken with important people, award certificates, and various other career mementoes are typically displayed prominently for visitors to see. There is nothing wrong with having a "love me" wall in your office, but do not over do it. For making a positive impression on employees and for gaining credibility with them, evidence of your achievements can serve a valuable purpose. However, when trying to encourage employees to open up and reveal their concerns, fears, issues, and problems, it is helpful to have a more inviting place to meet—one that is comfortable and not all about you. A good rule of thumb for decorating your office is: three walls for visitors and one for you.

VERBAL COMMUNICATION

Effective verbal communication ranks close in importance to effective listening. Even in the age of high technology, talking is still by far the most frequently used method of communication. This is why leaders in organizations should strive to continually improve their verbal communication skills. Being attentive to the following factors will help improve the quality of your verbal communication:

- *Interest.* When speaking with employees, show interest in your topic. Show that you are sincerely interested in communicating your message to them. Demonstrate interest in the receivers of the message, as well. Look them in the eye, or if in a group, spread eye contact evenly among all receivers. Speakers who sound bored, ambivalent, or indifferent concerning their own message cannot expect receivers of the message to be enthusiastic about it.

- *Attitude.* Maintaining a positive, friendly attitude can enhance verbal communication. This is because people are more open to listening to someone who is friendly and positive. A caustic, superior, condescending, disinterested, or argumentative attitude will shut down communication. To increase the likelihood that your messages will be received in a welcome or at least open-minded manner, be positive, be friendly, and smile.

- *Flexibility.* People who come across as dogmatic and dictatorial in their verbal communication run the risk of having their message rejected by receivers. Flexibility and a willingness to hear other points of view will usually improve the chances that people will receive your message in a positive manner. For example, if during a team meeting you present a case for solving a problem, let employees know that you would like to hear any ideas they might have. Even if no one has an alternative idea to propose, the fact that you are flexible enough to ask will improve the reception your idea receives. In fact, an effective tactic is to ask for their ideas before presenting your own. Sometimes when a leader presents his ideas first, employees are reluctant to raise issues that might appear to challenge or contradict him.

- *Tact.* Tact is an important ingredient in verbal communication, particularly when delivering a sensitive, potentially controversial, or unwelcome message. Tact has been referred to as the ability to hammer in the nail without breaking the board. The key to tactful verbal communication is to think before speaking. Tact does not mean being less than forthright. Rather, it means finding a way to candidly say what has to be said without adding insult to injury.

- *Courtesy.* Being courteous means showing appropriate concern for the needs and feelings of the receiver. Calling a meeting as employees are walking out the door at the end of a workday is inconsiderate and will inhibit communication. Courtesy also dictates that you avoid monopolizing conversations. When communicating verbally, give receivers ample opportunities to ask questions for clarification and to state their own points of view. Leaders in organizations should remember that one-sided conversations are not really conversations at all. They are broadcasts.

COMMUNICATING CORRECTIVE FEEDBACK

Executives, managers, and supervisors occasionally need to give corrective feedback to employees. In fact, this is an important responsibility of organizational leaders at all levels. Corrective feedback is provided to help employees improve their performance. Effectively given corrective feedback will do so. But in order to be effective, corrective feedback must be communicated properly. The following guidelines will help enhance the effectiveness of corrective feedback:

- *Be positive.* To actually improve performance, corrective feedback must be accepted and acted on by the employee. This is more likely to happen if it is delivered in a positive manner. Corrective feedback that is delivered in a less than tactful manner may cause the receiver to become defensive. If this happens, you are more likely to get excuses than improved performance. Give the employee being corrected the necessary feedback, but do not focus solely on the negative. Find something positive to say. For example, assume a team member has arrived late for work twice in one week. One approach would be to confront the tardy employee and say, "I'm glad you could show up today. I certainly hope this job isn't interfering with your social life." The employee would certainly get the message about coming to work on time, but he might also be offended by the sarcasm in the feedback. Also, if there is some legitimate reason for his tardiness, the employee might resent the assumption that his social life is the cause. A better approach would be to say, "Is everything OK? I noticed that you have been late twice this week." This approach lets the employee know that his tardiness has been noticed, but it also gives him the benefit of the doubt by assuming there is a legitimate reason for it. Another positive approach would be to say, "Mark I am really proud of the work you did on the ABC Project. Now let's talk about how you can do an equally good job of getting to work on time." The latter two examples let the employee know that his tardiness is unacceptable but without creating resentment or defensiveness. Remember, the goal is to correct and improve, not to punish.

- *Be prepared.* Before giving corrective feedback, do your homework. Then when giving the feedback, focus on facts. Give specific examples of the behavior that needs to be improved. A normal human response to corrective feedback is to view it as criticism and become defensive. For example, return to the case of the employee who was late for work two days in one week. If this employee becomes defensive he might try to deny being late. However, if he knows that his supervisor has the facts, this is less likely to happen. A supervisor who is poorly prepared might say, "Mark, you have been late a couple of times this week." The vagueness of this statement might encourage Mark to challenge it. However, if the supervisor says, "Mark, you were 30 minutes late on Monday and 20 minutes late on Tuesday," he will know better than to challenge the statement.

- *Be realistic.* When working to improve the performance of employees, there is always a temptation to rush, to get in a hurry. Leaders in organizations who want peak performance from employees can be forgiven for wanting it right now. Unfortunately, employee development is seldom immediate. Improvement can take time and often does. Consequently, when giving corrective feedback for improving performance it is important to be realistic. First, use your experience to determine how much improvement is realistic to expect over a specific period of time. Then be realistic in setting improvement goals. Second, make sure the performance you want to improve is within the control of the employee. Never make the mistake of expecting an employee to correct something over which he has no control. Explain the situation to the employee, ask for his input, and listen carefully. If there is an inhibitor standing in the way of the desired improvement, removing that inhibitor is the leader's job.

Communication is an imperfect, but essential process. Without effective communication, employees cannot achieve peak performance and continual improvement, nor can leaders facilitate the process. Consequently, investing the time and effort necessary to become an effective communicator is a worthwhile endeavor for leaders in organizations.

GROUP TRAINING ACTIVITIES

1. Mark is having communication problems in his department. When he first became the departmental supervisor, Mark simply told his team members what he wanted them to do and when they had to complete their assignments. But he soon noticed that people sometimes misinterpretted his instructions. Consequently, of late he asks team members to repeat his instructions to make sure they have heard him and understand. This approach has cut down on the communication problems in his department somewhat, but it has not eliminated them. For example, just this morning he told a team member to complete a project by the end of the day. When the employee had not brought the completed work to him by the end of the day, Mark stopped by his cubicle to inquire only to learn that this team member was gone for the day. "I don't get it," mumbled Mark to himself. "I told him I needed that project completed today, and I know he heard me and understood what I said." If Mark was a friend of yours, what advice would you give him to improve communication in cases like this?

2. Mary's team members complain constantly that she does not listen to them. One employee summed up the feelings of the entire team when he said: "Sure her door is always open when we need to talk. But that does not mean she listens. She interrupts constantly, jumps ahead to where she thinks you are going, and continues to do paperwork instead of concentrating on what you say." Is Mary

a good listener? Would you like to be a member of her team? What advice would you give Mary about listening to her team members?

3. Steve's office is an impressive place—if you want to be impressed about Steve. The walls in Steve's office are covered with every plaque, certificate, and degree he has ever received. There are trophies and photographs covering the exploits of his entire career on every surface in the office. There are several chairs in the office, but the only comfortable chair is the one behind Steve's desk. What non-verbal messages does Steve's office give to people who visit him there? What kinds of problems might Steve encounter when using his office to meet with employees who want to make a complaint or recommendation?

Nine

TEAMWORK

Best Practice Number 9: *Become an effective team builder and team leader and help employees become good team players*

A team is a group of people working together to accomplish a common mission. In organizations some teams are functional units such as human resources, sales, marketing, accounting, receiving, shipping, information technology, etc. These are permanent teams. Others are temporary or ad hoc in nature. These teams are formed to accomplish a specific objective. Having done so, they are disbanded. Regardless of the type of team, effective teamwork is critical to organizational success. It is less difficult for organizational leaders to equip, enable, and empower employees for peak performance and continual improvement in an environment of effective teamwork.

THE BASIS OF EFFECTIVE TEAMWORK

Having a common, collective mission is essential to effective teamwork because the very basis of the concept is a group of people committing to the accomplishment of a common mission. Effective teamwork is easy to define, but it can be difficult to achieve. In fact, ensuring that all members of a given team buy into its collective mission is one of the most difficult challenges for leaders in organizations. Of course, there is more to effective teamwork than just committing to a common mission, but once all members of a team have made a commitment the other ingredients will fall in place more readily.

People are naturally individualistic and this especially true of Americans. The rights of the individual are spelled out in the U. S. Constitution, and more specifically in the Bill of Rights. Respect for the individual is deeply ingrained in the American psyche—it's in our blood. Our heroes tend to be rugged individuals who triumph over adversity. Consequently, convincing people in organizations to put their natural individualistic tendencies aside for the good of the team is a difficult undertaking. This is one of the primary reasons that teambuilding is not a destination but a process that never ends. It is something that leaders in organizations must work on constantly. Organizational leaders should understand that with teambuilding the job is never done.

TEAMBUILDING

Part of building an effective team is choosing team members wisely. If the team is a functional department, team members are chosen through the staffing process. This is why I encourage leaders in organizations to consider not just education, experience, and other "paper" credentials when hiring employees for their departments, but also fit. During the interview process it is important to consider how well prospective employees will fit in with their fellow team members. An otherwise talented employee who is a poor team player can undermine the performance of an entire team.

An employee who disrupts or inhibits effective teamwork is not worth the investment no matter how well-qualified he might be for his individual job. It is also important to consider fit when selecting team members for ad hoc teams. Remember, teams in organizations are like sports teams—it matters who the players are. Before choosing team members, the team being formed must have a mission statement so that the members selected will know the team's purpose.

Developing a Mission Statement for the Team

Before choosing team members, the individual who will serve as the team leader should develop a mission statement. This is a critical step in the formation of a team. The mission statement explains the team's reason for being. A mission statement is written in terms that are broad enough to encompass everything the team will be expected to do, but specific enough that progress can be measured. Achieving the proper balance between broadness and specificity can be a challenge. Do not be concerned if it takes several drafts to get the mission statement suitably written. It probably will. The following mission statement is provided as an example that meets the broadness and specificity requirements:

> The purpose of this team is to identify ways to improve productivity in the XYZ department while simultaneously improving quality.

This statement is broad enough to encompass a wide range of activities. It gives team members plenty of room in which to operate. The statement does not specify how much productivity and quality will be improved. This level of specificity comes in the goals set by the team. Goals come after the mission statement and explain it more fully and in quantifiable terms. Although written in broad terms, this sample mission statement is specific enough that team members will know they are expected to simultaneously improve productivity and quality. It also meets one other important criterion: simplicity. Any employee could understand this mission statement. It is brief and to the point, but comprehensive.

Team leaders should keep simplicity as well as balance between broadness and specificity in mind when developing mission statements. A good mission statement is a tool for communicating the team's purpose, both within the team and throughout the organization. Consequently, it should be understandable, not just to team members but to any member of the larger organization.

Choosing Team Members

Once the team's mission statement has been written, it can be used as a communication tool when choosing team members. Before choosing the members of an ad hoc team, identify all potential team members. This is important because there will often be more potential team members than the number of members actually needed. After the list of candidates has been compiled, the selection process can begin. Having a list of all potential team members will allow you to consider not just qualifications, but fit. In choosing team members, care should be taken to ensure a broad mix. This rule of thumb should be adhered to even if nobody volunteers to serve and team members must be drafted, something that occasionally happens with ad hoc teams.

Another challenge to achieving effective teamwork is that team leaders are not always able to choose the members of the team's they are asked to lead. Sometimes the team has already been formed or the members are chosen by higher management. Whether leaders inherit or select the members of their teams, the information presented in the rest of this chapter still applies.

Responsibilities of Team Leaders

Becoming a team leader is often the first step up the career ladder to higher leadership positions in an organization. In fact, team leadership is excellent training for higher leadership. Consequently, when an opportunity arises to lead a team it is important to get it right. What follows are typical responsibilities of team leaders:

- Serve as the team's representative to higher management.

- Serve as the official record keeper for the team. Records include minutes, correspondence, agendas, and reports. Typically, the team leader will appoint a recorder to take minutes during meetings. However, the team leader is still responsible for distributing and filing minutes and making sure they are accurate.

- Participate in team discussions and debates, but take care to avoid dominating.

- Implement team recommendations that fall within the team leader's realm of authority, and work with higher management to implement those that fall outside of it.

Developing Positive Working Relationships in Teams

A team works most effectively when individual team members form positive, mutually supportive peer relationships. Positive working relationships can be the difference between having a high-performance team and having one that is mediocre. Learning to develop positive relationships in teams is important for organizational leaders.

- Help team members understand the importance of being honest and reliable. Effective teamwork is not possible in an environment of mistrust.

- Help team members develop an attitude of mutual support. Team members should be supportive of each other as they struggle with the challenges of getting the job done. Further, team members should help each other deal with the stress of the job.

These are the basics. Competence, trust, communication, reliability, and mutual support are the foundation on which effective teamwork is built. Any time devoted to improving these factors is a good investment for leaders in organizations.

FOUR-STEPS TO EFFECTIVE TEAMBUILDING

Good teamwork does not just happen. It takes commitment, patience, and hard work. Effective teambuilding is a four-step process. The steps are:

1. Assess

2. Plan

3. Execute

4. Evaluate

Specifically, the process of teambuilding proceeds as follows: a) assess the team's strengths and weaknesses to identify factors that need to be improved as well as those that can be capitalized on, b) plan teambuilding activities based on the results of the assessment, c) execute the planned teambuilding activities, and d) evaluate results. These steps are explained in greater detail in the following sections.

Assessing Team Strengths and Weaknesses

If you were the new coach of a baseball team about which you knew very little, what is the first thing you would want to do? Most coaches in such situations would begin by assessing the abilities of their team members. They would identify specific strengths and weaknesses.

With this done, the coach would have an accurate picture of what he needed to do to turn the team into a winner or to improve on an existing winning record.

This same approach can be used in any kind of organization. A mistake often made by team leaders is beginning teambuilding activities before determining what kinds of activities are really needed. Resources in most organizations are limited. Even in those rare cases where they are not limited, leaders cannot justify wasting resources. It is important to use them as efficiently and effectively as possible. Team leaders who begin teambuilding activities without first assessing strengths and weaknesses run the risk of wasting resources trying to strengthen areas that are already strong, while at the same time overlooking areas that are weak. Accurately assessing the strengths and weaknesses of teams is an important aspect of teambuilding.

For teams in organizations to be effective and productive, several factors must be present. At a minimum these factors include the following:

- Clear direction that is understood by all members (e.g. mission, goals, ground rules).

- Team players on the team (e.g. team first—me second).

- Fully understood and accepted accountability measures (e.g. evaluation of performance).

What follows are specific criteria in each of these three broad areas that can be used for conducting an assessment of a team's strengths and weaknesses.

Direction and Understanding

People in teams need to know where the team leader is trying to take them and what the team is supposed to accomplish. In other words, they need to have direction and fully understand it. The following criteria can be used to determine if a team has direction and if it understands that direction:

- Does the team have a clearly stated mission?

- Do all team members understand the mission?

- Do all team members understand how and where the team fits into the overall organization?

- Does the team have a set of broad goals that translate its mission into more measureable terms?

- Do all team members understand the goals?

- Does the team have a schedule and deadline for achieving each goal?

- Do all members of the team understand the schedule and deadlines?

Characteristics of Team Members

Effective teamwork requires that team members be good team players. While it is necessary for members of teams to think independently and critically, once decisions are made they must act as a team in implementing them. The following criteria can be used to determine if a team's members are good team players:

- Are all team members open and honest with each other all the time?

- Do all team members trust each other?

- Do all team members put the team's mission and goals ahead of their personal agendas all the time?

- Do all team members know they can depend on each other?

- Are all team members committed to accomplishing the team's goals?

- Are all team members willing to take responsibility for the team's performance?

- Are all team members willing to cooperate with each other to accomplish the team's mission?

- Do all team members take the initiative to ensure the best possible performance of the team?

- Are all team members patient with each other?

- Are all team members resourceful in finding ways to get the job done in spite of obstacles?

- Are all team members punctual for work, meetings, assignments, and in meeting deadlines?

- Are team members tolerant of individual differences among members of the team (i.e. intellectual, racial, cultural, gender, political, and religious)?

- Are all team members willing to persevere when the job gets hard?

- Are all team members mutually-supportive of each other?

- Are all team members comfortable stating their opinions, pointing out problems, and offering constructive criticism in team meetings?

- Do all team members support team decisions once they are made?

Accountability

People in teams need to know how the team's performance will be evaluated—what accountability measures will apply. The following criteria can be used to determine if team members understand how the team will be held accountable for its performance:

- Do all team members know how team progress/performance will be measured?

- Do all team members understand how success is defined for the team?

- Do all team members understand how ineffective team members will be dealt with?

- Do all team members understand how team decisions are made?

- Do all team members know their respective responsibilities?

- Do all team members know the responsibilities of all other team members?

- Do all team members understand their authority within the team?

- Do all team members know what to do when unforeseen problems cause them to miss a deadline?

Conducting a Team Assessment

An efficient and effective way to assess the strengths and weaknesses of teams in organizations is to turn the criteria listed in the previous sections into an assessment instrument that can be distributed to all team members. Ask team members to complete the assessment without attribution and return it to the team leader for compilation and analysis. Better yet, load it with survey software and ask employees to complete it on line.

Turning the criteria into an assessment instrument can be easily accomplished by adding two items: 1) a rating scale, and 2) a set of instructions. A rating scale that has proven effective over time assigns numerical values to the following possible responses for each criterion:

Completely true	(6)
Somewhat true	(4)
Somewhat false	(2)
Completely false	(0)
Do not know	(X)

A briefly-stated set of instructions can be added to explain how to apply the rating scale to each criterion based on the individual's personal perceptions. The following instructions are provided as an example:

To the left of each criterion is a blank for recording your perception of that item. For each item record your perception of how well it describes your team. For example, if the statement is completely true, record a "6." If it is completely false record a "0." You may record fractional answers (e.g. 3.5, 2.7, 4.3, etc.). If you do not know how to rate a given criterion record an "X."

Once all team members have completed the assessment, the team leader computes the average score for each criterion. If the survey is loaded onto the Internet using survey software, the software will perform the computations automatically. Any criterion that receives a team average of less than "4" or "somewhat true" represents a weakness that should be singled out for improvement. Any criterion that receives a team score higher than "4" represents a strength that can be exploited to maximize the team's performance. When manually computing the average score for each criterion do not count any that are marked with an "X" or the team average for that criterion will be skewed.

Developing a Teambuilding Plan

Teambuilding activities are planned based on the results of the assessment of strengths and weaknesses. For example, assume the assessment shows that the team is floundering because it lacks direction. Clearly, part of the process of building this team must be developing a clear and comprehensive mission statement. If the team in this case already has a mission statement one of two things is certain: 1) the mission statement has not been properly explained to team members, or 2) the mission statement is vague or confusing and needs to be rewritten. Regardless of what the assessment reveals about the team, the findings of the assessment are used as the basis for developing a teambuilding plan for enhancing the team's performance.

Executing Team-Building Activities

Team building activities should be implemented on a just-in-time basis. This means it is best to provide teambuilding activities once a team has actually been formed. Training all personnel in an organization in anticipation of eventually putting them on a team is not an effective approach. Like any kind of training, teamwork training will be forgotten unless it is put to use immediately. Consequently, the best time to provide training to correct weakness identified in the assessment is after a specific team has actually been formed. In this way, team members will have the opportunity to focus on specific weaknesses and immediately apply what they learn during the training.

Teambuilding is an ongoing, never-ending process. The idea is to make a team better and better as time goes by. Consequently, teamwork training should be provided as soon as possible after a team is formed, and it should be based on an assessment of the team's strengths and weaknesses. All subsequent teambuilding activities should also be based on the results of an assessment. Leaders in organizations should never make the mistake of training blindly. Assess first and then base decisions concerning what training to provide on the results of the assessment.

Evaluating Team-Building Activities

If teambuilding activities have been effective, weak areas pointed out by the assessment should be strengthened. A simple way to evaluate the effectiveness of teambuilding activities is to give the team sufficient time to improve its performance and then conduct the assessment again. If this assessment (evaluation) shows that sufficient progress has been made, nothing more is required for the time being. If not, additional teambuilding activities are needed. If a given teambuilding activity appears to have been ineffective, get the team together and discuss it. Use the feedback from team members to identify problems with the training and use the information to improve subsequent teambuilding activities. Involving the team in evaluating teambuilding training is itself an effective teambuilding activity in and of itself.

TEAMS SHOULD BE COACHED

Organizational leaders should know that if employees are going to work together as a team, they have to be coached. Just being the "boss" will not ensure effective teamwork. Leaders in organizations need to understand the difference between bossing and coaching. Bossing, in the traditional sense, involves giving orders and evaluating performance. Bosses approach the job from a perspective that can be summarized as follows: "I'm in charge—do what I say."

Coaches, on the other hand, are team leaders who approach the job from a *follow-me* perspective. Their overriding goal for the team is consistent peak performance and continual improvement. Consequently, they work with individual team members and the team as a whole to help them do better and get better every day. Leaders in organizations can become effective coaches by doing the following things:

- Giving their team a clearly defined charter (mission, goals, and ground rules) and making sure that all members understand the charter.

- Making team development and teambuilding on-going activities that never end.

- Mentoring individual team members or providing mentors for them.

- Promoting mutual respect between and among team members as well as between themselves and team members.

- Working to make human diversity within a team an asset.

- Setting a positive example of being an effective and productive member of the organization's management team.

Coaching and the Team Charter (Mission, Ground Rules, and Goals)

You can probably imagine a baseball, football, basketball, soccer, or track coach calling his team together and saying, "This year we have one overriding purpose—to win the championship." In one simple statement this coach has clearly and succinctly defined the team's mission—the first component of a team charter. From this statement, team members should immediately realize that everything they do will be aimed at winning the championship. The coach's statement of the mission was brief, to the point, specific, and easily understood. Coaches of work teams should be just as specific in explaining their team's mission, ground rules, and goals to team members. Writing a mission statement for a team was explained earlier in this chapter.

Developing the Team Charter

A team charter is a document consisting of three major components: 1) mission statement for the team, 2) ground rules for team members, and 3) team goals. It is used to provide direction for team members and to make sure they understand where the team fits into the overall organization. The mission statement and goals are developed by the team leader. The ground rules are developed by the team members with the assistance and guidance of the team leader.

Developing the mission statement

This section reviews and augments the information presented earlier in this chapter concerning writing a team's mission statement. The mission statement for the team is a brief summary of the team's purpose. It should be a subset of the larger organization's mission statement and show where the team fits into the organization. Some team leaders like to include the organization's mission statement in their team charters to make sure that team members understand the connection between the respective missions of the organization and the team. A well-written team mission statement is brief (no more than a short paragraph), but comprehensive and easy to understand. The following examples—one for a private-sector and the other for a public-sector organization—meet these criteria and can be used as examples when developing mission statements for any kind of organization:

- *Private-sector organization.* The following team mission statement is for the quality management team of an organization that manufactures kitchen appliances: *The Quality Management Team's mission within the organization is to: 1) ensure superior value for customers, and 2) ensure continual improvement of the quality of XYZ, Inc.'s processes and products.*

- *Public-sector organization.* The following team mission statement is for the training unit of a county Sheriff's Department: *The Training Unit's mission is to provide high-quality customized training that continually updates and expands the job-related knowledge and skills of the Sheriff Department's personnel.*

Developing the ground rules

A team's ground rules answer the following question: As we work together to accomplish our team's mission, how are we to interact with each other? Developing the ground rules for a team presents the team leader with an interesting challenge. On one hand it is important that all team members accept the ground rules as their own—rules they established rather than rules that have been imposed on them. On the other hand it is important for the team leader to exercise a modicum of control over the process. The ground rules are established to help encourage peak performance and continual improvement. It is the team leader who is ultimately accountable for that performance. The buck stops with the team leader.

An effective way to maintain control of the process of developing team ground rules while still achieving buy-in from team members is to begin the process with a *menu* of potential ground rules. The menu should contain 15 to 20 ground rules that represent factors that are widely-known as necessary for peak performance and continual improvement in teams. The menu is distributed to all team members. Individual team members are asked to circle the ten items on the menu they think are most important, and return the marked up menu to the team leader without attribution.

The team leader then compiles the top ten items for the team. If there are items that are important to the team leader that do not make the top ten list, she retains the right to add them to the list. A team will typically have from eight to twelve ground rules. Any more than this and some of them probably need to be combined. Asking teams to select their top ten ground rules from the menu gives team leaders room to add items when necessary. When conducted in this manner, the process gives team members sufficient involvement to ensure buy-in while still giving the team leader control over the process.

What follows is a list of possible ground rules for team charters. This list can be used as a guide in developing a menu of potential ground rules for any kind of team in any kind of organization:

- *Honesty.* Team members will be open and honest with each other at all times.

- *No personal agendas.* Team members will put the team's needs ahead of their personal agendas in all cases.

- *Dependability.* Team members will conduct themselves in ways that show they can be depended on.

- *Enthusiasm.* Team members will be enthusiastic about accomplishing team goals.

- *Responsibility.* Team members will take responsibility for their individual performance as well as the team's performance.

- *Mutual support.* Team members will be mutually-supportive in carrying out their responsibilities in the team.

- *Initiative.* Team members will take the initiative in helping the team accomplish its mission.

- *Patience.* Team members will be patient with each other as new processes, procedures, methods, and skills are learned.

- *Resourcefulness.* Team members will be resourceful, innovative, and creative in finding ways to get the job done in spite of obstacles.

- *Punctuality.* Team members will be punctual in arriving at work, team meetings, and other scheduled activities as well as in meeting deadlines.

- *Tolerance/sensitivity.* Team members will be tolerant of and sensitive to individual differences in other team members.

- *Perseverance.* Team members will persevere in getting the job done when difficulties arise and during times of adversity.

- *Conflict management.* Team members are encouraged to express opinions, make recommendations, point out problems, and offer constructive criticism, but with tact. When team members disagree, they will do so without being disagreeable. In addition, team members will solve differences among themselves in a responsible, professional manner that contributes to team morale and performance.

- *Decisions.* Team members will participate in the decision-making process by offering thoughtful input before the decision is made. Once a team decision has been made, all members will support it fully and do their best to carry it out, even if they do not agree with it (unless, of course, there are ethical problems with the decision).

Putting Together the Final Team Charter

Once the team's mission statement has been finalized and the team's ground rules selected, the team charter can be finalized. It will contain the team's name, mission, ground rules, and goals. The first three of these components are relatively static. Although these components should be reviewed from time to time if the team is permanent in nature (e.g. a functional department), they will not change much over time unless the nature of the team itself changes. The team's goals on the other hand may change frequently as existing goals are accomplished and new ones are added. Team goals are established by the team leader and higher management.

Coaching and Team Development

Work teams should be similar to athletic teams when it comes to team development. Regardless of the sport, athletic teams practice constantly. During practice, coaches work on developing the skills of individual team members and the team as a whole. Team development activities should be continual and they should go on forever. A team should never stop getting better. Coaches of work teams should follow the lead of their athletic counterparts. Developing the skills of individual team members and building the team as a whole should be a normal part of the job—a part that takes place regularly and never stops.

Coaching and Mentoring

Organizational leaders must be good coaches, and good coaches must be good mentors. This means they must establish nurturing, developmental relationships with team members. Developing the capabilities of team members, improving the contributions individuals make to the team, and helping team members advance their careers are all mentoring activities. Organizational leaders who are mentors help team members by:

- Developing their job-related skills

- Making sure they understand all components in the team's charter

- Helping them build character

- Helping them learn to be good team players

- Teaching them the organization's corporate culture

- Teaching them how to get things done in the organization

- Helping them understand other people and their points of view

- Teaching them how to behave in unfamiliar settings or circumstances

- Giving them insight into the differences among people

- Helping them adopt values that support peak performance and employee excellence

Coaching and Mutual Respect

It is important for team members to respect their coach, for the coach to respect team members, and for team members to respect each other. Organizational leaders can use the following strategies to earn the respect of employees and to show them how to earn the respect of each other:

- *Trust made tangible.* Trust is established by a) setting a positive example of being trustworthy, b) honestly and openly sharing information, c) explaining personal motives, d) avoiding making personal criticisms and doing personal favors, e) giving sincere recognition for a job well done, and f) being consistent in the application of discipline. Doing these things will build trust and mutual respect.

- *Appreciation of people as assets.* Even in this age of advanced technology, people are still an organization's most valuable asset. This fact is the underlying principle upon which this book was written. To achieve peak performance and continual improvement, employees must be treated like assets that can increase in value if properly developed over time. Appreciation for people is shown by a) respecting their thoughts, feelings, values, and fears, b) respecting their desire to lead and follow, c) respecting their individual strengths and differences, d) respecting their desire to be involved and to participate, e) respecting their need to be winners, f) respecting their need to learn, grow, and develop, g) respecting their need for a safe and healthy workplace that is conducive to peak performance and continual improvement, and h) respecting their personal and family lives. Most organizations will claim that people are their most valuable asset, but too few actually follow through and treat employees like valuable assets. Words are not enough. Leaders in organizations must develop employees in ways that continually increase their value to the organization.

- *Communication that is clear and candid.* Communication can be made clear and candid if coaches do the following: a) open their eyes and ears—observe and listen, b) be tactfully forthcoming, c) give continual feedback and encourage team members to do the same, and d) confront conflict in the team directly and immediately before it can fester and blow up. People in teams want to be informed and they want to know that the information they are given is accurate and dependable.

- *Unequivocal ethical standards.* Ethical standards can be made unequivocal by: a) adopting the organization's code of ethics at the team level or, if the organization does not have one, working with the team to develop its own code of ethics, b) identifying ethical conflicts or potential conflicts as early as possible and acting to resolve them, c) recognizing and rewarding ethical behavior, d) correcting unethical behavior immediately—never ignoring it, and e) making new members of the team aware of the team's code of ethics. In addition to these strategies, coaches must set a consistent example of living up to the highest ethical standards themselves.

Coaching and Human Diversity

America is the most diverse country in the world and this diversity is reflected in its workforce. Diversity in all of its forms—racial, gender, cultural, political, religious, and intellectual—can be a tremendous asset to organizations or it can be the cause of constant conflict. The difference is in how organizations handle diversity. This is why organizational leaders must invest the time and effort necessary to make diversity an asset to their teams and to the overall organization.

Sports and the military have typically led American society in the drive to embrace diversity, and both have benefited immensely as a result. To list the contributions to either sports or the military made by people of different genders, races, cultures, religions, and political persuasions would be a gargantuan task. Fortunately, leading organizations in the United States are following the positive examples set by sports and the military. The best-led organizations have learned that most of the future growth in the population from which they recruit their employees will consist of women, minorities, and immigrants. These people will bring new ideas and new perspectives to their jobs, precisely what organizations need if they are going to stay fresh, current, and able to maintain a state of excellence.

In spite of the progress that has been achieved in making the American workplace both diverse and harmonious, some people—consciously and unconsciously—still erect barriers between themselves and people who they view as being different. This tendency can quickly undermine the trust and cohesiveness on which teamwork is built, especially when the team has a diverse membership. To keep this from happening, organizational leaders can apply the following coaching strategies:

- *Identify the specific needs of different groups.* Those who lead teams in organizations should ask women, ethnic minorities, and older workers to describe the unique inhibitors they face in trying to achieve peak performance and continual improvement. Make sure that all team members understand these barriers, and then work together as a team to eliminate, overcome, or accommodate them.

- *Confront cultural clashes.* When diversity-based conflict occurs in teams, confront it immediately. This approach is particularly important when the conflict is based on such issues as religion, culture, ethnicity, age, and/or gender. Because these issues are so deeply personal to individuals, they are potentially more volatile than everyday disagreements over work-related concerns. Consequently, conflict that is based on or aggravated by human diversity should be dealt with quickly and effectively. Few things will polarize a team faster than diversity-related disagreements that are allowed to fester and grow. When this happens more of the team's productive energy will be devoted to the conflict than to achieving peak performance and continual improvement.

- *Eliminate institutionalized bias.* Organizations that have done things a given way for a long time can suffer from institutionalized bias. This is a situation in which the bias—although not necessarily intended—results from a failure to match changes in the composition of the workforce with corresponding organizational changes. Consider the following example. An organization that has historically had a predominantly male workforce now has one in which women are the majority. However, the organization's facility still has 10 rest rooms for men and only two for women, a circumstance left over from how things used to be. This is an example of institutionalized bias. Teams can find themselves unintentionally slighting their members simply out of habit, tradition, or unwitting circumstances. When the demographics of a team change but its habits, traditions, procedures, and work environment stay the same, the result can be unintended discrimination. Eliminating institutionalized bias is important because failing to do so will undermine a team's morale and performance. If the bias applies more broadly than to just one team, it will ultimately undermine organizational excellence.

An effective way to eliminate institutional bias is to circulate a blank notebook and ask team members to record—without attribution—instances and examples of it they have encountered.

After the initial circulation, repeat the process periodically. The input collected will be helpful in identifying institutionalized bias that can then be eliminated. By collecting input directly from team members and acting on it promptly, leaders in organizations can ensure that discrimination by inertia is not creating or perpetuating resentment among personnel who need to be focused on peak performance and continual improvement.

Handling Conflict in Teams

Conflict will occur in even the best teams. Even when all team members agree on a goal, they can still disagree on how best to accomplish it. Organizational leaders should know that effective teamwork will be undermined unless conflict is confronted promptly and resolved in a positive manner. People in teams have sufficient energy to pursue peak performance or to pursue conflict, but not both. Conflict can sap the energy of a team and undermine its performance.

Potential Human Responses to Conflict in Teams

Conflict in organizations is probably inevitable. Consequently, it is important for leaders in organizations to understand the various ways in which people respond to conflict and how to ensure that their responses are team-positive and resolution-oriented. The various responses to conflict all fall into one of the following categories:

- *Escape responses.* Escape responses represent one extreme of the continuum of possible responses to conflict. Escape responses are negative—they hurt the organization, the team, and the person in question. They include denial, flight, and suicide. People who respond to conflict in any of these ways are so averse to it that they will take an extreme approach to avoiding it. All escape responses are harmful. Consequently, team leaders should be vigilant in observing team members and in acting quickly if they notice any who might take an escape response to conflict.

- *Attack responses.* Attack responses represent the other extreme of the response continuum. They are negative in that they hurt the organization, the team, the victims, and the person who perpetrates the attack. They include litigation, assault, and murder. One team member filing a grievance or, worse yet, a lawsuit against another can tear a team apart. Only assault or murder would be more devastating to team cohesion. When any of these attack responses happen, team members take sides. When team members take sides, the conflict spreads and becomes more intense. Consequently, team leaders must stay closely connected to their team members so they can anticipate the potential for an attack response and move quickly to prevent it.

- *Resolution responses.* Resolution responses are positive in that they can lead to a resolution that is good for the organization, the team, and the individuals involved. Although all of the responses explained in this bulleted item are resolution responses, it is important to understand that they are not all equally positive. Consequently, the various resolution responses are listed in order of preference. People in conflict can overlook, reconcile, negotiate, mediate, or arbitrate to arrive at a resolution. Often the best way to resolve conflict is for those involved to simply *overlook* what brought it on in the first place and move on. This occurs when both parties realize that fighting over a certain issue is going to get them nowhere, so they agree to drop it and move on. When this option does not work, *reconciliation* is the next option. Reconciliation is the forgive-and-forget response. This means that those involved sit down as responsible professionals and work out their differences. When this option does not work the parties in question can *negotiate* some type of mutually-agreeable resolution. In this case, neither party gets everything desired, but each gives enough that both parties are willing to accept the resolution and move on. *Mediation* is the next option when the other responses have not worked and the parties involved bring their conflict to the team leader. In this case, the team leader serves as a referee and tries to guide the conflicting parties to a resolution that is in the best interests of the team and the organization. When this does not work, the only remaining positive response is *arbitration*. With arbitration, the conflict is brought before the team leader, as it was with mediation, but this time the team leader acts as judge rather than referee. She decides how the dispute will be settled and uses her authority to impose that resolution.

On one hand, effective teamwork is essential to organizational excellence. It is also essential to achieving peak performance and continual improvement since it creates an environment that encourages and supports both. On the other hand, achieving effective teamwork is one of the leader's most difficult challenges, and it is a challenge that never ends. However, with persistence and patience leaders in organizations can build and maintain teams that will bring out the best in employees and ensure peak performance and continual improvement, not just for individuals but the entire organization.

GROUP TRAINING ACTIVITIES

1. "My team members don't seem to get along. They bicker about everything," said Mack to his fellow supervisor, David. "I really need some help. Do you have any suggestions that will help me create a more harmonious environment in my team?" Put yourself in David's place and discuss various strategies Mack might use to prevent and resolve conflict in his team.

2. One day Mickey's boss surprised him by saying, "You would get a lot more out of your team if you would stop bossing and start coaching." Mickey wasn't sure what his boss meant, but he decided to find out. Assume he came to you for help. Discuss what the group would tell Mickey.

3. Anita is growing increasingly frustrated with her team. There seems to be constant petty bickering and discord among the members. She had always thought that diversity would be an asset, but the promise has not manifested itself in her team. All it has done in her team is cause problems. Discuss how Anita might go about turning diversity into an asset in her team.

Ten

CHANGE MANAGEMENT

Best Practice Number 10: Become proficient at managing change and help employees become positive change agents.

One of the keys to achieving and maintaining peak performance at the individual and organizational levels is continual improvement. People and organizations that excel never rest on their laurels. Rather, they do what is necessary to get better all the time. To get better all the time people and organizations must improve continually. In practical terms, continual improvement means continual change. Consequently, leaders in organizations must be effective change managers who can help employees become positive change agents.

Only through determined, committed leadership can an organization overcome a principle I call *organizational inertia*. Inertia is a concept from physics which states that a body at rest will stay at rest until sufficient force is applied to move it. Organizations are like the body at rest in physics. They will cling to the status quo until sufficient effort is put into making changes. The principle of organizational inertia can be summarized as follows: *An organization's culture, systems, processes, and procedures will tend to perpetuate themselves until sufficient leadership is applied to change them.*

IMPROVED PERFORMANCE—THE BEST REASON FOR CHANGE

While conducting research for my book *Effective Change Management* (Prentice Hall), I came across two other books on the topic that showed the great diversity of opinion surrounding the concept of organizational change. One of the books was titled *If It Ain't Broke Break It*. The other was titled *Stop All This mindless Change*. As the titles indicate, the former advocated constantly shaking up the status quo while the latter advocated putting on the brakes.

After studying these polar opposite perspectives, I concluded that they were not really as far apart as the titles suggest. Both books make some excellent points and are good reads for anyone interested in organizational change. For example, *If It Ain't Broke Break It* correctly attacks the tendency of organizations to continue doing things the way they have always done them. Breaking out of these ruts is really what the author means by "if it ain't broke break it." The author of *Stop All This Mindless Change* is not against change per se, just change for the sake of change.

This chapter offers a different point of view that incorporates some of both perspectives. The foundation of my philosophy of organizational change is that continual improvement is the best reason for change. In a competitive environment, the best reason to change something in an organization is to improve it. If an organizational change will not result in some kind of improvement, why make it?

Organizations that excel change constantly, but they do so for the purpose of improving their people, processes, and products or the environment in which they operate. Improvements to people, processes, products, and environments, in turn, make organizations more competitive. Organizational leaders need to understand that the most effective change initiatives are tied directly to the continual improvement of performance. If the rationale for change is anything but improvement, organizational leaders need to step back and analyze their motives.

Organizations excel by identifying, adopting, and deploying best practices. These practices should never be changed on a whim, to eliminate boredom, to provide variety, or just to see what might happen. The only reason to change best practices is to improve them, and before the new-and-improved version is adopted and deployed as the new best practice leaders in organizations should make sure that it actually results in improvements. Improved best practices should never be adopted without first running them through sufficient trials to know that they really will bring improvements. The *change-to-improve* philosophy is the theme of this chapter and a best practice of executives, managers, and supervisors who are developmental leaders.

NEED FOR LEADERSHIP IN ORGANIZATIONAL CHANGE

In a highly-competitive environment organizations are constantly looking for ways to catch up, keep up, or stay ahead. To play a positive role in the process, leaders in organizations must be positive change agents and effective change managers. Positive change agency and effective change management are important leadership responsibilities. When you are responsible for implementing a major organizational change or a significant part of one, the change-management model explained in the following sections will help.

Step 1: Develop the Change Picture.

For most people, the unknown breeds fear. This is one of the main reasons that people in organizations tend to resist change: because they fear the unknown. Even when people do not like conditions as they currently exist, they take comfort in at least knowing the conditions and being familiar with them. Because of their comfort with the familiar, employees often adopt an attitude toward change that is best summarized by the old maxim, *the devil you know is better than one you don't know.* Consequently, when making a major change it is important for leaders in organizations to eliminate fear of the unknown. This is the first step in the change-management model.

To eliminate fear of the unknown, eliminate the unknown. The unknown can be turned into the known by developing a compelling, informative change picture. A change picture is a written explanation of how things will be after the change. The key to making a change picture compelling is to develop it from the perspective of those who will be affected by the change. Change is personal to people. Consequently, the first thing they always want to know about change is how it is going to affect them. A good change picture answers this question by providing the following information about the change initiative: what, when, where, who, why, and how.

A good change picture explains the nature of the change (*what*), *when* the change will occur, *where* the change will occur, *who* the change will affect, *why* the change is being made, and *how* it will affect all stakeholders. This final consideration—how the change will affect stakeholders—is the most important to employees because they are typically major stakeholders in organizational change.

A good change picture will explain the "how" element in terms that are personal to stakeholders. For example, if there will be layoffs, new hires, mandatory training, changed work hours, different working conditions, or anything else that will affect employees, the change picture should explain it in terms that are open, honest, candid, and easily understood. Leaders in organizations who keep employees guessing about how a change will affect them run the risk of losing their best personnel while damaging the trust and morale of those who remain.

Step 2: Communicate the Change Picture to all Stakeholders

Once the change picture has been written it must be communicated to all stakeholders, especially those who will have to help implement it. I am often asked if the change picture should be provided in person or just emailed to stakeholders. My answer is always the same: "Both and more." I recommend that leaders in organizations use a variety of mediums for communicating the change picture, and the more the better. However, no matter what communication methods are used, it is imperative that there be a feedback loop so that stakeholders can ask questions, express concerns, point out problems, or just vent. This is why I recommend that face-to-face meetings be part of the communication mix.

An important part of communicating the change picture to employees involves conducting what I call a *roadblock analysis*. The roadblock analysis involves meeting with employees and asking them to consider the change in question and identify potential roadblocks that might derail its implementation. A roadblock analysis can be accomplished by email or even telephone, but the best approach is face-to-face. By asking people who are closer to the nuts and bolts of the change for their observations, leaders in organizations can identify roadblocks that might undermine a successful implementation. Once they have been identified, the roadblocks can be removed or, at least, mitigated before beginning the implementation phase of the change management model. Removing or mitigating roadblocks is explained in a later step.

Step 3: Take Responsibility for the Change

Organizational change never just happens—it requires commitment and a lot of energy, both mental and physical, from a lot of people. More than anything, it requires people who will step forward and take responsibility for doing their part to make the change succeed. Although some people in organizations will react to change by openly resisting it, many will exhibit a more passive form of resistance. One of the more common forms of passive resistance is the wait-and-see attitude. Employees who adopt a wait-and-see attitude do not necessarily work against the change, but they do not work for it either. They might say all the right things about supporting the change, but in reality they put no effort into making it succeed.

The wait-and-see crowd can be even more detrimental to change initiatives than those who openly oppose the initiatives. This is because making organizational change is like pushing a boulder up a hill. The organization needs all of its personnel pushing together in a coordinated and concerted effort. Those who openly oppose the change can be neutralized by isolating them from the implementation process. But those who act like they are helping when in fact they are not can pose serious roadblocks to the change. When trying to push a boulder up a hill, a lot of people are needed who will push with all their might.

People who act like they are pushing when they really aren't make the task more difficult for those who are. This is why people in organizations do not have to openly work against changes they oppose. All they have to do is sit back and let them fail for lack of commitment and effort. However, in spite of the wait-and-see crowd, if those who are doing their part can manage to get the boulder over the crest of the hill, things will get easier from that point on. When this happens, those who contributed nothing to getting the boulder up the hill typically join the parade of people following it down the other side, all the while acting as if they had pushed with all their might. On the other hand, if the boulder bogs down and fails to make it up the hill, members of the wait-and-see crowd will be quick to join the naysayers who openly opposed the change.

Organizational change succeeds only when the people responsible for implementing it are willing to: 1) take responsibility for pushing the boulder up the hill, and 2) commit to doing what is necessary to push the boulder over the crest of the hill. Once the organizational inertia has been broken and the boulder is moving, responsible personnel cannot let up or rest until it is over the crest and momentum is working on their behalf.

Step 4: Enlist Influential Personnel

Every organization has employees who are more influential than others. Their influence might result from seniority, talent, popularity, strength of personality, or a variety of other reasons. Regardless of why they are influential, other employees look to them for direction and approval. These influential employees can contribute significantly to the success or failure of a change initiative. For this reason, it is important to enlist them on the side of making the change succeed. Enlisting influential personnel can be a challenge because they might initially be opposed to the change. Consequently, before enlisting influential personnel it is important for leaders in organizations to have face-to-face, one-on-one conversations with them.

During these conversations, leaders should determine where influential employees stand concerning the change. Are they for it, against it, or just waiting to see what will happen? If they are against the change, do they intend to throw up roadblocks or just sit back and to see what will happen? If influential personnel are against the change or in wait-and-see mode, leaders have two options: 1) isolate them from the implementation process to limit their negative influence, or 2) enlist them in the effort by giving them responsibility for some aspect of the implementation plan. Sometimes giving an influential employee specific responsibilities relating to the change is enough to convert him into a supporter.

When an influential team member is enlisted in this manner, it is important to apply appropriate reinforcement methods. Typically this means applying both the carrot and the stick. In other words, a *carrot* is provided in the form of incentives the individual will receive when the change succeeds and a *stick* in the form of consequences if it does not succeed. Assurance of full cooperation should be gained before putting an influential employee to work on behalf of the change otherwise you may be putting a fox in the henhouse.

Step 5: Eliminate or Mitigate Roadblocks

An earlier step in this model involved conducting a roadblock analysis to identify any obstacles that might impede a successful implementation of the change initiative. In this step, the obstacles identified are either eliminated or mitigated. In order to explain the change management model in a step-by-step manner, it is necessary to put this step here. However, in reality, removing or mitigating roadblocks begins as soon as they are identified. This step can be carried out in parallel with those that have already been explained.

More often than not the obstacles identified are internal impediments decision makers have not thought of. Here are a few examples of change initiatives I have been involved with that contained roadblocks that had to be eliminated or mitigated. The first case involved my company expanding into a new business line that depended on the expertise of one highly-specialized engineer. This was the change initiative, adding a new business line. As it turned out, this engineer was about to submit his resignation to accept another job. This was the roadblock—something I was unaware of but that his team mates knew about. The engineer's impending departure came up during the roadblock analysis. As a result we postponed the change initiative until he could be replaced.

Another change initiative involved replacing the organization's fleet of cars with pickup trucks to gain more room for transporting materials. Changing from cars to trucks was the change initiative. The trucks ordered would be equipped with standard transmissions, saving the company a substantial amount of money. An issue that came up during the roadblock analysis was that only a few of our personnel knew how to drive standard-transmission vehicles. To eliminate this roadblock it was necessary for the company to provide driver training classes for the personnel who would drive the trucks. In these examples, stakeholders who were closer to the problem were able to point out the roadblocks and management was able to eliminate them before they derailed the implementation process.

Step 6: Develop a Step-by-Step Implementation Plan with Assignments

Once the roadblocks to a successful implementation have been removed or mitigated, a step-by-step implementation plan is developed. The plan lists every action—no matter how small—that must be accomplished get the change initiative successfully implemented. Every action that is to be taken is then assigned to a specific individual—not a group or a team, but an individual. This is important. Even if a team must accomplish a given action step, the team leader is given the responsibility. Avoiding confusion over accountability is essential to a successful implementation. It prevents a situation in which everyone looks at each other and says, "I thought you were going to do that."

Step 7: Establish Progress Points, Monitor Progress, and Adjust as Necessary.

One of the reasons so many change initiatives falter is that leaders fail to monitor progress. Assigning responsibility for specific tasks is important but doing so is no guarantee of a successful implementation. To ensure a successful implementation, leaders in organizations must roll up their sleeves and stay involved. This means assigning deadlines for completion of each action step that is assigned to someone, establishing incremental progress points that precede these deadlines, monitoring regularly to ensure that satisfactory progress is being made, and making adjustments when unanticipated problems pop up.

It is almost guaranteed that problems will arise that even the roadblock analysis did not anticipate. When this happens, leaders need to know about it and take immediate action. In other words, they need to adjust as necessary to keep the implementation on track and the momentum working for the change rather than against it. Monitoring and adjusting continues until the change initiative is successfully implemented and has become the new normal.

Case: Recovering from a Poorly Handled Change Initiative

I was once asked to help an organization climb out of the hole it had dug for itself by mishandling a major change initiative. The change involved transitioning the organization from a well known word-processing software package to another that was just emerging as a major competitor, but would eventually become the undisputed market leader. The way the organization handled the transition is instructive, at least in a negative sense. Its information technology (IT) department had decided that the new software was better in several key ways and would save the organization money in the long run. The IT director convinced the organization's executives of this and was given the go ahead to proceed with making the change. This is where the trouble began.

The IT department chose a Friday afternoon to send out a company-wide message that read: "The IT Department will upgrade your word-processing software over the weekend. The upgrade will be completed by the time you arrive for work Monday. If you experience any problems with the upgrade, contact an IT technician." As you might suspect, when Monday morning rolled around there was an avalanche of calls to the IT department. In the first place, only a few people had even read the message from IT. Late Friday afternoon is not a good time to send an important message. The few employees who had read the message thought little of it, their attention by then focused on the upcoming weekend. Consequently, on Monday when employees turned on their computers, most of them experienced an unpleasant surprise.

Little work was accomplished that Monday as confusion, then frustration, and finally anger became the order of the day. There were so many panicked pleas for help that the IT technicians simply stopped answering their phones. A near employee revolt resulted in a stern call from the company's CEO to the IT director. That night all of the company's IT personnel—including the director—worked until the new software had been removed and the old software re-installed. This is where things stood when I was brought in as a consultant.

The company faced an interesting dilemma. The new software had been paid for and, in truth, was superior to the old. Making the change in software was the right thing to do. The problems were all short-term in nature and were aggravated by a botched implementation. The new software was not the problem. I convinced the CEO that the change could be made, but that the implementation process would have to be much different the second time around.

We began by developing a comprehensive change picture that explained the what, who, when, where, why, and how of the change from the perspective of the user. This task took some work because the company's IT personnel saw the change only from their limited perspective—lower costs, easier maintenance, and more frequent updates. These were important benefits for the company and the IT department, but less so for everyday users. Users all had the same question: How is the change going to make things better for me?

To break the logjam caused by IT personnel who could see the change only from their limited perspective, I arranged for one influential individual from every office—mostly administrative assistants—to observe a demonstration of the new software. I insisted that the demonstration be given by an actual user, not a member of the vendor's sales team. The vendor hired an administrative assistant from another organization that had adopted its software. She was given a two-day contract to demonstrate the software, answer questions, and help my client's personnel see the benefits of the change. These hands-on users then helped me develop a change picture that answered the what, who, when, where, why, and how questions from the perspective of users.

Before communicating the change picture to stakeholders companywide, I met with all of the company's management and supervisory personnel. Each manager and supervisor was given a copy of the change picture and an in-depth explanation of its contents. I then provided the group with a list of the questions that were most likely to be asked by employees, along with recommended answers. I compiled this list of questions and answers during the demonstration that was made for influential users. When I was sure that executives, managers, and supervisors understood the what, who, when, where, why, and how of the change from the perspective of employees, I asked them to do two things: 1) accept personal responsibility for ensuring a successful implementation in their respective teams and departments, and 2) call team and departmental meetings to communicate the change picture to their personnel face-to-face.

In the meantime, I had already met with the influential users who had observed the demonstration of the new software. After convincing higher management to award them small incentive bonuses as compensation for their commitment, support, and assistance, I enlisted these influential users on the side of making the change succeed. This turned out to be one of the most effective of the various change-implementation steps. These influential users had the power to convince their colleagues to accept or reject the new software. By enlisting them on the side of success and giving them a measure of responsibility for achieving it, the change initiative was able to gain acceptance at the grassroots level where it was essential.

During each team and departmental meeting called to communicate the change picture to stakeholders, leaders conducted a roadblock analysis. Because the influential personnel we enlisted to help with the implementation had been working their magic, most roadblocks had already been identified and eliminated. The one concern raised universally in the roadblock sessions was the need for training. Training was arranged and all personnel were asked to participate, including those who claimed they did not need it.

To pave the way for making the training mandatory, the CEO and executive management team participated in it. The reason I insisted that training be mandatory is that some personnel—especially those who had been the acknowledged experts on the previous software—might not want to admit that they needed it. Status in the eyes of peers is important to people in organizations and should never be ignored when implementing change initiatives. It is always better to provide training to someone who does not need it than to risk not training someone who does.

One of the reasons change initiatives fail is closely related to training. Every organization has personnel whose status among their peers is tied to their expertise. For these personnel, admitting that they need training can be a blow to the ego. The most effective way I have found to deal with this phenomenon is to make training mandatory and then spread the following message: "We understand that some of you do not really need the training, but your participation will be helpful to your peers." This approach typically eliminates ego problems while creating a common experience—the training—among the organization's personnel that can increase camaraderie by giving them something they went through together.

Following the training sessions, the IT department re-installed the new software. Things went much smoother this time around. However, this does not mean there were no problems. Anticipating this—since when making a major organizational change Murphy's Law always applies—I asked all managers and supervisors to closely monitor the progress of the implementation in their teams and departments. The key was for them to act immediately whenever problems arose, which they did.

A number of minor problems popped up and were dispensed with in short order, but only one major obstacle presented itself. There were a number of projects in the pipeline that had been going back and forth between the organization and its customers when the software change was made. Because the old software and the new were not compatible, the organization had to find a way to complete several projects using the old software. Several customers that still used the old software themselves demanded that their projects be completed on it.

After discussing the situation with the personnel responsible for the projects in question and the company's IT director, we settled on a solution. The solution involved establishing a temporary office for the projects that, for whatever reason, needed to be completed on the old software. Of course, we could have simply loaded both software packages on the computers of the personnel assigned to the projects in question but decided against this. Our concern was that if both software packages were readily accessible the personnel in question would opt for the familiar and never use the new.

With a separate office equipped with the old software, personnel had to make an extra effort if they wanted to use it. This approach allowed the projects in question to be completed on the old software without the down side of perpetuating the dependence of personnel on it. In a relatively short time, the old-software office was eliminated and the new software became the norm. After a rocky start, the organization enjoyed a successful implementation.

The model for implementing organizational change presented in this chapter will help executives, managers, and supervisors become effective change managers. It will also help them equip, enable, and empower employees to be effective change agents and contributing participants in the on-going change process. In turn, it will help organizations improve continually. Remember, continual improvement, which is essential to organizational excellence, requires continual change. The more effectively the change process is managed, the better the performance of individual employees and the organization as a whole.

GROUP TRAINING ACTIVITY

Each member of the group is to choose a major organizational change he or she is familiar with that did not go well. All members explain their initiatives in detail to the group. Examples may come from the organizations of participants, from past employers, or from any other source. The goal of the activity is to identify the most poorly-handled change initiative possible. Using this worst-case change initiative as the group's subject, decide how the change-management model could have been used to produce a better result.

Eleven

PERFORMANCE APPRAISAL

Best Practice Number 11: *Make sure the performance-appraisal process is used to actually improve performance.*

In organizations striving for excellence, continually improving the performance of employees is paramount. This is because in a competitive environment, the performance bar is always being raised. What passes for peak performance today will not suffice tomorrow. In other words, the concept of peak performance is fluid. What is considered excellence today might be considered mediocre tomorrow. Competitors that are hungry and driven will always find ways to ensure that their personnel become increasingly productive all the time. This means that leaders in organizations must go beyond just facilitating peak performance in employees. They must ensure that employees continually improve their performance. This fact makes having an effective performance-appraisal process essential for organizations. For this reason, executives, managers, and supervisors must make sure that the performance appraisal process in their organizations actually encourages and facilitates improved performance.

The management adage—*If you want something to improve, measure it*—is the rational for performance appraisals. If done well, the performance appraisal can be an effective tool for promoting peak performance and continual improvement. A performance appraisal is just what the name implies: an appraisal of how well an individual employee is performing as measured against specific performance criteria. An effective performance-appraisal process can help organizations ensure that employee performance improves continually—an absolute necessity in a competitive environment.

PURPOSE OF PERFORMANCE APPRAISALS

The primary purpose of a performance appraisal is simple: to improve performance. The results of performance appraisals are often used for other purposes such as in making decisions about promotions, incentive pay, and recognition. They are also used as documentation when there is a need for employee discipline or to terminate a problem employee. But the primary purpose of the performance appraisal is to improve performance. Unfortunately, performance appraisals do not always satisfy this purpose. The performance appraisal is like any tool. Unless used it is properly, it will not do the job it was designed to do.

Problems with Performance Appraisals

Too often, performance appraisals do not produce the desired result—improved performance—because they are ineffectively conducted. One of the more common reasons for the ineffective use of the performance appraisal is that many leaders in organizations view the process as an inconvenience, something they have to do but would rather not. Supervisors often dread doing performance appraisals.

There are several different performance-appraisal methods that have been developed in an attempt to overcome the problems presented in this section. Some organizations use the 360 degree appraisal process wherein the evaluation includes input from peers, the supervisor, management, and, in some cases, customers. Others use the two-way appraisal process in which employees evaluate their supervisors while the supervisor is evaluating them. Most organizations still use the traditional method in which supervisors evaluate their team members. All of these methods have their strengths and weaknesses, but none of them solve the fundamental problems that cause supervisors to approach the process as an unwanted obligation rather than an opportunity to improve performance. These problems include the following:

- *Aversion to Confrontation.* Some supervisors are not comfortable telling employees they need to improve. Employees can become defensive, upset, and occasionally even angry when confronted with performance-appraisal results that suggest a need for improvement. Supervisors who are averse to confrontation might rate employees higher than they deserve as a way to avoid having to deal with frustration or anger.

- *Aversion to disappointment.* Most people would rather give others good news than bad. With performance appraisals, this tendency can lead to artificially inflated ratings. Some supervisors are not comfortable disappointing employees they work with every day. Supervisors who do not want to disappoint their team members would rather given them artificially inflated performance ratings than risk hurting their feelings.

- *Insufficient management support.* Some organizations undermine the performance-appraisal process by failing to: 1) put any teeth in it, and 2) support supervisors who do the appraisals. If supervisors believe they will not be supported by higher management when they assign ratings—good or bad—the process becomes nothing more than an obligatory box to check off. When supervisors come to believe that their recommendations for improvement or corrective action made during performance appraisals will not be backed up by higher management, the process loses its credibility and becomes a meaningless exercise. If the performance-appraisal process lacks credibility with supervisors, it will not contribute to the improvement of performance.

- *Insufficient understanding of the "why" and "how" of performance appraisals.* Some organizations make the mistake of assuming that supervisors will automatically understand why the performance-appraisal process is important as well as how to properly conduct performance appraisals. Conducting performance appraisals is one of the more difficult responsibilities of supervisors. Organizations should invest the time and effort necessary to ensure that supervisors understand why performance appraisals are important and how to conduct them properly. Providing training on how to conduct all aspects of the performance appraisal is essential, especially for new supervisors.

Unless these problems are dealt with, it will not matter if an organization adopts the two-way, 360, or traditional approach to performance appraisals. It is not the method used that undermines the value of performance appraisals. Rather, it is how well the method is used. In order for performance appraisals to serve the intended purpose of improving performance, organizations must take the process seriously and supervisors must understand how to play their role in it. That role consists of much more than sitting down once a year and filling out a performance-appraisal form for each team member. The critical role of the supervisor is explained in the next section.

SUPERVISOR'S ROLE IN THE PERFORMANCE-APPRAISAL PROCESS

In the current context, the term "supervisor" applies to any individual in an organization who supervises other personnel. Hence, the information in this section applies to executives, managers, supervisors, team leaders, and anyone else who oversees direct reports . Supervisors play a critical role in the performance-appraisal process. In fact, the supervisor's role is the most important role in the process. Performance appraisals will not help improve performance unless supervisors play their role effectively. The supervisor's role in the performance-appraisal process consists of a list of interrelated tasks that can be divided into three categories: 1) preparing for the appraisal, 2) doing the appraisal, and 3) following up after the appraisal.

Preparing for the Appraisal

The performance-appraisal process involves more than just filling out a form once a year. The first step in the process is preparation, and each component of this step should be completed well before the appraisal forms are actually completed. Preparation for the performance-appraisal process consists of the following tasks:

- Writing or updating job descriptions

- Reviewing and recommending revisions to performance-appraisal forms

- Making sure that employees know what is expected of them and how they will be evaluated

Writing or updating job descriptions

Before conducting a performance appraisal, it is important to ensure that the supervisor and the employee fully understand what the job entails. One of the reasons the performance-appraisal process breaks down in some organizations is that the performance criteria used do not match the actual job requirements. In other words, the job requires one thing but the appraisal measures another. To prevent this problem, supervisors should work with their organization's human resources personnel to write job descriptions if they do not already exist and update them if they do. Specifically, supervisors should ensure that:

- Every employee has an up-to-date job description

- Job descriptions are an accurate summary of what is actually expected of employees

- Performance criteria contained in the appraisal form match the job description and performance expectations of the employee

Reviewing and recommending revisions to performance-appraisal forms

This step is a corollary to the previous step. It is undertaken to ensure that the performance criteria in the appraisal form match what is actually expected of employees. The performance-appraisal process loses credibility when there is a mismatch between actual expectations and appraisal criteria. Supervisors who allow this to happen are like the teacher who teaches one thing and then tests on another. Not only will a mismatch between expectations and appraisal criteria fail to improve performance, it can dampen morale and, in turn, undermine performance.

Informing employees of what is expected of them and how they will be evaluated

There should be no surprises when employees see their performance appraisals. Employees should know well in advance of an appraisal what is expected of them. They should also know how they will be evaluated. This means that an important part of the unit-level orientation is the supervisor reviewing job descriptions and the performance-appraisal form with employees. Both documents should be up-to-date and accurate. The supervisor should also explain when performance appraisals are conducted (e.g. on the 60 or 90-day anniversary date for new employees, every six months, annually, on the anniversary of the employee's first day on the job, etc.).

Reviewing the job description and performance-appraisal form with employees gives supervisors an excellent opportunity to explain the purpose of the process: continual improvement of performance. Supervisors should never assume that employees automatically understand the challenges faced by organizations that operate in a competitive environment or how their individual performance affects the organization's ability to compete. During unit-level orientations is the time to explain these concepts and to underscore the role of performance appraisals in helping organizations stay competitive.

Doing the Appraisal

At the appointed time, the performance-appraisal form should be completed. The ratings given should be an accurate reflection of the employee's actual performance during the appraisal period. Some supervisors make the mistake of basing their ratings on what they have observed during only the last several months. This is a mistake. Ratings should reflect performance during the entire rating period, even if it has improved significantly of late. Occasionally, low-performing employees who know that an appraisal is coming up will make a special effort to temporarily improve their performance until the process is completed for another year. Once the appraisal process is completed, their performance reverts to its usual lower level. Supervisors who allow this to happen will make no progress when it comes to improving performance.

One of the reasons that some supervisors base their ratings on just the last few months is that they fail to document performance—good and bad—throughout the entire rating period. Consequently, when the time comes to do performance appraisals, all they can remember is the last few months. To ensure that a performance appraisal accurately reflects the entire rating period, supervisors should document their daily observations as well as any out of the ordinary performance issues—good or bad. In this way, the ratings earned by the employee are an accurate reflection of his performance.

When doing a performance appraisal, two factors are especially important: 1) being objective in assigning ratings, and 2) properly conducting the appraisal interview (including giving corrective feedback to employees and being aware of the legal issues that apply in this situation). Procedures for assigning ratings and conducting the appraisal interview are explained in the paragraphs which follow.

Being objective when determining ratings

Human beings are not objective by nature. We are all subject to emotions, biases, experiential limitations, and preconceived notions. We tend to favor others who look, talk, think, and believe as we do. This is normal and nothing to be ashamed of, although it is something we to be worked on constantly. These human tendencies make it difficult to be objective, but supervisors must make the effort because objectivity is especially important when doing performance appraisals.

Supervisors who let their emotions, biases, and preconceived notions affect the ratings they give during the performance-appraisal process decrease the value of the process. As hard as it is for human beings to be objective—and the truth is people are never completely objective—objectivity is important from the perspective of improved performance as well as from a legal perspective. Strategies that can help supervisors increase their level of objectivity when doing performance appraisals include the following:

- *Base ratings on facts.* When assigning a given rating, supervisors should step back, reflect, and ask themselves if the rating is based on documented facts or personal feelings, biases, preconceived notions, or other non-objective human factors. Documentation is important for all ratings that indicate a need for improvement, but it is just as important for high ratings. Simply taking a moment to reflect and then asking the *objectivity question* before assigning a rating can help supervisors overcome a lack of objectivity. A word of caution is in order here. Some performance-appraisal forms give supervisors the opportunity to check "insufficient information to give a rating." This box should never be checked as a way to avoid assigning a real rating—either low or high. There are times when a supervisor will not have sufficient information to assign a rating for a given criterion. But those times should be rare. The "insufficient information" box should never be used by supervisors as an escape mechanism.

- *Avoid personality bias.* Supervisors are just like anyone else—they occasionally have personality clashes with people. Most people have experienced trying to deal with an individual whose personality grated on them. Supervisors sometimes find themselves in this situation and the person in question is one of their team members. When this is the case, it can be easy to let personality differences affect performance-appraisal ratings. When evaluating an employee whose personality is bothersome, supervisors must make a special effort to focus on performance. Before assigning a rating for any criterion, take a moment to review your thoughts and then ask if the rating reflects performance or negative feelings about the individual's personality.

- *Beware of both extremes when assigning ratings.* Some supervisors develop reputations as being tough evaluators. Others are known as soft touches. Neither is appropriate. If supervisors develop a reputation for how they assign performance ratings, it should be one of objectivity and fairness. Although some employees perform so poorly that they deserve ratings at the bottom extreme, they are few. The few who are consistently rated at the bottom extreme should be candidates for either focused development or termination. On the other hand, few employees perform so well that they deserve all top ratings. After all, there is room for improvement with even the best employees. Supervisors who assign most ratings at either extreme of the performance scale should step back and reassess.

- *Avoid the halo effect.* The halo effect is a phenomenon that can influence the ratings supervisors assign to certain employees. It happens when a given employee performs extraordinarily well on a certain aspect of the job. Supervisors can become so impressed by the employee's excellent performance in this one area that they put a "halo" on her and assign top ratings on all appraisal criteria. This is an easy trap to fall into, but it should be avoided. Assigning employees high marks in one area because they perform well in another will not improve performance.

- *Avoid pecking-order bias.* In every team there is a pecking order. Based on their level of criticality to the mission, some jobs are more important to supervisors than others. These critical jobs are higher in the pecking order than others, at least in the mind of the supervisor. Consequently, when doing performance appraisals, supervisors must make an extra effort to evaluate employees in these high-in the pecking-order jobs on the basis of actual performance. They must avoid rating them higher simply because the job they do is more important. The ratings should reflect actual performance in the job, not the relative importance of the job. If a given job is more important to the team's mission than another, employees in that job should earn a higher wage or salary. This is the proper way to acknowledge the relative importance of jobs. When doing a performance appraisal, supervisors are rating individuals on their actual performance in their respective jobs, not on the relative importance of their jobs.

Properly conducting the appraisal interview

The appraisal interview is the most critical part of the performance-appraisal process. In this step supervisors show employees the completed appraisal form and discuss the ratings they have assigned. This part of the process must be handled well if the appraisal is going to lead to improved performance. The steps in conducting the appraisal interview are: 1) review the purpose of the performance appraisal, 2) explain the assigned ratings and give reasons, 3) solicit feedback from the employee, 4) set goals for improvement, and 5) abide by the rules of thumb that will prevent legal problems.

- *Review the purpose of the performance appraisal.* The purpose of the performance appraisal should have been thoroughly explained to all employees during their unit level orientation. However, the beginning of the appraisal interview is a good time to review that purpose. Supervisors can never over-emphasize the fact that the purpose of the performance-appraisal process is to improve performance. It is one thing for employees to understand this purpose in a theoretical sense, but it is quite another to understand it when faced with ratings that suggest the need for improvement. If it is difficult for supervisors to be objective when assigning ratings, imagine how difficult it is employees to be objective when receiving those ratings. For the supervisor, the ratings assigned are supposed to represent an objective reality—nothing personal, just business. But for the recipients, the ratings received on performance appraisals are very personal. Employees tend to view their ratings not just as a reflection of their performance, but as a reflection of themselves as individuals. Because of this, a brief review of the purpose is always a good way to start the appraisal interview.

- *Explain the assigned ratings and give corrective feedback.* Once the purpose of the performance-appraisal process has been reviewed, it is time to explain the ratings that have been assigned for each criterion. This is going to be what the employee is most interested in, so supervisors should not prolong their suspense. There are two schools of thought concerning this step. One is that the first time employees should see their ratings is during the interview when the supervisor is present to explain them. The other school of thought is that employees should receive the completed appraisal form at least 24 hours prior to the appraisal interview so they have time to consider their responses and decide if they wish to challenge any of the ratings. It is important for employees to have sufficient time to reflect upon their ratings. To ask employees to sign an appraisal form they have not had time to review can create a perception that the supervisor just wants to get the process over with as fast as possible without giving employees opportunities for reflection or inquiry. Consequently, if the first approach is used, supervisors should give employees time to reflect—typically 24 hours after the appraisal interview—before asking them to sign the appraisal form. When discussing ratings with employees, supervisors should remember the following strategies for giving corrective feedback: 1) be positive, 2) be prepared, 3) be realistic, 4) make feedback a two-way process, 5) listen attentively, and 6) discuss positives and negatives.

- *Solicit feedback.* During the appraisal interview, supervisors give employees feedback on their performance in the form of ratings. They should also explain how they arrived at the ratings. Then they should solicit feedback from employees. It is important that the appraisal interview be a two-way process. Not only should employees be given opportunities to comment on the ratings, they should be encouraged to challenge any ratings they disagree with. It is important for supervisors to determine how employees would rate themselves on all of the criteria. One way supervisors can make sure they know how employees rate themselves is to ask. During the appraisal interview, as each rating is discussed supervisors can ask employees how they would rate themselves on each criterion. Another approach is to ask employees to complete the appraisal form themselves and bring it to the interview. In this way supervisors can compare their ratings with those of employees. Supervisors and employees should discuss ratings, but not for the purpose of negotiating. The appraisal interview is not a bargaining process wherein the supervisor says "I'll give you a five on this criterion if you will accept a three on that one." The purpose of two-way communication is to ensure that: 1) employees fully understand where and how they need to improve, and 2) supervisors hear from employees on any factors they might have overlooked. Ideally the supervisor and employees will agree on all ratings assigned by the end of the appraisal interview, even if an employee does not like a given rating. Of course, this is not always possible—employees will always find it difficult to accept low ratings objectively. However, supervisors and employees will come closer to reaching full agreement if there is two-way communication than if employees are simply shown their ratings and asked to sign the form. The process should accommodate those instances in which the supervisor and employee do not agree by adding a qualifier such as this after the signature line on the appraisal form: *By signing this form the employee acknowledges having reviewed it. The employee's signature does not necessarily indicate agreement.*

- *Set goals for improvement.* This is an important step in the appraisal interview, a step that is sometimes overlooked. It is not enough to assign ratings that document the need for improvement. Supervisors and employees need to collaborate on setting goals for making needed improvements. Setting improvement goals will generate dialogue about related issues such as training, mentoring, and other activities that might be necessary to facilitate improvement. Improvement goals should be specific and measureable. This means that improvement goals should be results-oriented rather than process-oriented. For example, assume an employee needs to improve her customer service skills as measured by customer satisfaction feedback cards. It is not sufficient to set an improvement goal that says: *The employee will complete a customer service seminar.* This is a process goal. The employee in question might complete the required seminar but still deliver poor customer service. A better rendering of this goal would be: *The employee will receive at least 90 percent "satisfied" ratings as measured by customer satisfaction survey cards over the next four quarters.* This is a results-oriented goal that explains how much improvement is expected, the period of time allowed for improvement, and how the progress will be measured.

- *Know the legal rules of thumb.* In today's litigious environment, it is important for supervisors to know the legal aspects of performance appraisals. Supervisors do not need to be attorneys, but they do need to approach the performance-appraisal process objectively and fully informed. The following rules of thumb will help supervisors keep the performance-appraisal process within the law: 1) keep comprehensive records relating to employee performance (do not set up a second set of records—keep records in the employee's file in the Human Resources Department), 2) focus on performance, not personality or other non-performance-related factors, 3) be positive, constructive, and specific in giving feedback to employees (the process is to help them improve, not to punish them), 4) be honest, equitable, and impartial, and 5) apply the appraisal criteria objectively, consistently, and uniformly.

Following Up after the Appraisal Interview

Completion of the appraisal interview is not the end of the performance-appraisal process. Rather, it is the beginning of a new phase that continues until the next performance appraisal. Improvement goals have been set. Now the employee's progress toward achieving these goals must be monitored. It is a mistake to simply set goals and wait until the next round of performance appraisals to determine if they are being met. Supervisors should monitor the progress of employees continually and intervene wherever necessary to remove obstacles, give encouragement, and help facilitate improvements. Follow-up continues until the next round of performance appraisals. In this way, there are no surprises next time—for employees or supervisors. Further, when handled this way the process is more likely to result in real improvements.

GROUP TRAINING ACTIVITY

The group is to select two members to act the parts of supervisor and employee. Assume that the supervisor has completed a performance appraisal form for the employee and the ratings indicate a need to improve in three areas: customer service, teamwork, and on-time attendance. The *supervisor* and the *employee* are to act out the appraisal interview. Other members of the group are to critique the supervisor's performance and offer constructive feedback for improvement. Then a new member of the group plays the role of the supervisor until all members have had their turn.

Twelve

TIME MANAGEMENT

Best Practice Number 12: *Become proficient at time management and help employees develop time management skills*

Time management is important in organizations that are striving for excellence. Employees who are expected to achieve peak performance and continual improvement must be good time managers. The same is true of organizational leaders. People in organizations who fail to manage their time effectively can cause a number of problems including wasted time (theirs and others), added stress (on them and others), lost credibility, missed appointments, poor follow through on commitments, poor attention to detail, ineffective execution, and poor stewardship. Further, organizational leaders who are poor time managers will not be able to help employees become good time managers. Time management is critical to peak performance, continual improvement, and organizational excellence.

HOW POOR TIME MANAGEMENT CAN UNDERMINE PERFORMANCE

The following scenario shows how poor time management can undermine performance. Jane is a team leader in her organization. Although she has excellent credentials, Jane's team never seems to meet its deadlines or perform at peak levels. The main reason for her team's mediocre performance is Jane's poor time management. Because she is a poor time manager, Jane's bad example contributes to poor time management among her team members as well as to other performance problems.

Because she is always running late, Jane never gets to spend much one-on-one time with team members. She claims to have an open-door policy, but in reality she is always so busy trying to catch up that she has no time to listen when her team members have complaints, recommendations, suggestions, or concerns. As a result, she typically just ignores their input and feedback. Her most frequent response when team members need a few minutes of her time is "I'll get with you later. I don't have time right now."

Unfortunately for Jane, her team, and the organization, complaints that are put off until later or are just simply ignored often become problems that snowball over time. The longer they are ignored, the bigger the problems become. Jane and her team suffer from the snowball effect all the time, which means that the organization suffers from it too. Poor time management at any level is the enemy of peak performance, continual improvement, and organizational excellence.

TIME MANAGEMENT PROBLEMS: CAUSES AND SOLUTIONS

Does the following situation sound familiar? You prepare a list of things to get done at work today, but before you can get to the first item on the list you are interrupted by minor emergencies that need immediate attention. By the time you have put out all the fires that demanded your attention the work day is over and your to-do list is sitting on your desk untouched. For many people, this type of day happens all the time. The reasons people spend too much time putting out fires and too little time working on planned activities vary, but most of them are predictable.

The most common causes of time management problems are: unexpected crises, telephone calls, poor planning, taking on too much, unscheduled visitors, poor delegation, disorganization, inefficient use of technology, failing to say "no," and inefficient meetings. Organizational leaders must learn to overcome these time wasters and help employees learn to be good time managers. Effective time-management strategies are explained in the remainder of this section.

Unexpected Crisis Situations

Crisis situations are a part of the job for people in organizations, no matter what the job happens to be. People in organizations will never completely eliminate crisis situations—there are just too many causal factors that cannot be controlled. However, there is a correlation between planning and crisis situations that can be stated as follows: *better planning equals fewer crises*. This is the good news. The bad news is that even with good planning, crisis situations will still occasionally happen.

A crisis, by definition, is a situation that must be dealt with right away. Consequently, when crises occur they take precedence over other obligations. This is why it is important to limit the amount of time devoted to dealing with crisis situations or, said another way, *putting out fires*. The following strategies can help minimize the amount of time people in organizations must devote to putting out fires:

- *Schedule loosely.* Anyone who has been to a doctor's office is familiar with the concept of overbooking. Physicians tend to schedule appointments so tightly that more often than not by mid-morning the doctor's work is hopelessly backed up. Too often the doctor's appointment log is more of a dream sheet than a realistic schedule. Physicians who schedule too tightly are guilty of ignoring the management adage that *most things take longer than you think they will.* All it takes is one crisis with a patient, and the rest of the day is thrown off schedule. People in organizations are often like physicians in that they schedule more appointments and activities in a day than they can realistically handle. The solution to this problem is to schedule loosely. This means scheduling more time than you think appointments will require and, then, trying to complete them on schedule. If you think an appointment will take 15 minutes, schedule 20 or even 30 minutes for it. Then try to finish it in 15 minutes. Also, if someone says, "I just need five minutes of your time," do not take this literally. People rarely take just five minutes of your time. Schedule 10 or 15 minutes. Scheduling loosely also means leaving catch-up time in between appointments. Often there is follow-up work that needs to be done at the conclusion of an appointment. Leave sufficient time between appointments to get this work done immediately. Work that is left undone will add up throughout the day and become tomorrow's crisis.

- *Do not be an amateur psychologist.* Leaders in organizations must be open to listening when employees have ideas, concerns, recommendations, or complaints relating to their jobs. This is the point of the five-minute rule explained in an earlier chapter. However, it is not uncommon for team members to ask for time to discuss personal problems that are not the responsibility of supervisors, managers, or executives. In such cases, there is nothing wrong with making a helpful referral. In fact, providing this type of assistance is recommended. But a referral is as far as your help should go in such cases, especially during work hours. Leaders in organizations should not try to be amateur psychologists when their team members are having personal problems. There are several reasons for this, but in the current context the main reason is that getting overly involved in the personal problems of team members can be a time consuming enterprise. Problems that relate to the job should receive your full and immediate attention. However, the personal problems of team members are best handled by referral to human resource professionals who are better equipped to deal with them.

Telephone calls

The telephone can be one of the biggest time wasters in your life. Spending time on hold, listening to irritating answering-machine messages, and playing telephone tag are all major culprits, but they are not the biggest time wasters when it comes to telephone use. I once conducted a study about telephone conversations at work. One of the study's conclusions was that approximately 38 percent of the time spent on the telephone was unrelated to the purpose of the call. The unrelated 38 percent consisted of talk about such topics as politics, sports, children, grandchildren, spouses, and the weather. Although I do not believe that all such unrelated chit-chat is necessarily a waste of time, even allowing for the usual courtesies, there is still a lot of time wasted on telephone calls.

The various types of cellular telephones and their extended capabilities—text messaging, Internet access, photography, and numerous other applications—have only compounded the problem. On the other hand, if used wisely cellular telephones can help solve the problem of time wasted by the telephone. The following strategies will help minimize the amount of time in your day that is wasted by the telephone.

- *Use e-mail instead of the telephone whenever appropriate.* One of the best ways to avoid wasting time on hold, playing telephone tag, or listening to recorded messages is to use e-mail instead of the telephone whenever appropriate. Of course, e-mail is not always a feasible option. However, when it is you can simply type a brief message, click "Send," and move on to your next task. With email there is no pressing one for this option or two for that option, no talking to answering machines, and no being put on hold. In addition, people are often more prompt about returning e-mail messages than they are about returning telephone calls or responding to phone messages.

- *Categorize calls as important, routine, and unimportant.* Leaders in organizations will find that time invested in helping administrative assistants learn to distinguish between important and unimportant telephone calls and between important and routine calls will be time well spent. One of the ways to do this is to provide administrative assistants with a list of people you always want to talk to. Within reason, these calls should always go through. On others, the administrative assistant can take a message, let the caller leave a recorded message, or even suggest sending an e-mail message. If administrative assistants are going to take written telephone messages, train them to be comprehensive and detailed. In addition to who called and when, a good telephone message will contain the caller's telephone number, reason for calling, and a good time to return the call. It will also let the intended receiver know if the caller was angry, upset, etc. This type of information will help you determine which calls should be returned, in what order, and at what time.

- *Use your cellular telephone to return calls between meetings and during breaks.* On one hand, cellular telephones can be obnoxiously intrusive. How many times have you been interrupted by the inopportune ringing of a cellular telephone, yours or someone else's? On the other hand, cellular telephones can help you turn time that might otherwise be wasted into productive time. You can save valuable time by taking telephone messages to meetings with you and using your cellular telephone to return them during breaks and between meetings. You can also use them to return calls from your car while traveling to your next meeting, provided that you have the appropriate "hands-off" technology or that your car is off the road and parked. Do not be one of those people who drives with his knees while text messaging or making cellular telephone calls.

- *Block out time on your calendar for returning telephone calls.* Telephone tag is one the most persistent and frustrating time wasters in the workday. Assume that e-mail is not appropriate and you really need to talk to someone. You place the call, but the person you need is not available. You leave a message. She calls back, but now you are tied up in a meeting. She leaves a message. You call her back, but just miss her. This frustrating situation known as "telephone tag" repeats itself every day in organizations. To minimize the amount of time you waste playing telephone tag, block out times on your calendar for returning calls and let the times be known to callers who leave messages. An effective approach is to schedule two 30-minute blocks (at least) in each day: one in mid-morning and one in mid-afternoon. Block these times out on your calendar as if they are appointments. Make sure that the people who take your messages (and your recorder) let callers know that these are the times during which you typically return calls. In this way, if callers really need to talk with you, they will make a point of being available during one of these times. In fact, they can make connecting even easier by indicating which time they prefer. Another version of this strategy is to send an e-mail that asks either: 1) What is a good time for me to call you today?, or 2) Will you call me at _____ today?

- *Limit unrelated chatting.* One of the reasons telephone calls are such time wasters is the human propensity for unrelated chitchat. You can save a surprising amount of time on the telephone by simply getting to the point, and by tactfully nudging callers to do the same. There is certainly nothing wrong with a few appropriate comments on the latest ball game, movie, or news item, but the amount of time devoted to unrelated issues should be kept to a minimum. Stay focused, stay on task, and tactfully nudge callers do the same.

Poor Planning

The correlation between planning and crises has already been stated. There are crisis situations that simply cannot be avoided, and there are those that result from poor planning. A good rule of thumb to remember is this: The more effort you put into planning, the less time you will waste putting out fires. The following strategies can help improve your planning and cut down on the number of crisis situations you have to deal with:

- *Spend the last ten minutes of each day planning the next day.* Devoting just 10 minutes at the end of each work day to reviewing what you have accomplished and what still needs to be done and then using this information to plan the next day can save valuable time. One of the best ways to minimize the number of crisis situations you have to deal with is to know what is on your plate when you arrive for work each day. Three of the most persistent causes of crisis situations are forgotten meetings, overlooked obligations, and missing paperwork. You can eliminate these causes by using the last ten minutes in the day reviewing the next day's meetings and obligations, retrieving any paperwork or other documentation that will be needed the next day, and creating a *to-do* list with the items listed in order of importance. By tending to just these few tasks, you will be able to begin the next day well-prepared.

- *Remember that most tasks take longer to complete than you think they will.* This is a good rule of thumb to follow. No matter what you have planned, experience shows it will probably take longer than you think it will to complete. Consequently, it is wise to build a little extra time into your schedule. For example, if you think a task will take 30 minutes, allow 45 minutes, and then try to finish in 30. In this way, you will have extra time, if it is needed, without having to rush. If the task happens to be completed on time, you can always put the time gained to good use getting a head start on other obligations.

Taking on Too Many Responsibilities

One of the reasons successful people are successful is that in any given situation they take the initiative and seek responsibility. In military parlance, they run to the sound of the guns, not away from it. There is both good news and bad news in this fact. The good news is that taking the initiative and seeking responsibility promotes peak performance, continual improvement, and organizational excellence. The bad news is that doing so too often can overload your schedule. When you are a person who takes the initiative and seeks responsibility, it is easy to fall into the trap of taking on too much. This is a common problem among leaders in organizations. When this happens, the following strategies can help get your schedule back in balance:

- *Make a list of all current and pending obligations.* Make a list of all of your obligations and commitments. For each entry on the list, ask the following questions: 1) What will happen if I do not do this? and 2) Is there someone else who could do this? Invariably you will find things on your list that really do not have to be done. These items sounded like good ideas when they were put on the list, but in retrospect they do not really need to be done or, at least, not now. In addition, going through this exercise will often reveal that you are doing things that could and should be delegated. Asking these two simple questions will usually reveal ways to pare down the list. Once the list has been pared down to what has to be done and which items you need to do yourself, prioritize the remaining items.

- *Take stock of your after-work activities.* People who perform well enough at work to become organizational leaders are typically involved after work in civic clubs, chambers of commerce, economic development organizations, professional associations, coaching little league, and various other activities. Participation in these and other outside activities is an excellent way to grow as a leader and to benefit your organization. However, it is easy to fall into the trap of joining too many outside organizations or taking on too many outside activities. Balance is the key. For leaders in organizations, outside activities are like food. The right amounts of the right types are essential, but too much—even of the right types—can be harmful. When I am asked to help organizational leaders who find themselves over extended, I always start with outside activities. Leaders who overburden themselves with too many outside activities are just creating a situation that will distract them from what they need to be doing to facilitate peak performance and continual improvement.

Unscheduled Visitors

It is important for leaders in organizations to maintain an open-door policy for employees. On the other hand, unscheduled visitors can take up a lot of time. I encourage organizational leaders to find the right balance between maintaining an open-door policy and requiring visitors to have appointments by applying the five-minute rule that was explained in an earlier chapter. To review, with this rule an employee can have a five-minute audience any time unless you happen to be tied up with something pressing. However, within that five minutes employees are expected to state their problem and recommend a well-considered solution. If the employee has thoroughly prepared before asking for an audience, five minutes is plenty of time for most workplace issues.

If an issue cannot be handled in five-minutes, employees may make an appointment so the necessary time can be blocked out on your calendar. Using the five-minute rule and requiring appointments for issues requiring more than five minutes will lessen the problem of people just dropping in unannounced to chat, although it will not completely eliminate it. After all, some of the people who just drop in might be superiors in the organization or even customers. Consequently, it is important for leaders in organizations to understand how to minimize the amount of time taken up by drop-in visitors. The following strategies will help:

- *Do not allow drop-in visitors during peak times.* Some days are busier than others and some times of the day are busier than other times. During these peak times, it is best to ask drop-in visitors to come back at another time when you can give them your undivided attention, unless they are: 1) bringing you critical information that needs to be conveyed immediately, 2) informing you of an emergency, or 3) someone who must be seen right away no matter what else is going on in your day.

- *Train administrative support personnel to rescue you.* You can minimize the intrusions of drop-in visitors by working out an arrangement with administrative support personnel to rescue you after a pre-arranged amount of time, say five minutes. It works like this. Whenever a drop-in visitor has been in your office for five minutes or so, the secretary buzzes you or looks in and says "it's time to place that important call." This will tactfully let the drop-in visitor know that you have work to do.

- *Remain standing.* One way to convey the message that you are busy without having to actually say it is to remain standing when an unannounced visitor walks into your office. Once visitors sit down and get comfortable, it can be difficult to uproot them. By continuing to stand, you tactfully convey the message that, "I can give you a few minutes, but only a few."

Poor Delegation

Poor delegation is one the easiest time-wasting traps to fall into. Some leaders find it difficult to let go of work they are accustomed to doing themselves. In addition, some think that nobody can do anything right but them. These two phenomena can result in poor delegation, a major time waster. Tasks that do not require your level of expertise should be delegated. If subordinates cannot perform the tasks in question satisfactorily, you have a training problem, and training problems cannot be solved by refusing to delegate work. Leaders who continue to do work subordinates should be doing because they do not like to delegate will contribute little to peak performance, continual improvement, or organizational excellence. If an employee who should be doing certain work cannot do it properly, he should be trained and mentored or replaced.

Personal Disorganization

You can waste a lot of time rummaging through disorganized stacks of paperwork looking for the folder, form, or document needed. I once worked with an individual who had the unfortunate habit of never putting files, documents, or forms in the same place twice when he was done with them. Wherever this person happened to be when he finished with a file is where he would leave it. As a result, this otherwise talented professional could be counted on to waste valuable time looking for "missing" paperwork. He eventually earned a reputation for being habitually disorganized—a reputation that hurt his career. Organizational leaders use the following strategies to help decrease the amount of time wasted because of personal disorganization:

- *Clean off your desk or work station.* This strategy sounds so simple that you might be tempted to ignore it. But before doing so, look at your work area. Check your in-basket and your stack of pending work. Do not be surprised if you find paperwork sitting in your in-box that is so old it is no longer relevant. Go through everything on your desk or in your work area and get rid of anything that is no longer pertinent. When you decide to get organized, one of your best organizational tools will be a large trashcan.

- *Re-stack your work in priority order.* Go through your in-box or stack of pending work and re-organize everything in order of priority. Paperwork is often stacked in the order it comes in, especially when you are in a hurry and do not have time to organize it. Because this can happen so frequently, it is a good idea to occasionally stop what you are doing long enough to go through your work stack and re-organize everything by priority. It's an even better idea to screen work as it comes in, placing your work in priority order from the outset.

- *Categorize work folders.* Organize your paperwork in folders by category. Have a *Read Folder* for paperwork that should be read, but requires no writing or other action. Have a *Correspondence Folder* which contains correspondence that requires some action on your part. Have a *Signature Folder* for paperwork that requires your signature (correspondence, requisitions, etc.). Organizing work in this way will save time and increase efficiency.

Inefficient Use of Technology

Even in the age of technology there are still people in organizations who are guilty of the inefficient use of technology. Timesaving technologies save time only if you know how to use them. Computers, cell phones and other handheld communication devices, facsimile machines, and other electronic devices will save you time only if you know how to efficiently use their various features. No matter what kinds of technologies you use in doing your job, learn how to use it effectively and efficiently.

Unnecessary and Inefficient Meetings

In spite of their value in bringing people together to convey information, brainstorm, plan, and discuss issues, meetings can be one of the biggest time wasters in organizations. Organizational leaders can minimize the amount of time wasted in meetings by: 1) making sure that all standing meeting are actually necessary, and 2) keeping the meetings that are necessary as short as possible. Strategies that will help minimize the time wasted in meetings follow:

- *Understand what causes wasted time in meetings.* Much of the time spent in meetings is wasted. The principal reasons for this are poor preparation, the human need for social interaction, idle chitchat, interruptions, getting side-tracked on unrelated issues, no agenda, people who love the sound of their own voice, and no prior distribution of back-up materials. In addition to these time wasters, there is also the *comfort factor.* Coffee, soda, tea, water, goodies, and social interaction can create a comfortable environment that people are reluctant to leave. Make a point of eliminating these time wasters from meetings, especially those meetings you chair.

- *Ask if regularly-scheduled meetings are necessary.* Most organizations have regularly-scheduled weekly, bi-weekly, and monthly meetings of various groups and teams. When these meetings were established they probably had a definite purpose, and that purpose might still be valid. However, it is not uncommon to find people in organizations meeting only because they have always met on a given day at a given time. Sometimes meetings are perpetuated out of habit rather than need. If you call or attend regularly scheduled meetings, ask the following questions about each meeting: 1) What is the purpose of the meeting? 2) Is the meetings really necessary? 3) Could the meeting be scheduled less often (e.g. Can weekly meetings meet twice a month instead? Can monthly meetings meet quarterly instead?), and 4) Could the purpose of the meeting be satisfied some other way (e-mail updates, written reports, etc.)?

- *Hold impromptu meetings standing up.* Impromptu meetings that should last no more than 10 minutes can be kept on schedule by holding them standing up. These are typically meetings without an agenda called on the spur of the moment to quickly convey information to a select group or to get input from that group. These types of meetings are best held in your office rather than in a conference room. It will be hard to keep participants from pulling up chairs and settling in if the meeting is held in a conference room.

- *Complete the necessary preparations before meetings.* For sit-down, scheduled meetings, have an agenda that contains the following information: purpose of the meeting, starting and ending time, list of agenda items with a responsible person for each, and a projected amount of time to be devoted to each agenda item. Set a deadline for submitting agenda items and stick to it. Require all back-up material to be provided at the same time as the corresponding agenda items. Distribute the agenda, back-up material, and the minutes of the last meeting at least a full day before the meeting. If you distribute meeting materials too far in advance participants will simply put them aside and forget about them. In addition, you increase the likelihood of cutting off the submittal of agenda items too soon. On the other hand, if you wait until during the meeting to distribute materials you will waste time handing them out and waiting while participants read them. Ask all participants to read the agenda and back-up materials before the meeting. This is why they are distributed beforehand. In other words, insist that people come to meetings prepared.

- *Begin meetings on time, stick to the agenda, and stay focused.* When you conduct meetings, begin on time. Waiting for latecomers only encourages tardiness. If participants know you are going to start on time, most will eventually discipline themselves to arrive on time. Have someone take minutes. In the minutes, all action and follow-up items should be typed in bold face so they stand out from the routine material. Make the minutes of the last meeting the first item on the agenda. In this way the first action taken in the meeting is following-up on assignments and commitments made during the last meeting (those items that appear in boldface in the minutes). Stay focused. Keep participants on the agenda and on task. The last agenda item should always be either "New Business' or "Around-the-Table" comments. Such an agenda item gives participants an opportunity to bring up issues that are not on the agenda without getting the meeting sidetracked before agenda items have been disposed of. However, it is important to make sure that participants know that only critical issues that have arisen since the agenda was finalized are to be brought up as a new business. Further, around- the-table comments should be limited to minor matters that do not warrant a place on the agenda, require no discussion, and will take very little time—matters such as announcements. If you allow participants to get into discussions of items not on the agenda, they will begin to bring up all of their issues in the new business portion of the meeting rather than devoting the time and effort necessary to get them on the agenda. Ask participants to turn off cellular telephones during meetings. Interruptions from cellular telephones can be a major distraction and time waster in meetings.

- *Follow-up meetings promptly.* Have the minutes of the meeting typed and distributed electronically right away—ideally on the same day the meeting occurred. Allow an appropriate amount of time for participants to act, then follow-up on action items from the minutes. If you call meetings, never wait until the next meeting to ask about progress made in completing the action items from the previous meetings. Between meetings, use e-mail or telephone calls to monitor progress on action items.

The strategies recommended in this chapter will help leaders in organizations take control of one of their most valuable assets—time. They will also help leaders teach employees how to be good time mangers. When leaders and employees are good time managers, they benefit and the organization benefits because well-managed time that is used productively contributes to peak performance, continual improvement, and organizational excellence.

GROUP TRAINING ACTIVITIES

1. The group is to complete the following assignment: develop an annotated checklist for ensuring that managers at XYZ, Inc. can maintain an open-door policy for employees without letting it rob them of the time they need to perform other duties.

2. The group is to complete the following assignment: Make a list of all standing meetings each of the members must attend (weekly, bi-weekly, monthly, quarterly, etc.). Analyze all of these meetings and decide if they are: 1) really necessary, 2) could meet less frequently, and 3) could be handled in some other way.

Thirteen

CUSTOMER SERVICE

Best Practice Number 13: Become a customer-service champion and help employees develop customer-service skills.

In a globally competitive environment, the customer is king. In order to excel, private-sector organizations must out-perform the competition every day. Public and non-profit organizations, also under pressure to perform, must achieve maximum efficiency and effectiveness. Organizations in all sectors are graded by the toughest judge on earth—the customer. Consequently, every individual in an organization, regardless of his position or status, must share one critical characteristic: a commitment to customer satisfaction. People in organizations that are striving for excellence must understand that the customer is king and approach their work accordingly. This is why organizational leaders must be customer-service champions and why they must do what is necessary to help employees develop customer-service skills.

THE CUSTOMER FOR YOUR ORGANIZATION

Customers go by a variety of names depending on the type of organization. Healthcare organizations call their customers patients. Legal firms call their customers clients. Magazine and newspaper publishers call their customers subscribers. Government firms call their customers taxpayers. Regardless of what they are called, customers are entities with which your organization exchanges something of value.

Service-sector firms provide services of value to their customers and, in return, their customers provide something of value to them—money. Manufacturing, processing, and other technology companies provide products of value to their customers and, in return, their customers provide something of value to them—money. Public- sector organizations provide services to their customers and, in return, their customers support them with taxes. Non-profit organizations provide services to specific groups in the community and, in turn, the community supports them through donations. This mutually-beneficial exchange of value is the heart and soul of the provider/customer relationship, regardless of the type of organization.

External and Internal Customers

When the term "customer" is used, most people are referring to those people and organizations that use their products or services. These are external customers. External customers are an organization's most important customers. However, there are also internal customers. An internal customer is simply one employee whose work depends to some degree on that of another employee. Team members in organizations are typically internal customers for each other. It is important for leaders in organizations to understand the concepts of external and internal customers and use this understanding to guide their actions and decisions. It is also important for leaders to make employees aware of the concepts of the internal and external customer.

IMPORTANCE OF A CUSTOMER-DRIVEN PERSPECTIVE

Customer satisfaction is critical in a competitive environment, regardless of the type of organization. In the private sector, if customers dislike your organization's products or services they can take their business elsewhere. In the public sector, if customers are unhappy about by how your organization treats them they can complain to elected officials. With non-profit organizations, dissatisfied customers can simply withhold their donations. When one of your customers leaves unhappy, your organization loses and, often, some other organization wins. Being customer-driven is important because customer-driven behavior is the best way to ensure customer satisfaction, and customer satisfaction is essential to an organization's survival. On the other hand, creating unhappy customers is the surest way to guarantee failure.

Consider the following widely-known facts about unhappy customers, facts that apply to all types of organizations:

- Unhappy customers do more than just take their business elsewhere, they tell other potential customers about their dissatisfaction.

- Only a relatively few unhappy customers will give an organization a chance to correct their problem. Instead, most will simply take their business elsewhere or, in the case of public-sector organizations, complain to elected officials.

- Once unhappy customers migrate to a competitor, it is very difficult—some believe impossible—to get them back.

- It typically costs an organization at least five times more to attract new customers than to retain existing customers.

These facts show that being a customer-driven organization is essential in a competitive environment, regardless of the type of organization. Customer satisfaction is one of the key measures of organizational excellence.

CUSTOMER-SATISFACTION STRATEGIES

Being a customer-driven organization is about more than attitude. Attitude is important. In fact, it is critical. But the proper attitude toward customers must be translated into action to do any good. Consequently, being customer-driven is about attitude and action. What follows are a number of specific strategies organizational leaders can use to translate a customer-driven attitude into action.

Expect Employees to Take Responsibility for Customer Problems

Ensure that employees never respond to customers in ways that could be perceived as giving them the runaround. Train all employees to take ownership of customer problems regardless of who in the organization is responsible for the problem in question. This does not mean that employees should try to solve problems that are outside of their authority or beyond their expertise. Rather, it means that anyone and everyone in the organization should be prepared to *adopt* customers who have problems and take the initiative in getting them to the appropriate person or department.

Consider the following scenario. An employee in your organization's accounting department answers a telephone call that should have been routed to the shipping department. The person calling is a customer with a shipping problem. This type of thing happens all the time in organizations. The accounting employee responds to the customer by giving him the *brush off.* "That is a shipping problem. You need to call back and ask for the shipping department." The brush-off response is bad customer service. To a customer, any person who answers the telephone in your organization IS the organization. Telling customers to hang up and call another department gives the impression that the organization does not want to be bothered with them.

A better option is what I call the *ownership* response. With this response any employee who answers the telephone takes ownership of the situation regardless of who is ultimately responsible for solving the customer's problem. The individual who takes ownership connects the customer with the right person or department. Until the customer is definitely being served by the right person, the employee who took ownership maintains responsibility for the customer. This means that he takes responsibility for guiding the customer to the right party in the organization and making sure the connection is made. An employee who takes ownership of a customer's problem becomes an internal emissary on behalf of the customer.

Rather than telling the customer to hang up and call another number, the original employee should have said: "Thanks for calling. This is the accounting department, but I am going to connect you with the shipping department right away. But just in case you have a problem of any kind, my name is _____ and my telephone number is _____. I will make sure that you are taken care of." The call is then transferred to the right person, but the *ownership* does not stop there. The employee who has taken ownership stays on the line until he is sure that the right person in the organization is on the telephone and understands the customer's problem. Employees should never just press the transfer key and hang up. Chances are that doing so will send the customer to an answering machine, thereby making her feel as if she is getting the run around.

If the person who can solve the customer's problem is not available, the original employee asks the customer to explain the problem in detail and takes comprehensive notes, including a telephone number and email address. The individual who can solve the customer's problem is then tracked down and asked to contact the customer right away. If it is going to be more than a few minutes before the customer's call can be returned, this fact is explained and a convenient time for returning the call is worked out.

Regardless of the nature of the call, the person who answers it takes ownership until the problem is either solved or has been definitely fielded by the responsible person in the organization. This also applies to walk-in customers. Remember, customers often do not know the name of the appropriate person in your organization or the proper channels for their complaint. They just want their problem solved. Having any and all personnel prepared to take ownership of customers will make a more positive impression than responding in a way customers perceive as getting the runaround.

Teach Employees that Temporary Solutions are not Satisfactory

A major issue in customer service is the *I'm-too-busy syndrome.* On one hand, employees are usually already busy with other responsibilities when customers call or drop by with complaints. On the other hand, customers with complaints typically want their problems solved right now. These competing situations can cause employees to respond by arranging quick but temporary solutions to customer problems so they can get back to the other pressing issues they face. Even when employees are not particularly busy, pressure from customers for a quick fix to their problems can cause them to arrange fast but temporary solutions. A temporary solution is not necessarily a bad thing. However, forgetting to follow up with a permanent solution is, and this happens frequently in organizations.

The problem with expedient temporary solutions is that once they are implemented the original problem still exists, but is often forgotten about as problem solvers move on to other pressing matters. Consequently, leaders in organizations should never be satisfied with temporary solutions to customer problems and should make sure that employees are never satisfied with them. Even if a temporary solution is the best approach at the moment, employees should be taught to establish a timetable for finding a permanent solution. Permanent solutions often take longer to put in place, but they are *permanent*. Once applied they stay applied. A temporary fix that is not replaced by a permanent solution will allow problems to resurface just making customers more angry or frustrated than they were originally.

Treat Customers Right Even When They are Wrong

Most people have heard the maxim that *the customer is always right.* Although I agree with the intent behind this philosophy, the maxim itself does not translate well in practical terms. People in organizations are constantly confronted with situations where customers who complain have created their own problems. For example, think of customers who buy a new computer, attempt to set it up without reading the instructions. And then complain when it does not work.

Because of this type of situation, when leaders tell employees the customer is always right it creates an instant credibility gap. For this reason, I developed my own customer-service maxim. This new maxim satisfies the intent of the old one but has more credibility with employees who have to apply it on a daily basis. My customer-service philosophy is: *Even when customers are wrong, they should be treated right.* By "right" I mean with courtesy, respect, and a sense of urgency to get their problem solved.

For example, a customer might not have read the instructions for a given product or service correctly and, as a result, created a problem. This happens all the time. Clearly, in this case the customer is not right and, in fact, is the cause of his own problem. However, he is still a customer. Assuming that your organization wants him to continue to be a customer, preferably a satisfied customer, employees should treat him with courtesy, respect, and a sense of urgency to help. This means that employees must be willing to help customers even when the customers are the source of their own problems. Leaders in organizations should remember this unchanging fact of life in a competitive environment and teach it to employees: if an organization will not help its customers, its competitors will.

Value the Customer's Time

One of the most valuable possessions customers have is their time, a fact people in organizations must never forget because their customers won't. One of the worst things an organization can do to customers is waste their time by forcing them to wait. As a rule, people do not like to wait. Invariably, customers who are made to wait will use the time to conjure up grievances against your organization. Consequently, it is important for leaders in organizations to help employees learn to deal with customers in a timely manner. The key to timely customer service is preparation.

Part of the preparation, especially for walk-in customers or those who call on the telephone, is the *ownership* principle explained earlier in this chapter. When the first person to wait on a customer or answer a customer's telephone call takes ownership of the situation, timely customer service is more likely to be achieved. For customers who make appointments, the key to timely customer service is preparation. Leaders should train employees to prepare for appointments with customers by doing their homework, organizing their paperwork, and planning their agenda, all well in advance of the meeting.

Making sure employees know that they are to be are prepared when meeting with customers will help avoid time-wasting situations such as leaving customers cooling their heels while employees look for pertinent paperwork or files. It will also give employees time to consider solution options before actually dealing with the customer. Customers who have their time wasted by your organization will sooner or later migrate to a competitor that respects their time.

Make Customers Feel Welcome and Appreciated

Organizations that excel make their customers feel welcome and appreciated. Consequently, leaders should understand and ensure that employees understand that customers are why the organization exists. They should also ensure that customers are treated accordingly. Employees should be trained to welcome telephone calls and face-to-face visits from customers. This is important because customers can sense when they are appreciated as well as when they aren't. The minute customers sense they are not welcome they will begin looking for a competitor that will appreciate them.

Eliminate the Little Things that Bother Customers

When customers visit your organization is there ample parking for them? Is the parking lot convenient and near the facility? When customers call your organization, do they get tied up in an endless loop by the telephone answering system or can they talk to a human being? Does your organization have a welcome "feel" to it for customers who visit? Does your organization make the process as convenient as possible when customers need to visit restricted-access areas? Does your organization have a comfortable place for customers to wait when they show up early for meetings? Are the customers' needs and preferences considered when setting up meetings? These questions might seem trivial to you, but they aren't to customers. In fact, it is often the little things that either impress or bother customers most. Consequently, leaders should learn to view the organization through the eyes of the customer and help employees learn this important skill.

Often it is an organization's frontline employees who observe first-hand the little things that bother customers. Consequently, it is important to teach employees to make note of customer irritants and pass the information along to a supervisor so that corrections can be made. Leaders in organizations should keep a master list of customer irritants and work constantly with higher management to eliminate them. Although all personnel in the organization should be on the lookout for customer irritants, the process typically works like this: 1) employees identify the irritants, and 2) leaders take the necessary action to eliminate or mitigate the irritants. This is because the people closest to the customer—frontline employees—are more likely to observe the problems caused by customer irritants.

Promise Small but Deliver Big

One of the worst mistakes people in organizations can make when dealing with customers is to promise big but deliver small. Failing to keep promises is a sure way to lose customers. Some people are just flippant in their dealings with others and do not give sufficient thought to what they are promising. In other cases, over promising can occur because of the demands of a customer. People will sometimes overpromise as a way to placate temporarily a difficult customer. Customers can certainly be demanding, and their demands will occasionally be unrealistic. When this is the case, employees may try to mollify them by promising to respond in a way they know is unrealistic. This is a mistake.

While over promising—regardless of the motive—might temporarily satisfy a demanding customer, when the promise is not fulfilled the problem will just return. When this happens, the customer's dissatisfaction will be even worse than it was originally. This is why organizational leaders should teach employees to promise small and deliver big. For example, assume someone in your organization is talking on the telephone with a customer who is demanding that his order be filled and shipped no later than the end of the work day. The customer is angry and insistent. Realistically, the order can be filled and shipped by Noon the following day, but not by the end of the current work day. This situation is ripe for a major customer service error. Under pressure the employee might decide to promise to ship the order by the end of the day just to mollify the demanding customer.

This will get the customer off of the telephone and give the employee some temporary breathing space. However, when the customer goes on-line to check his order's progress he will know it has not been shipped. Now the customer is going to be doubly angry. Not only did your organization fail to deliver his order on time, it failed to deliver on its promise. When this kind of situation is allowed to occur, both parties lose. The customer loses because his order has not been shipped and the organization loses because the customer's trust has been broken. Customer trust is the foundation upon which good customer service is built. Once lost, customer trust is difficult to regain.

Rather than turn a demanding customer into an unhappy customer who no longer trusts the organization, the employee in this situation should have promised small and then delivered big. For example, she could have told the customer that the order would be filled and shipped by the end of the following work day. This would have been promising small. Delivering big would have been filling and shipping the order by Noon the next day—which was the realistic option in the first place.

In this way, when the customer goes on-line and finds that his order will arrive earlier than promised, his impression of the organization goes from bad to good. The customer might still grumble a little because the package could not be delivered when he originally wanted it, but he will know that when the organization makes a promise it keeps it.

Let Customers Know about Organizational Changes

Customer loyalty is one of the goals of good customer service. This is because loyal customers tend to be repeat customers. Customers become repeat customers because: 1) like the way the organization does things, 2) they like the organization's products/services, and 3) they like the way people in the organization treat them. Consequently, when an organization makes a change that will affect customers in anyway, it is important to let them know about it *before* the change is implemented. Surprising repeat customers who are accustomed to doing things a certain way is bad business.

Customers become accustomed to an organization's personnel, procedures, products, services, and environment. They learn how to deal with an organization, who to call when they have a problem, and other things that make them comfortable. For example, if your organization's contact information—e-mail address, telephone number, mailing address, or web site—is going to change, let customers know well before it happens. If a long-time employee who is popular with customers is going to retire or leave, let customers know before it happens. When any change in the organization is contemplated, ask the following question: Will this change affect customers and if so how? Once this question has been answered, inform customers about the change and take the steps necessary to mitigate any discomfort or inconvenience it might cause them.

The employee's role in preventing unwanted surprises for customers is to: 1) use their proximity to customers to make leaders in the organization aware of when and how changes will affect them, 2) help the organization make customers aware of changes, and 3) use their relationships with repeat customers to help win their acceptance of changes. Leaders in organizations should make sure that employees are aware of the roles they can play with customers and that they are equipped, enabled, and empowered to play these roles effectively.

Treat Customers like Partners

An excellent way to encourage continual improvement in an organization is to treat customers like partners who are part of the continual improvement-process. The judge who determines the value of the products and services an organization provides is the customer. Consequently, as the organization works to continually enhance its value to customers, it makes sense to involve them in the process. Organizational leaders and employees can play a key role in making customers into partners if they are given the challenge and appropriate training.

Many organizations ask for customer feedback—an after the fact approach to involving customers. This can be an important part of the continual-improvement process. But organizations that excel do more than rely on customer feedback. They take the initiative to ask for customer input. In other words, they involve customers at the front end by securing customer input during transactions. This can be done formally, through conversation, or by simply observing customer reactions.

In addition to monitoring customer satisfaction in real time, organizations that excel involve customers *before* introducing or changing a product or service. In this way, they know firsthand how the broader customer base will react to the changes. If the reaction is positive, the new idea can go forward. If the reaction is negative, the new product or service can be revised or replaced with something better. Because employees are on the frontline of interaction with customers, they should be trained to play a key role in soliciting, observing, and collecting customer input.

Organizations that excel become adept at soliciting customer input through a variety of means. Some use customer focus groups in which teams of customers are formed and asked to give their input concerning a product or service that is under development or revision. Some use customer surveys. Others select loyal customers who they trust and meet with them one-on-one. The actual method used is less important than the fact that organizations involve customers at every point in the developmental or revision process. Dealing with customers in these types of settings can be an excellent developmental experience for employees, an experience that will help equip, enable, and empower them for peak performance and continual improvement.

Establish an Infrastructure that Supports Customer Service

Organizations often make more noise than progress when it comes to delivering excellence in customer service. What is typically missing in these organizations is a solid foundation or infrastructure upon which to build a customer-friendly environment. As a first-step in establishing a customer-friendly environment in their organizations, organizational leaders should make a point of familiarizing themselves with the various components of a customer-service infrastructure. Employees are the first and most important component of such an infrastructure.

Before getting into the various components of an organization's customer-service infrastructure, the reader needs to understand a foundational principle about human behavior in organizations. This principle is that employees are more likely to do what the organization needs them to do when they are: 1) given specific expectations, 2) monitored to ensure that performance meets expectations, 3) held accountable for meeting expectations, and 4) recognized/rewarded for exceeding expectations. When leaders in organizations do these four things, employees are more likely to excel at doing their part to ensure customer satisfaction.

If an organization wants effective customer service, it must expect, monitor, evaluate, recognize, and reward it. The means by which these things are systematically accomplished make up the organization's customer-service infrastructure. An organization's customer-service infrastructure has the following components: strategic plan, job descriptions, performance appraisal system, daily monitoring by supervisors, and recognition/reward system.

If excellence in customer service is important, the organization's strategic plan should say so. The plan should contain at least one core value stating that customer-service excellence is a high priority in the organization. This is an excellent way to show all stakeholders that the organization's top management team is committed to excellence in customer service which, in turn, means that all personnel should make it a high priority.

In addition to including customer-service excellence as a core value in the strategic plan, it is important to include it as part of the job description for every position in the organization. In organizations that excel, customer service is everybody's job. Even in organizations that maintain a customer-service department, all personnel still have their individual roles and responsibilities relating to customer service. Including a statement about customer-service excellence in all job descriptions lets employees know that they have a role to play in achieving it.

If customer-service excellence is expected of employees, leaders in organizations should monitor the customer-service behaviors of employees continually. Employees are more likely to exhibit certain behaviors when they know that the behaviors are monitored. On the other hand, failing to monitor and immediately correct negative customer-service behaviors is the same as condoning them.

In addition to monitoring customer-service behaviors on a regular basis, it is important to formally evaluate them periodically. If an organization expects a certain type of behavior from its employees, that behavior should be part of the performance-appraisal process so that it is evaluated formally and systematically. Including customer-service behaviors in the performance-appraisal process is an effective way to hold employees accountable for what is expected of them in this critical area. It is also an effective way to ensure that the customer-service behaviors of employees improve continually. The management principle that says *if you want something to improve measure it* applies here.

Employees who consistently deliver excellent customer-service should be properly recognized and rewarded. Recognition can and should be both informal and formal. Informal recognition occurs during daily monitoring by executives, managers, and supervisors. When an employee is observed delivering excellent customer service, immediate public recognition such as "good job" or a pat on the back is in order.

Telling employees "good job" in front of their peers is one of the best forms of recognition and it can be a powerful way to reinforce positive customer-service behaviors.

Formal recognition of customer-service excellence is also important. When decisions are made about recognition awards such as employee of the month, quarter, or year, customer-service excellence should be one of the criteria applied. In fact, customer service is so important to the success of an organization, that some choose to recognize employees specifically for excellence in this critical area rather than just making customer-service excellence one of the criteria for broader performance awards.

To add the final building block in the infrastructure for customer-service excellence, organizations should reward positive customer-service behaviors. Rewards for customer-service excellence can come in several different forms. For example, consistently delivering customer-service excellence, when coupled with other considerations, should lead to promotions, salary increases, and incentive bonuses. Employees are likely to at least think—even if they do not verbalize their conviction—that if customer-service excellence is really important to the organization it will be rewarded in tangible ways. Employees who hold this conviction are right.

In a competitive environment the customer is king. Organizations that excel consistently deliver excellent customer service. Ensuring excellence in customer service is a critical responsibility for leaders in organizations. A major part of this responsibility is helping employees develop customer-service skills. The strategies explained in this chapter will help turn an organization's personnel into customer-service champions.

GROUP TRAINING ACTIVITY

Assume that your organization is having serious customer-service problems. Your group has been formed as an ad hoc committee to look into the situation and make recommendations for improvements. The organization has already taken several steps to promote customer-service excellence, but they do not seem to be working. These steps are: 1) the CEO sent an organization-wide email to all personnel stating that his highest priority is customer-service excellence, 2) customer-service posters containing catchy sayings have been displayed on the walls of every hallway in the organization's facility, and 3) employees have been encouraged to attend a customer-service seminar that is offered every Friday morning (attendance is optional). Your group's assignment is to develop a list of problems/issues/shortcomings that could be causing the organization's poor customer service and a corresponding list of recommendations for improving customer service. Both lists will be presented to the organization's CEO.

Fourteen

ATTITUDE

Best Practice Number 14: Maintain a positive can-do attitude and help employees develop one.

Many years ago while taking graduate classes at night I worked for a business that was an excellent learning laboratory. Every day at work I saw situations that supported and exemplified the theories we studied in my night classes. I also saw situations that either disproved or, at least, challenged some of these theories. One of the more memorable theories presented in my classes had to do with the powerful effect attitude can have on employee performance. A popular professor claimed over and over that attitude was one of the key determinants of the ultimate success or failure of individuals and organizations.

This professor was quick to clarify that attitude was not to be viewed as a substitute for preparation, effort, or talent but rather as a complement to these things. He claimed that when all other things are equal, an individual with a positive attitude will outpace one with a poor attitude. Further, he asserted that organizations that place a high priority on developing positive attitudes in their personnel will outperform competitors that overlook this important strategy. My experience at work during those years confirmed this professor's contention time and again. It continues to do so more than 40 years later. This is why organizational leaders should devote the time and effort necessary to help employees develop positive attitudes.

POSITIVE ATTITUDE DEFINED

A positive attitude is easy to recognize. Even people who cannot find the words to define the concept know a positive attitude when they see one. For example, consider this scenario from early in my career. I worked for a gloomy supervisor who just hated to hear about problems and was adept at finding the negative in any situation. If you walked into his office to simply ask a question, this supervisor would cut you off and say, "I don't want to hear it. Don't bring me your problems—I have enough of my own."

I greeted him one morning and before he could cut me off said, "I have no problems to report. I just stopped by to say hello." Rather than respond with relief, Mr. Raincloud treated me to a melancholy monologue about the shortcomings of his boss, our organization, his employees, and our customers. In every situation, this gloomy supervisor saw only the problems and potential threats. His doom-and-gloom attitude was so pronounced that his team members began to refer to him, ironically, as "Mr. Sunshine." Mr. Sunshine moped around under a dark cloud for another year, the very picture of despair. Then one day he simply wasn't there anymore.

His replacement could not have been more different. If you brought a problem to this new supervisor, he invariably smiled, rubbed his hands together in anticipation, and said, "Let's see how you and I can solve this problem." He was a breath of fresh air in our department and a calming influence in the midst of the inevitable storms that occasionally batter an organization. Nothing rattled him. Problems were challenges to be confronted, and finding the best possible solution in even the worse of circumstances was always his focus. His optimism was infectious and within just days it began to have an effect. The morale in our department quickly improved, and so did the performance.

What this new supervisor had that his predecessor lacked was a positive attitude. A positive attitude is simply a frame of mind possessed by people who exhibit a constructive, helpful outlook on life and work. A positive attitude should not be confused with artificial optimism in which people simply ignore uncomfortable realities that are obvious to everyone else. Rather it is a commitment to concentrating on solutions rather than problems, to facing up to challenges and saying "We can" instead of "We can't." It is a commitment to seeking the best possible solution in even the worst possible circumstances.

Characteristics of People with Positive Attitudes

A positive attitude is like courage. It shows up most prominently during difficult times. People with positive attitudes consistently do things in a certain way. In all situations they do the following:

- Focus on the positive in all situations

- Have positive expectations in all endeavors

- Associate with other positive people when they have a choice

- Concentrate on solutions rather than problems

- Look for lessons in the mistakes of others rather than pointing the finger of blame

- Take a *can-do* approach to new challenges

- Take the initiative in all situations

- Take a proactive approach to work and life

- Use bad situations as opportunities for teaching and learning

- Provide calm and reason in the middle of life's storms

There is nothing artificial about these characteristics, which is an important point for organizational leaders to understand. It is not uncommon to meet people who are perpetually smiling and always seem to be upbeat, but whose apparent positive attitude is really just a veneer of false optimism. Often these false optimists are an organization's most visible and vocal advocates of maintaining a positive attitude. Their office walls are typically plastered with uplifting posters containing catchy slogans, and their conversations are peppered with feel-good maxims. However, their act has no depth and, as result, quickly falters in the face of adversity, which is when a real positive attitude is needed most. False optimism is a surface-level phenomenon. A positive attitude comes from deep within.

POSITIVE ATTITUDE VERSUS FALSE OPTIMISM

I saw an excellent illustration of the crucial difference between a positive attitude and false optimism many years ago while playing high school football. My team was losing badly against a vastly superior opponent. Near the end of the game every member of my team was bruised, battered, and feeling like a loser. In fact, we were embarrassed and humiliated. All we wanted to do was get the game over with and get off the field. With just a few minutes left in the game, my team had the ball at mid-field.

We had one more chance to score, but this meant little to us. One touchdown—in the unlikely event we could even score one—is little consolation when you are behind by 40 points. Throughout the game our offense had failed to move the ball and our defense had failed to keep our opponent from scoring. You could count all of the first downs we had made on one hand and have fingers left over. As my team mates and I looked up at the time clock and silently urged it to move faster, our coach stepped in and exhibited what I now view as an excellent act of leadership.

Calling a timeout, he signaled for the offensive team to join him on the sideline. As we ran off the field, our cheerleaders were blissfully yelling to a rapidly dwindling crowd "We're going to win! We're going to win!" I can still remember thinking as I ran off the field, "Our cheerleaders are nuts." As we gathered around the coach, instead of yelling and exhorting as coaches sometimes do, he silently stared directly into our eyes. For what seemed an eternity, the coach did not say a word. The expression on his face was calm but determined. Finally, just as the silence was becoming unbearable our coach said: "You boys can hear what our cheerleaders are saying and you know it's not true. We are not going to win this game no matter what we do—at least not on the scoreboard." Then, pointing at his chest, our coach said, "But we can still win it in here."

The coach went on to explain that the game had been lost on the scoreboard since the first quarter. Normally, in a situation like this—with the game clearly won—the opposing coach would substitute some of his second-string players to give them experience. But our opposing coach was different. He had kept his first-string players on the field for the whole game in an attempt to run up the score and keep our team out of the end zone. Not only did he want to beat us by a lopsided score, he wanted to show that we could not score even one touchdown on his team.

With our entire team circled around him, our coach said (paraphrased): The game we are playing is no longer the one reflected on the scoreboard. The new game—the one our opponent is playing—is about humiliating our team by keeping us out of the end zone. He has already won the first game, but we can win this new game. You boys are getting ready to go back out there and put the ball in the end zone. You can do it. You are going to show that bunch of arrogant prima donnas across the field what you are made of. Then, after we score we are going to do an on-side kick. If we come up with the ball, we are going to score again. If they are able to field the on-side kick, we are going to keep them out of the end zone for the rest of the game. We can do this. It's a new game, and we can win it.

My team mates and I ran back on the field re-energized and possessing a whole new attitude. We had a renewed sense of purpose and were committed to scoring a touchdown. Up to now the game had been a breeze for the other team and, as a result, our opponent had become cocky and over-confident. Some of the opposing players had actually begun to taunt and mock us. What they failed to realize is that they were in a new ballgame against a new team with a new attitude.

When the ball was snapped, we flew off the line with such intensity and played with such tenacity that we could not be denied. It wasn't easy and it wasn't pretty, but we did finally score. Then, rather than kick the extra point our coach decided to put an exclamation point on our touchdown: we went for two points and scored again. The opposing players were flabbergasted. Several yelled "What's the point?" They didn't get it.

After we finally scored, there was still enough time left on the clock for the kickoff, but not much more. We executed the on-side kick perfectly and when we came up with the ball the change in momentum was palpable. Up to this point the players on the other team had played with an air of dismissive confidence. Now, all of a sudden, their arrogance had vanished. We could see it in their eyes. The eyes of the opposing players had a deer-in-the-headlights look in them. They began yelling accusations at each other and running around in frantic confusion over the unexpected turn of events. We began to grind out hard-fought yardage again and were well on our way to another score when the clock ran out on us. The final numbers on the scoreboard were still hopelessly lopsided—a clear loss to outsiders—but not to my team mates and I. Ironically, it was our team that ran off the field with heads held high. The so-called winning team, on the other hand, skulked off in a state of shock and embarrassment.

What our cheerleaders exhibited on this memorable night, although with the best of intentions, was false optimism. When you are behind by 40 points with just minutes to play, you are not going to come from behind and win, not even in a Disney movie. But what our coach exhibited was wise leadership and a positive attitude. He knew we could not possibly overcome a 40-point deficit in the little time that remained, and he knew that we were embarrassed and humiliated by our poor performance and the taunts of the opposing players.

Determined to find a way to let us walk out of that stadium with our heads held high and our self-worth undiminished, this good man simply invented a new game, a game we could win. Like people with a positive attitude typically do, he turned some sour lemons into sweet lemonade, and in so doing taught 50 boys a more important lesson than a victory on the scoreboard ever could have. If the other coach and his players were paying attention, they should have learned a valuable lesson too.

PRACTICAL BENEFITS OF A POSITIVE ATTITUDE

A positive attitude will enhance the performance of individuals and, in turn, organizations. In practical terms, this is one of the principal benefits of a positive attitude: it is a performance enhancer. The performance of individuals is the product of a number of different factors including knowledge, skills, talent, motivation, leadership, support, and a variety of intangibles. A positive attitude is a multiplier. It will enhance the value of all the factors that contribute to peak performance and continual improvement.

For example, an individual with a certain amount of knowledge who has a positive attitude will outperform an individual with an equal amount of knowledge who has a negative attitude. This same rule of thumb applies to all of the factors that affect peak performance and continual improvement. Other practical benefits of a positive attitude include the following:

- *Better attendance.* In organizations where positive attitudes are the norm, attendance is better. This is because positive attitudes reduce stress and stress is one of the most persistent causes of poor attendance. The proof of this assertion can be found in an individual's sick-leave record and, in turn, the collective sick-leave record of the organization. The higher the level of stress, the higher the average number of sick leave days taken by an organization's personnel. Negative attitudes have the effect of multiplying stress while positive attitudes have the effect of reducing it. Reduce the level of stress in an organization and you will improve attendance. A positive attitude is a stress reducer.

- *Better customer service.* Customers do not like to deal with grouchy, whiny, negative people. When customers need help or have a problem, they want to deal with someone whose attitude says, "You are important to me and I will take care of you." This is the approach of personnel with a positive attitude. Personnel with a negative attitude are likely to convey a much different message, a message that might cause customers to migrate to the competition.

- *Better leadership.* Leaders at all levels in an organization—executives, managers, and supervisors—will get better results from their personnel by consistently displaying a positive attitude. Employees are more likely to follow leaders who have a positive attitude. Nobody wants to follow a negative person. When trying to lead people to peak performance a positive attitude is essential. A positive attitude says, "We can." A negative attitude says, "We can't." Nobody wants to follow a leader whose attitude says, "We can't."

- *Better teamwork.* Effective teamwork is difficult to sustain. It requires a concerted effort under even the best conditions—conditions few organizations ever experience. There are so many factors that can undermine effective teamwork (e.g. the personal agendas, interests, personalities, and egos of team members; turnover; poor human relations; and the attitudes of organizational leaders). In order to establish and maintain effective teamwork, organizational leaders must exhibit positive attitudes toward their team members, each other, the work to be accomplished, customers, vendors, and other stakeholders. If an organization's leaders are not positive about these things, why should employees be? If employees are not positive about these things, the organization will not enjoy the benefits of effective teamwork.

- *Better attitudes among employees.* Attitudes are like the measles—we catch them from each other. When organizational leaders exhibit a positive attitude, employees will "catch" it from them. Of course, the obverse is also true. Consistently show employees a negative attitude and they will eventually "catch" one and follow your negative example. The most effective way for organizational leaders to promote positive attitudes is by example. This is also the best way to spread negative attitudes. Consequently, consistently displaying a positive attitude—even under the most difficult circumstances—is essential for organizational leaders.

- *Better human relations.* The attitudes of personnel at all levels will determine the quality of human relations in an organization. Do people like to come to work? Do people view the organization, their work, and each other in a positive light? Is there a spirit of camaraderie and cooperation in the organization? Is there a family atmosphere in the organization? The answer to all of these questions is typically "yes" in organizations that enjoy good, positive human relations. This is important because organizations with good human relations among their personnel are able to focus on peak performance and continual improvement instead of petty disagreements, jealousies, inter-departmental squabbling, office politics, and other counter-productive forms of human interaction. The better the attitudes of an organization's personnel toward each other and their work, the better the human relations in that organization. The better the human relations in an organization, the more talent and energy available to focus on achieving peak performance, continual improvement, and, ultimately, organizational excellence.

MAINTAINING A POSITIVE ATTITUDE

The point has already been emphasized that organizational leaders promote positive attitudes in employees by exhibiting positive attitudes themselves. Setting a consistent example for employees is an essential ingredient in helping them maintain a positive attitude. To help employees maintain positive attitudes, leaders must first maintain their own. The following strategies will help with this challenge:

- *Remember that you control your attitude.* There are so many factors that make a given workday good or bad over which people in an organization have no control. Problems occur unexpectedly, deadlines bear down, people become impatient with each other, critical personnel get sick, equipment breaks down, important customers migrate to a competitor, and on and on. You cannot control most of the factors that cause problems, but you can control how you respond to problems. In other words, you can control your attitude. Maintaining a positive attitude is a conscious choice, nobody can make you have a bad attitude and only you can choose to have a positive attitude.

- *Accentuate the positive.* Jobs have their good points and bad, their enjoyable aspects and those that are less enjoyable. It is easy to fall into the trap of focusing on the less enjoyable aspects of the job while taking the enjoyable aspects for granted. To maintain a positive attitude, stay focused on the enjoyable aspects of your job. When things are not going well, ask yourself this question: What do I like about this job? Better yet, on a day when things are going well make a list of the things you like about your job. Then, on days when things are not going well, pull out your list and remind yourself of the positive aspects of the job.

- *Be solution-oriented.* When you find that problems at work are dragging you down, stop focusing on the problems and start focusing on solutions. The tendency of people who are trying to accomplish any task is to focus on those things that are getting in their way, slowing them down, or impeding their progress. For example, assume your team is up against a deadline to complete a project and your organization's computers crash. It is almost certain that most of your team members are going to focus on the computer crash. If so, they are looking in the wrong direction. The positive approach would be to start looking for alternative ways to get the project completed on time. I was once involved in a situation similar to this and got to observe how an organizational leader with a positive attitude handles a crisis. We were working on a publishing project and were up against an unforgiving deadline when the organization's computers crashed. While everyone else fretted, fumed, and made disparaging remarks about computers, our team leader calmly asked two questions: 1) How many of you have your own laptop computers?, and 2) Where is the nearest Internet café? We all had laptops and there was an Internet café right up the street. Within minutes we were back in the saddle. Because a team leader with a positive attitude immediately started looking for a solution rather than complaining about the problem, our team completed the project on time.

- *Associate with positive people.* It has already been mentioned that people tend to *catch* each other's attitudes in the same way they catch the measles—by simply being around each other. Spend too much time around negative people and you are likely to catch a negative attitude. Consequently, organizational leaders should make a point of identifying positive people and spending as much time as possible with them. If there are no consistently positive people to associate with at work, find some outside of work. In addition to identifying positive people to interact with on a regular basis, read positive literature, listen to positive CDs, and watch positive DVDs. There will always be plenty of negative influences in your life, and you will not have to look far to find them. Negatives have a way of finding you. But positive influences are different. They are available, but more often than not you have to seek them out. Associating with positive people, literature, and other influences might take some work, but the results will be worth the effort.

ELIMINATING A NEGATIVE ATTITUDE

For some people a negative attitude is the norm. In addition, even the most positive people will sometimes succumb to negativity. In spite of your best efforts to maintain a positive attitude, the stress and pressures of the job may occasionally get the better of you. This can happen to anyone, and does happen to most. Do not be surprised to find negativity creeping into your attitude from time to time. When work becomes difficult, even the most positive person can slip into a negative frame of mind. In fact, you can just about count on this happening at some point in your life, and probably more than once. Whether negativity is your normal frame of mind or the result of the pressures of work, it must be eliminated. Organizational leaders with negative attitudes cannot lead effectively.

If you are usually negative or have recently slipped into it, do not despair. Negativity and attitudinal backsliding should be taken in stride. In spite of their best efforts to maintain a positive attitude, people are going to fall prey to a negative attitude from time to time. Negativity is a curable condition, but the prescription is different than that for maintaining a positive attitude. Organizational leaders who need to eliminate a negative attitude or help employees do so will find the following strategies helpful:

- *Help someone else whose attitude needs work.* Often the best way to eliminate a negative attitude is to help someone else eliminate theirs. Helping someone else will take your mind off of the factors that are pulling you down. It will also make the point that you are not alone in experiencing attitudinal challenges. Once you realize that you are not alone in your attitudinal dilemma, it will be easier to overcome it. If you notice colleagues or direct reports who have slipped into negativism, help them get refocused on solutions rather than problems, connect them with positive people they can associate with, and recommend positive literature, CDs, and DVDs that will help get them back on track. In helping them, you may help yourself.

- *Look for the good in others.* A sure sign of a negative attitude is seeing only the bad in others. If you find yourself focusing on the weaknesses, shortcomings, and human flaws of others, negativity has set in. When this happens, make a point of looking for the good in people. It is always easier to see the negatives in people, but positives can usually be found if you will look for them. Looking for the good in others is itself a positive act. This is an important point because eliminating a negative attitude is an action-oriented undertaking. You cannot just sit back and hope a negative attitude will just go away. It won't. You have to make a conscious effort to eliminate it. Looking for the good in others will help.

- *Recognize the efforts as well as the accomplishments of others.* A negative attitude is a self-centered phenomenon. In essence, a negative attitude says, "I want things to go my way and if they don't I am going to react in a negative way." To eliminate a negative attitude it is necessary to focus on things external to you. Recognizing not just the accomplishments but the efforts of others is a good way to start. Look for employees who are putting forth a good effort or who have accomplished something important and recognize them. The recognition does not need to be formal. A simple pat on the back or just saying "good job" is all that is necessary. This strategy has the double benefit of helping eliminate a negative attitude while at the same time reinforcing peak performance and continual improvement in others.

- *Look for things you appreciate about your job.* I will never forget an exchange that took place on an airplane several years ago. Two passengers sitting across the aisle from me were engaging in the usual kind of small talk that strangers on airplanes make.

After a few minutes, one passenger asked the other, "How are things going with your job?" This was an innocent enough question, but it elicited more of a response than might have been expected. The other passenger proceeded to deliver a scathing tirade about everything that was wrong with his job, colleagues, employees, and customers. To hear this man talk, there was nothing good about his job. The other passenger listened to this avalanche of negativity for a while but finally broke in and said, "I'll trade with you. I have been unemployed for nine months. I can't find anything and don't know what I am going to do." The message to his negative seat mate was clear. Be thankful you have a job. Some of us don't. On your worst day at work you can find things to appreciate about your job—even if all you can appreciate is the fact that you have a job. When the pressures and stress of the job are dragging you down, look for things you appreciate. They are right there behind that cloud of negativity you have created with your attitude.

Doing the things explained in this section will help organizational leaders eliminate their own negative attitudes. The same strategies can be used to help employees eliminate theirs. If colleagues or employees are suffering from negative attitudes, share the information in this section with them. Explain how you use these strategies to eliminate negativity in your attitude. The more people in an organization adopt and maintain positive attitudes, the easier it will be to achieve peak performance, continual improvement, and organizational excellence.

GROUP TRAINING ACTIVITY

John is known throughout his organization for having a positive attitude, but the people in his new department don't. John was recently promoted to manage a department full of people with decidedly negative attitudes. He wants to help his personnel eliminate their negative attitudes and adopt positive attitudes. Unfortunately for John, things seem to be going in the opposite direction—it's his attitude that is changing, and for the worse. The more John interacts with his new employees, the worse his own attitude is becoming. As John sees it, he has three challenges: 1) convincing his employees that a positive attitude is important to them personally, to their department, and to the organization, 2) maintaining his own positive attitude, and 3) helping his employees eliminate their negative attitudes. Your group's assignment is to develop a plan complete with illustrative examples that John can use to meet these three challenges.

Fifteen

DECISION MAKING, PROBLEM SOLVING, AND CRITICAL THINKING

Best Practice Number 15: Become proficient at decision making, problem solving, and critical thinking and help employees develop their skills in these critical areas.

If organizations are going to achieve peak performance and continual improvement, organizational leaders and employees must excel in the areas of decision making, problem solving, and critical thinking. The best way for organizational leaders to help employees become good decision makers, problem solvers, and critical thinkers is by example. In order to set a positive example for employees in these areas, leaders must first become good decision makers, problem solvers, and critical thinkers themselves.

In addition to setting a positive example, organizational leaders should involve employees in decision making and problem solving. People learn best by doing. Involving employees in making decisions and in solving problems while setting a good example for them—including an example of critical thinking—is one more step toward achieving peak performance and continual improvement.

Nothing happens in an organization until decisions are made. Once decisions are made, problems will inevitably occur that must be solved before decisions can be fully implemented. Effective decision making and problem solving are important to organizations. In both, critical thinking will improve the result. Consequently, effective decision making, problem solving, and critical thinking are essential to both peak performance and organizational excellence. This chapter will help organizational leaders become effective decision makers, problem solvers, and critical thinkers so that they can, in turn, help employees develop skills in these important areas.

DECISION MAKING AND PROBLEM SOLVING: THE PROCESS

Decision making is the process of choosing one option from among two or more potential options. Ideally, the option chosen will produce the best result or at least the best possible result under the existing circumstances. The best possible or most advantageous result under the circumstances is sometimes referred to as the *most acceptable result.* Understanding the concept of the most acceptable result is important because organizational leaders often face situations in which the time and resources available to them do not allow for a perfect decision or solution.

Every organizational leader deals with situations in which they must make an acceptable decision or settle for an acceptable solution. For example, assume that your car breaks down and is so worn out that repairs are no longer an option. You have to replace it. The problem in this situation is that without a dependable vehicle, you have no means of transportation. The obvious solution is to get another vehicle, but there are a lot of options to consider (e.g. Car, truck, or van? Large, small, or mid-sized? Foreign or domestic? Pay cash or finance? Purchase or lease? Traditional engine or hybrid? Expensive car or economy model?). Each option has its costs and benefits, its good points and bad.

How you plan to use the vehicle is the first consideration when dealing with the car-truck-van option. Gas mileage will come into play in choosing between a vehicle with a traditional or a hybrid engine. Dependability, accessories, appearance, and warranty options must all be considered in the decision-making process. However, if you are like most people the one overriding consideration will be cost. In other words, the limiting factor—the one that will guide the decision-making process toward the most acceptable solution rather than the perfect solution—is money. Your ideal vehicle might be a Lamborghini or a Rolls Royce, but when money is factored into the decision-making process you will probably have to settle for something less expensive.

Assume that you ultimately purchase a mid-range vehicle from an American automobile manufacturer. Although the decision did not lead to the perfect solution to your transportation problem, it did lead to the most acceptable solution.

Decisions and Solutions: Perfect or Most Acceptable?

In the previous example, the perfect solution was thought to be a Lamborghini or a Rolls Royce. However, the limiting factor of money forced the individual in question to decide in favor of the most acceptable solution rather than the perfect solution. This is how decision making in organizations often is. Numerous factors can force organizational leaders to choose the most acceptable rather than the perfect solution. It is important for organizational leaders to understand this. It is this fact of life that gave rise to what is now called *the 70 percent solution.* This concept asserts—accurately—that a solution which is only 70 percent of the ideal but is implemented on time is still better than a perfect solution implemented too late.

For example, assume that 10 managers from your organization are flying to New York for an important meeting. Because of a mix-up with reservations, only seven of them can be seated on the flight that will arrive in New York in time for the beginning of the meeting. However, if the group can wait a couple of hours there is another flight that will get the whole team to New York at the same time, albeit two hours late for the meeting. Ideally all ten members of the group would arrive on time for the meeting, but circumstances have rendered this impossible.

The 70 percent solution in this case is for seven members of the group to take the early flight and arrive on time with the other three following as soon as possible thereafter. After discussing the situation, the senior manager in the group decides to opt for the 70 percent solution. He knows that by carefully choosing which seven members of his team go on the first flight, he might be able to re-organize the group's presentation so that the other three still arrive in time for their parts. He also knows that waiting for the entire team to show up at the same time—two hours late—might cause his company to lose the contract that is the reason for the trip in the first place.

Factors that can force organizational leaders to select the most acceptable solution rather than the ideal when making decisions include time, money, material, environment, technology, processes, and personnel. In a career that has spanned more than 40 years, I can remember taking on few projects in which all the needed resources were available to the extent I would have liked. At least one of these factors was almost always lacking to some extent, and usually more than one.

It is not uncommon for people in organizations to lack the time necessary to do a job perfectly. For example, I have written more than 70 books but have never felt that I had the time to include everything I would have liked to include. There is always something that might have been added or something that might have been written differently if only there was time. When a publisher decides there is a need for a book, time is typically of the essence. In fact, timing is always a key consideration when releasing a new book. The publisher decides when the book should be released to gain maximum effect, and that date becomes the immoveable object that drives all subsequent decisions.

Once the release date has been set in stone, the time needed for editing, indexing, and printing are determined and subtracted from the time available to develop the book. Whatever time is left over is the time the author has for research and writing. This remaining period of time is seldom ideal—at least in the mind of the author—for producing the perfect product. In fact, I have never met an author who did not think he or she could have covered a few more topics or gone into a little more depth if just given the time. Consequently, many books on the shelves of bookstores are the most acceptable rather than the ideal products. This same type of thing happens in most organizations.

In almost all organizations, money is a limiting factor in decision making and problem solving. Here is a scenario that has happened to me many times. My company would bid on a contract and win it. That was the good news. The bad news was that in order to win the contract, our marketing personnel had to cut every corner possible. The net result is that the project team was given a job that would normally require six months to complete, but now it had to be done in just four months. This is a common situation in organizations.

Limitations on the availability of material can influence decisions and solutions. For example, a problem with material once forced me to select the most acceptable rather than the ideal solution. I needed a new supply of stationery for my company and had waited until my existing supply was almost depleted before placing an order. When I finally got around to calling the printer, he did not have a sufficient supply of the specific paper I wanted—a heavy grade pale blue paper. He could match the color but not the grade of paper I have always used for my company's stationery, unless of course I could put off ordering the new supply for three weeks. Delaying the order was not an option. Consequently, I had to choose the most acceptable solution: same color of paper but different grade.

Equipment and technology are often limiting factors when organizations make decisions. For example, assume that an organization has an opportunity to receive a substantial new contract that has the potential to double its business volume over the next ten years. Should the organization accept the contract? On the surface the answer to this question would appear to be obvious. However, there are some issues that must be dealt with before the decision is made. The equipment in the organization's facility is currently maxed out. In order to take on a substantial new contract, the organization will have to purchase new equipment.

The equipment needed is highly-specialized and expensive. Further, it is not clear that the organization will be able to find qualified technicians to operate the new equipment. As the organization's marketing personnel discuss the new contract with their counterparts from production, it becomes clear that the answer to whether the organization should accept the new contract is not as obvious as it first appeared. In fact, it is clear that much of the increased income the new contract would bring will be consumed by the cost of the new equipment, facility, and personnel. The new contract will come at a cost. Accepting the new contract will boil down to deciding if the equipment required will allow the company to bring in additional contracts that, over time, will produce significant profits. Because of the equipment issues, the organization's top leaders will be forced to weigh the costs and benefits of the new contract carefully before deciding.

An organization's processes often become a factor when decisions must be made. Every organization has processes for performing its work. There are processes for bringing resources into the organization, processes for doing the work of the organization, and processes for shipping products or delivering services. The quality and capabilities of these processes can become a factor in the decision-making process. For example, one of the ways organizations sometimes get themselves into trouble is by taking on work that falls outside of their core competencies—competencies that include their processes.

For example, I once worked for a pre-stressed concrete construction company that was purchased by a well-known manufacturing firm. The construction company's core competencies/processes were in designing and building large concrete structures such as football stadiums, condominiums, bridges, and commercial buildings. The manufacturer's core competencies/processes were in designing and manufacturing the mechanical components of nuclear reactors. The questionable reasoning of the manufacturing executives in deciding to purchase the construction company went like this: They design and build big things and we design and build big things. Not surprisingly, the purchase failed to meet the expectations of either party.

Designing and constructing pre-stressed concrete structures required processes and expertise that were radically different from those required for designing and manufacturing nuclear reactor components. The difference in core competencies/processes should have been viewed as a limiting factor in the decision-making process. It wasn't—a fact that led to a rocky merger followed by an inevitable parting of the ways.

Of all the factors that can force an organization to select the most acceptable rather than the ideal solution, the one I have had to deal with most often over the past 40 years is people. An organization can perform only as well as its personnel perform. Perhaps the best examples of this fact can be found in the world of sports. College and professional teams do not win games because they have superior game plans. They win because their personnel do a better job than the other team in carrying out their game plans. Of all the factors that influence organizational performance, the human factor is still the most critical—even in the most advanced high-tech firms.

Even the most advanced technologies that are designed to limit the influence of the human factor on performance depend on the ability of humans to operate and maintain them efficiently and effectively. Take the example of the personal computer in an office setting. A personal computer with the right software can turn an administrative employee into a productivity giant, but only if that individual knows how to efficiently and effectively make use of all of the computer's capabilities. Without a talented human being who knows how to run it effectively, a personal computer is just an expensive paperweight.

The abilities and limitations of personnel as well as their availability often force organizations to accept less than ideal solutions. For example, a customer wants his order filled and shipped in two days. However, with the personnel currently on hand the organization will need a week to complete and ship the order. This type of situation happens all the time. I once faced the dilemma of my organization being offered a large and potentially profitable contract if we could complete it in six months. My best estimate of the time needed based on the personnel available was 18 months.

The work in question was highly specialized. My organization could not just hire people off the street to do it, nor could our existing personnel be stretched far enough to complete 18 months of work in just six months. In the end, my organization went with the most acceptable solution which was to be a sub-contractor and accept part of the contract rather than being the general contractor and accepting all of it. This was not the perfect solution, but it was the most advantageous one we could manage under the circumstances.

Organizational leaders must be good decision makers. Part of being a good decision maker is recognizing when the most acceptable solution is the appropriate solution. I have known otherwise talented professionals whose contributions to their organizations where limited by their inability to make a decision until they had all of their ducks perfectly in a row. These types of decision makers often suffer from paralysis-by-analysis. They can aim the gun but can't bring themselves to pull the trigger. Instead they keep aiming (analyzing) trying to line up the perfect shot until the target is removed. In other words, they ponder and fret until the time for a decision runs out. Had the decision makers in this case simply pulled the trigger at the point where they had the best shot at the target—meaning the best information available in the time allotted to them—the result probably would have been an acceptable solution.

Accepting less than a perfect solution is not and never should be used as a substitute for careful analysis, thoughtful preparation, or extensive research. Decisions that are the most acceptable rather than perfect are not seat-of-the-pants decisions or blind stabs in the dark. They are decisions made within a prescribed time frame after careful consideration of all available information. Unfortunately, time is almost always limited and so is information. If by chance everything necessary for an ideal solution is available, decision makers should, of course, opt for the ideal. But since this will not always be the case, organizational leaders should be prepared to make decisions that will lead to the most acceptable solutions.

PROBLEM SOLVING AND DECISION MAKING: THE MODEL

Problems create the need for decisions. In fact, anything that requires a decision is considered a problem. For example, if you and several colleagues decide to go out for lunch, a decision will have to be made concerning where to go. The problem requiring a solution is where to go for lunch. Unless the problem in question is an emergency requiring a snap decision, the best way to solve problems is by applying a systematic decision-making model. The following four-step model is widely used by organizations that excel at decision making:

1. Identify the root cause of the problem

2. Consider the alternative solutions

3. Choose the best alternative and implement it

4. Monitor progress and adjust as necessary

Identify the Root Cause of the Problem

Problems have root causes and contributing causes. The root cause of a problem is the one causal factor without which the problem would not have occurred. Contributing causes can exacerbate the problem, but they do not cause it. Contributing causes are sometimes referred to as symptoms. Too often in organizations, people deal with problems by treating the symptoms—the contributing causes—rather than eliminating the root cause. They treat problems the way physicians treat the common cold.

Assume that you wake up feeling terrible one day. You have a runny nose, watery eyes, and a stuffy head. The doctor diagnoses a head cold and writes a prescription to clear up your runny nose, dry your watery eyes, and eliminate the stuffy feeling in your head. Has the doctor solved the problem? Not really. What he has done is treat the symptoms of the problem. Of course, treating the symptoms will bring a measure of relief, but only temporarily.

The problem in this case is that you feel terrible. The root cause is a head cold. Contributing causes to your feeling terrible (symptoms) are a runny nose, watery eyes, and stuffy head. The doctor provided a prescription that will temporarily lessen the symptoms (contributing causes) but will not eliminate the root cause—the head cold. Even though the medicine will provide some temporary relieve, unless the head cold is eliminated the problem will eventually return. This is what happens in organizations when its personnel treat the symptoms of problems rather than eliminating root causes: the problem returns and keeps returning until the root cause is eliminated.

Identifying the Root Cause of a Problem

Unfortunately it is often easier to observe the symptoms of a problem than the root cause. In fact, identifying the root cause of a problem is often the most difficult step in the problem-solving process. Various tools are available to help organizational leaders identify the root causes of problems. The following checklist is a simple but effective tool for identifying the root cause of a problem:

- Time

- Money

- Supplies

- Equipment/technology

- Material

- Policies

- Management policies/practices

- Employees

- Customers

- Suppliers

- Inventory

- Training

- Purchasing

- Conversion processes

- Shipping

- Receiving

- Quality management/control

- Scheduling

- Facility

- Environment

- External factors (laws, restrictive covenants, politics)

When trying to identify the root cause of a problem, each item on the list is posed as a question or a series of questions. Assume that your team is experiencing an on-going problem and needs to identify the root cause. As the team leader, you are using the checklist as a guide in conducting a brainstorming session with your team members. You begin with the first item on the list—time—and pose the following questions: 1) Could this problem have been caused by time—having too little or too much? 2) If time appears to be a cause, is it a contributing cause or the root cause? This same exercise would be repeated for each item on the list until the team is comfortable it has identified the root cause as well as all contributing causes.

I was once asked to help a manufacturing firm that was experiencing an on-going problem with the printed circuit boards it produced. The scrap rate for the boards had risen to a level that was unacceptably high. Too many were being rejected by the quality department because of defects. The manufacturing manager had investigated the problem thoroughly and corrected it—so he thought—more than once, but the problem kept returning. I was asked to help the company's printed circuit-board team identify the root cause.

I asked the company's manufacturing manager to select a small group of his best printed-circuit board personnel to work with me. We sat in a conference room and reviewed the checklist presented in this section. For each item on the list, I posed a question and asked the others in the room to add any questions they thought might be pertinent. We were getting well into the list without identifying anything that might be the root cause of the increased scrap rate when we came to *environment.* Before asking questions, I requested an explanation from the experts concerning how the environment in the manufacturing shop could affect either their processes or their product.

It turned out that the environment in the shop was a critical factor in the manufacturing process. The temperature and humidity in the shop had to be maintained at prescribed levels or problems could result. One of the team members explained that the temperature and humidity were set at the proper levels and checked periodically throughout the day by selected team members. This team member said that as far as he knew the temperature and humidity had stayed within the prescribed range over the last month. I asked how often they were checked and at what specific times.

It turned out that the temperature and humidity in the printed-circuit board shop were checked at the beginning of the day, noon, and late afternoon. The company in question is located in Northwest Florida where the temperature and humidity soar during the summer months. I had a hunch and played it. Asking the team what months of the year had the highest scrap rate, I was told July and August. We discussed the possibility of environmental factors being the root cause, but could not agree since the temperature and humidity in the shop were routinely checked. Still playing my hunch, I asked that the temperature and humidity in the shop be checked every hour of the day for the next week rather than just three times a day (this occurred in August).

By the end of the following week, the problem-solving team and I were zeroing in on a possible root cause. We had found that between 1:30pm and 3:00pm the temperature and humidity in the shop were consistently falling outside of acceptable limits, a fact that was not picked up when they were checked at noon and then not again until 4:00pm. By checking the scrap records, the problem-solving team was able to determine that most of the defective boards rejected by the quality control technicians were manufactured between 1:30pm and 3:00pm. After checking a few other possibilities from the list, the team members felt certain that the root cause was environmental.

Once the temperature and humidity situation was corrected, the company's scrap rate went right back down to its previous acceptable level and stayed there. We had eliminated the root cause of the problem. Consequently the problem disappeared. In the process of identifying the root cause of the increased scrap rate, the problem-solving team also identified a few other potential problems. Two machine operators had not completed some essential updating training, a shortcoming that could lead to operator errors. Further, one box of solder—a critical material in the manufacturing process—was found to be defective. Had it been fed into one of the company's wave-soldering machines, all of the boards that passed through that machine would have been defective.

Identifying other problems before they happen is one of the side benefits of using the checklist presented in this section. It will help organizational leaders identify the root cause of an existing problem so that the cause can be eliminated, but it will also help identify potential new problems before they occur. Hence, the checklist is effective for both problem solving and problem prevention.

An especially valuable side benefit of this process was that the employees involved learned how to approach and solve problems systematically.

They participated in the process of identifying the root cause of the increased reject rate for printed-circuit boards and, by so doing, became skilled at using the checklist. Teaching employees to be good decision makers and problem solvers is one of the reasons it is important for organizational leaders to become effective in this regard and to set a positive example for employees to follow.

Consider Alternative Solutions

Once the root cause has been identified it must be eliminated before the problem in question can be solved. This typically requires a decision, and often more than one. How should the team go about eliminating the root cause? There will usually be more than one answer to this question and each alternative will have its own costs and benefits. When deciding which alternative to select for solving a problem, several considerations come into play. The cost of each potential solution must be weighed against the benefits.

When conducting a cost/benefit analysis for a given alternative, it is important to go beyond just the direct financial costs and benefits. Any applicable ethical ramifications should also be considered, as should those relating to employee morale and public relations. Of course not all decisions have ethical, public-relations, or morale- related aspects. However, decisions that do can quickly go awry if organizational leaders overlook these factors.

Inexperienced problem solvers sometimes make the mistake of applying one-hundred dollar solutions to ten-dollar problems. Making sure that decisions do not result in this kind of solution is one the main reasons for conducting a thorough cost/benefit analysis for each alternative solution considered. Depending on the complexity of the problem, a cost/benefit analysis can be nothing more than a simple mental exercise or it can involve extensive research.

Regardless of whether the cost/benefit analysis is formal and complex or informal and simple, it should be comprehensive enough to include consideration of all costs and benefits (i.e. personnel, facilities, equipment/technology, materials, ethics, morale, and public relations, etc.). For example, if a given alternative will require hiring new personnel, all personnel costs and benefits should be considered—not just the direct financial costs and benefits. In addition to salary-and-benefit costs, there will be costs associated with recruiting, orienting, and training the new personnel as well as with providing equipment and office space for them. All of these costs should be considered and weighed against the expected benefits.

Having considered the direct and indirect financial costs and benefits of a given alternative, organizational leaders should then consider the critical factors of ethics, morale, and public relations. Sometimes these factors will be irrelevant, but never make the mistake of assuming this is the case. Are there ethical concerns associated with any of the alternative solutions? Alternatives that involve questionable ethics should be ruled out even if they pass the financial test. What about morale? How will the alternative in question affect the morale of the organization's employees? Poor morale can undermine productivity and lead to turnover problems. What about public relations? How will customers, suppliers, and the general public perceive the alternative chosen? A negative public perception of an organization can be crippling.

A solution that appears attractive from a financial perspective but fails the ethics, morale, and/or public-relations tests will often just cause worse problems in the long run. Because of this it is important for organizational leaders to consider all cost and benefit factors—money, ethics, morale, and public relations—when conducting the cost/benefit analysis for a solution alternative. In fact, when there are ethical, morale, and/or public relations aspects to a solution alternative, these factors can actually magnify the financial considerations.

Case: Problem Solving in a Crisis

Perhaps the most famous case in support of the comprehensive approach to problem solving is the original Tylenol recall of 1982. It is still held up as the classic example of considering all factors when solving problems. Product recalls are now a common problem-solving strategy for organizations—partially because of the lessons learned many years ago from the Tylenol case. Prior to the Tylenol case, organizations were less inclined to consider the ethical, morale, and public-relations aspects of potential solutions.

In September 1982, a young girl died after taking a dose of Extra-Strength Tylenol. Within days, several other people from the same region— the suburbs of Chicago—died after taking Tylenol. It was soon determined that a disgruntled individual had gone into several different drug stores, stolen Tylenol from the shelves, took the containers to a different location, used potassium cyanide to contaminate the contents, and returned the altered bottles to the drug stores. In all, eight bottles were eventually found to have been contaminated.

The makers of Tylenol, Johnson & Johnson, were faced with a problem of crisis proportions—a problem that if handled poorly could lead to the deaths of additional customers and possibly the demise of the company. Any decision made by Johnson & Johnson executives had financial, ethical, morale, and public-relations implications. Taking into account all of these factors, the organization's leaders took the following steps: 1) issued a nationwide recall of all Tylenol products (31 million bottles of the medicine worth more than one billion dollars), 2) issued warnings to hospitals and distributors of Tylenol nationwide, 3) stopped production and advertising of Tylenol, 4) advertised in major media outlets nationwide warning consumers not to use any Tylenol products they had already purchased, and 5) pioneered the development of the tamper-proof cap for medicine bottles.

Johnson & Johnson chose a solution—complete disclosure and aggressive action to protect public safety—that cost the company more than a billion dollars in the short run but probably saved the company from bankruptcy in the long run. Had the company's executives chosen a minimalist approach in confronting the problem, Johnson & Johnson might have won the battle but lost the war. The problem the company faced was correctly perceived not as just making sure there were no more poisoned pills on the shelves of drug stores but as maintaining public trust in Johnson & Johnson and its products. The key to maintaining the public's trust was implementing a solution that protected the public rather than the company's bottom line and that would clearly be perceived as such in the media.

National media outlets, typically skeptical of the actions and motives of large corporations, were favorably impressed by how Johnson & Johnson handled the Tylenol crisis. In fact, media organs were so impressed with the organization that their coverage was almost uniformly positive, a fact that might have saved Johnson & Johnson. The company not only survived the crisis, within a few years Tylenol had become the most popular over-the-counter pain killer on the market. Had Johnson & Johnson's executives overlooked even one of the pertinent considerations, this might not have been the case.

In today's age of Internet communication, blogs, social networking, email, and other forms of instant communication, the pressure on organizations to consider all aspects of potential solutions has been magnified well beyond anything the executives of Johnson & Johnson faced during the original Tylenol crisis. Organizational leaders can now expect to face an unprecedented level of public scrutiny when making decisions and solving problems. In fact, leaders who are making major decisions and solving major problems are well advised to proceed as if they are on camera where everything they say and do is being recorded. Chances are this is true.

Because of the way Johnson & Johnson's decision makers handled the Tylenol crisis, they were able to do more than just reclaim Tylenol's market share, they were able to increase it. In any case, the lesson in this situation is clear. Approaching problem solving and decision making in a way that can be perceived by the organization's personnel, customers, suppliers, or the general public as self-serving rather than responsible can result in long-term costs that far outweigh any short-term benefits.

Choose the Best Alternative and Implement It

Once decision makers have decided how they intend to solve a problem, the alternative selected should be implemented. This is the point where the problem-solving process often breaks down. Organizational leaders who have put so much energy into identifying the root cause of the problem and choosing the best possible solution often fail to give an equal amount of attention to implementing the solution. They often tell their personnel, "Here is the solution we have chosen. Go implement it." Then they assume that the problem will be solved. Unfortunately, this approach often breaks down. To ensure that the solution chosen is effectively implemented, especially when dealing with complex problems, organizational leaders should develop an implementation plan. Developing an implementation plan was covered earlier in this book. A brief review of that material is presented here.

The implementation plan consists of a comprehensive breakdown of all tasks that must be completed for the solution to be fully implemented. These tasks are then assigned to specific individuals and given deadlines for completion. Before the work of implementation begins, all personnel with specific assignments are convened in a meeting to conduct a *roadblock analysis.* This step involves asking the following question: What roadblocks might inhibit the progress of the implementation? All potential roadblocks are identified. Then the organizational leader responsible for solving the problem in question works to eliminate or at least mitigate the inhibitors. This step can prevent the implementation from getting derailed before it even gets started.

Monitor Progress and Adjust as Necessary

Murphy's Law—anything that *can* go wrong *will* go wrong—often comes into play when implementing change in an organization. This is true even after implementation assignments have been made, deadlines have been set, and roadblocks have been eliminated or mitigated. Consequently, it is important for organizational leaders to monitor the progress of the implementation continually and make adjustments as necessary. Whenever Murphy's Law becomes a factor, leaders should act immediately to make adjustments before the implementation loses momentum.

CREATIVITY IN DECISION MAKING AND PROBLEM SOLVING

What comes to mind when you hear the term *creativity*? People typically think of painters, sculptors, singers, dancers, musicians, and actors. Of course, creativity is important in the fine and performing arts. However, creativity is not limited to artists, actors, and entertainers. Some of the most creative people in the world are those who make decisions and solve problems in organizations. They have to be. Competitive pressures make innovation, and creativity in decision making and problem solving essential for organizations. To perform at peak levels organizations need more than just good decisions—they need the best possible decisions. They also need solutions to problems that are creative, innovative, and improvement-oriented.

Creativity as a Concept

There are many different points of view regarding the concept of creativity. For example, people debate endlessly about whether creativity is the result of nature or nurture. In the current context, creativity should be viewed as an approach to problem solving and decision-making that is imaginative, original, and innovative. These three concepts—imagination, originality, and innovation—are important in helping employees become creative problem solvers and decision makers.

This definition shows that the concept of creativity applies more broadly than to just the fields of art and entertainment. It also settles the question of nature versus nurture. Imagination, originality, and innovation can be applied in any field. Architects are creative in their designs of buildings. Engineers are creative in their solutions to human problems. Business people are creative in how they structure deals. Coaches are creative in developing their game plans. I cannot speak for such fields as art and entertainment, but I can say with certainty that the kind of creativity needed in problem solving and decision making in organizations can be learned.

The Creative Process

To help employees become creative in solving problems and making decisions, organizational leaders need to understand that the concept involves more than just sudden insights that come to mind out of nowhere. Rather, creativity is a process that can be approached systematically and in phases. Creativity comes into play in the second step of the problem-solving process, when considering alternative solutions. Creativity can add alternatives to the list that others might not have thought of. The six phases in the creative process are preparation, perspiration, incubation, inspiration, validation, and implementation. These phases are explained in the following paragraphs:

- *Preparation.* Many people think that creativity reveals itself in a momentary flash of insight that simply arrives out of the blue. Perhaps it does work that way in some settings, but when it comes to problem solving and decision making in organizations, creativity begins with preparation. Preparation in this context means learning, gaining experience, and collecting information in the field or discipline associated with the problem. Creativity in problem solving and decision-making requires that the people involved be prepared. For example, you would not expect a person who has never worked as a surgeon to solve a complex problem relating to brain surgery. There are cases when an individual with no experience in a given field might offer insights that can be helpful in arriving at a creative solution to a problem, but these cases are the exception not the rule. Typically, preparation is essential. Preparation for creatively solving problems in a given field involves gaining education, training, and experience in that field. It also involves staying up to date and familiarizing oneself with all of the pertinent information about the problem in question. The key is learning to use the intuition that can come from blending knowledge and experience rather than letting knowledge and experience limit the imagination.

- *Perspiration.* Some people think that good ideas just fall down from the sky and land in the minds of creative people. This situation, when it does happen, is the rare exception. Typically the best and most creative ideas for solving problems are the result of a determined effort. People typically have to work hard (perspiration) to find creative solutions to problems. The creative process can involve exhaustive research and much trial and error. Organizational leaders should make this point when working with employees to solve problems.

- *Incubation.* Incubation involves giving ideas time to bump around in one's head for a while. An incubation period gives partially-formed ideas that are still fuzzy time to clarify themselves—a mental process that can be frustrating because of its ambiguity, but is necessary. Ideas typically incubate best when people get away from the issue in question and give their minds time to sort things out. Incubation is often a subconscious phenomenon. This is why some the best ideas seem to pop up when you are engaged in an activity unrelated to the problem in question (e.g. driving, showering, sleeping, playing golf, walking, running, or reading a book, etc.). Consequently, organizational leaders should always be prepared to immediately jot down notes when an incubating idea begins to take shape. Fortunately, cell phones and other similar technologies often have note-taking capabilities. Organizational leaders who do not use these types of technologies should keep a small note pad nearby at all times (e.g. on the dashboard of their car, in their pocket, on the bed stand, next to the recliner, etc.). Ideas that are incubating can begin to take shape at any time, but they can also be fleeting in nature. They can be like air bubbles in water that float to the surface only to burst and go away. In addition to being prepared at all times to make notes themselves, organizational leaders should teach employees to be prepared.

- *Inspiration.* This is the phase in the process most people associate with creativity. Inspiration occurs when an idea that has been incubating finally bubbles to the surface in one of those ah-ha moments. It is when things appear to have finally fallen into place and a workable solution appears to have been found. When an inspired idea finally reveals itself, the temptation is to immediately move to the implementation phase. Inspiration rarely occurs without going through the previous steps in the process. Further, an inspired idea should still be validated before being implemented.

- *Validation.* Most people have experienced jumping out of bed in the middle of the night with an idea that sounded great at the time only to find problems with it upon more informed reflection. For this reason, validation is an important part of the creative process. This is the phase when your creative ideas must undergo a reality check. This phase in the creative process matches the third step in the problem solving process: choose the best solution from the list of alternatives. Validation involves reviewing the idea to determine if it will actually work. Non-creative activities such as feasibility studies, cost-benefit-analyses, and budget calculations come into play in this phase. Validation is the phase in the process where creativity and reality must mesh in order for an idea to be accepted and acted on.

- *Implementation.* This phase of the creative process is the same as the implementation step in the problem-solving model presented earlier. Once a creative solution has been arrived at and validated, it must be implemented. Implementing a solution arrived at through the creative process is no different than implementing a solution that was obvious from the start. The same methods presented earlier in this chapter apply.

CRITICAL THINKING IN PROBLEM SOLVING AND DECISION MAKING

The most effective organizational leaders and employees are good critical thinkers. Critical thinking is essential to peak performance and continual improvement. There are several factors that make critical thinking essential in organizations: 1) things in organizations are not always what they appear to be on the surface, 2) advice—no matter how well-intended—is not always good, and 3) information provided from even the best sources is not always accurate. Consequently, failing to think critically can lead to costly errors, ineffective strategies, counterproductive policies, bad decisions, and unnecessary disputes.

Inaccurate assumptions, biased input, and inaccurate or incomplete information—things that would be recognized by critical thinkers—can cause organizational leaders and employees to make decisions that not only fail to solve the problem in question, but actually make it worse. Critical thinking amounts to applying sound reasoning, rationale judgment, and an appropriate level of skepticism when making decisions and solving problems.

Becoming a Critical Thinker

The fastest way to become a critical thinker is to do what critical thinkers do. Critical thinkers apply sound reasoning, rational judgment, and carefully-measured skepticism in all situations. In practical terms this amounts to such behaviors as the following: (1)

- Identifying bias in the advice, recommendations, explanations, and information received from others.

- Silently but objectively evaluating the motives of those who give you advice, explanations, recommendations, or information.

- Objectively distinguishing facts from opinions.

- Objectively distinguishing explanations from rationalizations.

- Getting to the heart of a matter by separating significant information from inconsequential input.

- Taking an objective 360-degree view of problems for both the short and long term.

- Doing the homework necessary to be well-prepared to participate effectively in the problem-solving process.

- Considering potential solution alternatives with an open mind.

- Confronting difficult problems head-on and persevering in finding optimum solutions.

- Distinguishing between long-term solutions and short-term expedients.

- Silently examining the opinions, actions, and motives of people rather than just accepting what you are told or what you observe at face value.

- Using facts to patiently chip away at ambiguity.

These types of behaviors distinguish critical thinkers from non-critical thinkers. Organizational leaders are well-advised to internalize this list of behaviors as if it is an assessment checklist. Doing the things in this list is the fastest way to become a critical thinker. Making sure that employees see you doing these things is an excellent way to help them become critical thinkers.

Behaviors Critical Thinkers Must Avoid

Organizational leaders who want to be critical thinkers should emulate the behaviors listed in the previous section, but they should also avoid certain behaviors and teach employees to avoid them. The behaviors to avoid are those that are common to *noncritical thinkers.* They include the following: (2)

- Being closed-minded, inflexible, and stubborn when discussing issues and problems.

- Being too willing to accept opinions at face value.

- Being arrogant and overly confident about your own opinions.

- Letting ego overrule facts and common sense (e.g. stubbornly sticking with an idea just because it is your idea).

- Accepting the latest opinion heard without bothering to validate it.

- Reacting to problems and issues out of emotion rather than facts, reasoning, and sound judgment.

- Ignoring the details of an issue.

- Failing to question or consider motives, opinions, and so-called facts.

- Quickly accepting another person's opinion without giving it an appropriate level of scrutiny.

The behaviors in this list are commonly seen in noncritical thinkers. Consequently, these are behaviors for organizational leaders to avoid. Leaders who find themselves exhibiting any of these behaviors should step back, reflect, and consciously take control of their actions. Remember that if employees see you exhibiting these behaviors they are likely to follow your example.

Better decisions and better solutions lead to better performance—for leaders, employees, and the organization. This is why organizational leaders should invest the time and effort necessary to become effective decision makers and problem solvers who think critically and creatively. But they should not stop there. Organizational leaders should also help employees develop into good decision makers and problems solvers. Then they can empower employees to use their critical thinking skills and creativity to make decisions and solve problems in ways that contribute to peak performance and continual improvement.

GROUP TRAINING ACTIVITY

It took Toyota Motor Company almost half a century to surpass General Motors as "king" of the world's automobile manufacturers. Beginning in the mid-1980's, no company was more closely associated with quality than Toyota. Toyota was the innovator when it came to transforming Japanese manufacturing from an entity that once produced cheap "junk" into the world's standard bearer for quality. Then, one day, the unthinkable happened. Toyota was forced to recall eight of its models for various quality problems, among them a gas pedal that allegedly would stick and had already been blamed for several serious accidents. Almost overnight the king of quality found itself trying to repair chinks in its armor.

Assume that your group is the problem-solving team Toyota established to recommend a solution to this problem. Develop a comprehensive, step-by-step plan for solving the problem and preventing it from ruining Toyota's reputation for quality and, in turn, its long-term viability as a company.

ENDNOTES

1. Daniel A. Feldman, *Critical Thinking*, (Crisp Learning, Menlo Park, CA, 2002), 3-24.

2. Ibid.

Sixteen

CONFLICT MANAGEMENT

Best Practice Number 16: *Become proficient at managing conflict and help employees develop conflict management skills.*

To teach employees to be good conflict managers, organizational leaders have to be good conflict managers themselves. Conflict management involves both preventing and resolving conflict. Leaders in organizations that excel are typically good at managing conflict. They have to be because most organizations operate in competitive environments, and competitive environments are stressful. As a result, they can be virtual breeding grounds for human conflict. This situation is complicated further by the diverse composition of the American workplace.

An organization's workforce will reflect the diversity of society. Consequently, people in organizations can be different in many ways including background, culture, race, age, agendas, ambition, opinion, perspective, and level of education to name just a few. Handled properly, these differences can make an organization stronger and more competitive. But if handled poorly, human differences can lead to conflict. Add ego and self-interest to the mix and the potential for conflict in organizations just increases.

The potential for conflict in organizations has always existed, even without considering human differences. Human diversity in all of its various forms—racial, cultural, intellectual, religious, and political—just magnifies the potential. Diversity is a two-sided coin. Organizations that handle diversity well benefit from it. However, those that handle it poorly often find that their workforce has divided itself up into counterproductive cliques. A major part of handling diversity well is learning how to manage conflict effectively. This is important because certain factors in contemporary society have increased the potential for conflict in organizations, as well as the nature of conflict itself. In the past, conflicts in organizations were typically verbal shoving matches or passive-aggressive encounters involving the gamesmanship of office politics. Human conflict in organizations still manifests itself in these ways, and always will. However, in contemporary society conflict all too often leads to violence, and no organization is immune to this trend.

WHY CONFLICT MANAGEMENT IS IMPORTANT

People who become angry will sometimes act out their anger in counterproductive and even violent ways. It is not uncommon to turn on the nightly news and hear about a shooting in a school, business, university, or some other kind of organization. For some reason or, more likely, for a variety of reasons, many people in contemporary society are angry. These angry members of society are increasingly prone to express their anger in counterproductive ways, including even violence.

People who harbor deep-seated anger often view those who disagree with them in surprisingly negative terms. Without actually verbalizing it, some angry people subconsciously think, *"If you disagree with me, you are not just wrong—you are bad and a threat to me."* The logical extension of this type of thinking is twofold: 1) if you are bad you must be punished, and 2) if you are a threat you must be eliminated. This type of thinking is clearly at odds with peak performance, continual improvement, and organizational excellence.

Because some people tend to see those who differ with them as being wrong, bad, or a threat, conflict that in the past would have been limited to a verbal exchange might now lead to violence. Even if it does not become violent, unresolved conflict in an organization is counterproductive. Consequently, if not properly managed conflict can get out of hand. When this happens, the organization can become so bogged down in negativity that it cannot perform at a competitive level. I've seen organizations that are so consumed by conflict that the work environment is *toxic*. Organizations such as this do not excel. This is why learning how to prevent and resolve conflict and, then, teaching these skills to employees is critical for organizational leaders.

How Poorly Handled Conflict can affect Organizations

In order to achieve peak performance and continual improvement, organizations need their executives, managers, supervisors, and employees to work cooperatively toward achievement of the same goals. This does not mean they always have to agree, quite the contrary. Differences of opinion about how best to achieve the organization's goals, if managed effectively, can lead to better strategies, and better strategies are essential in a competitive environment. One person's opinion about the best way to do something might sharpen the opinions of others and vice versa, provided those involved are able to discuss their differing opinions intelligently, maturely, and without rancor, anger, or hurt feelings.

On the other hand, if conflict is allowed to turn negative it can quickly become counter-productive. When this happens, human energy that should be devoted to achieving peak performance and continual improvement gets diverted and ends up being wasted on pointless internal squabbles. If this is allowed to happen, the organization's performance can go downhill fast. In order to excel, organizations need to ensure the free flow of ideas as part of the problem-solving and decision-making process. In order to ensure the free flow of ideas without generating conflict, organizations must have personnel who can disagree without being disagreeable. People who are good at managing conflict know how to keep disagreements on the high road that leads to better ideas as well as how to pull them up from the low road that leads to anger and strife.

HUMAN RESPONSES TO CONFLICT

People respond to conflict in different ways, some positive and some negative. Positive responses are those that lead to better ideas, better solutions, and stronger interpersonal relationships. Negative responses are those that undermine the organization's performance and competitiveness. There are a variety of potential negative and positive responses to human conflict.

Positive Responses to Conflict

Ideally people in organizations would be able to disagree without being disagreeable, and some can. However, human differences—whether they are differences of opinion, race, culture, gender, religion, politics, age, or other factors—always contain the seeds of conflict. In even the best organizations conflict is going to occur. After all, conflict occurs even in close families in which the people involved love each other.

When conflict occurs in an organization, those involved can choose to: 1) apologize and move on, 2) resolve it through discussion, 3) ask the supervisor to "referee," or 4) ask the supervisor to be the "judge." These options are presented in order of their desirability from the perspective of peak performance, continual improvement, and organizational excellence.

Apologize and Move On

Even the best team players will stumble occasionally and let conflict get out of hand. Sometimes the best response to conflict is to understand that people can get caught up in a situation and say things they wish they had not said or give in to anger and become disagreeable. For this reason people in organizations should learn to overlook occasional lapses in behavior on the part of team mates. If a discussion becomes heated and unpleasant words are exchanged, an appropriate response is for the parties involved to cool down, apologize to each other, and move on. In fact, the ability to do so is critical to the well-being of organizations and the success of their personnel. Harboring grudges and bad feelings will eventually undermine individual and organizational performance.

Resolve Conflict through Discussion

If team members have a disagreement and are not yet willing to apologize and move on, the next best approach is for them to step back from the conflict, cool down, and work out their differences by discussing them in the context of performance and the organization's mission. When individuals can work out their differences without involving others, they, the team, and the organization benefit. Because of this, it is important for organizational leaders to let employees know that they are expected to interact like responsible adults and work out their conflicts without involving others. Part of doing so means working out differences in a mature and professional manner without trying to get other team members to take sides and without taking the conflict up the chain of command.

This expectation that differences should be worked out in a mature and professional manner without involving others should be included in the job descriptions of all personnel at all levels. There should also be an evaluation criterion covering this expectation included in the organization's performance-appraisal form(s). Further, organizational leaders should make sure that employees understand that their willingness to resolve conflict without involving others is a high-priority expectation. Team members in conflict should never approach others in the organization and ask them to take sides. Further, they should understand that every time they take their unresolved conflict up the chain of command, they are failing to live up to expectations—not a good way to succeed or to help an organization excel.

Ask the Supervisor to "Referee"

Employees who cannot or will not work out their differences on their own have two options: 1) continue the conflict, or 2) ask their supervisor to referee (mediate). While it is best for employees to resolve conflicts without involving someone higher in the chain of command, it is better to involve the supervisor than to allow conflict to go unresolved. Unresolved conflict will just fester and escalate. Conflict that is allowed to escalate without resolution will eventually blow up.

Organizational leaders who are asked to mediate conflicts should serve as "referees," not judges. This means they are to help those in conflict find a satisfactory resolution, not decide the issue for them. Supervisors should not issue judgments in conflict situations unless and until this step—mediation—has been tried and failed. Although it can be frustrating for supervisors to take time out of their schedules to mediate disputes, doing so is important. Conflict that is left unresolved almost always escalates, spreads, and gets worse.

Organizational leaders who are called upon to referee disputes between and among their personnel will find the following mediation strategies helpful:

- Find a private place to hold the mediation meeting and ensure against any interruptions.

- Give each individual the opportunity to state his or her case in five minutes or less without comments, questions, corrections, or interruptions from the other party to the dispute.

- After hearing what each party has to say, conduct a dialogue to identify the root cause of the dispute.

- Once the cause has been agreed on by both parties, ask each, in turn, to propose a solution.

- Do not dictate the resolution. Rather, guide both parties toward a solution that is in the best interests of the team and the organization.

The goal of this option is to have those involved resolve the conflict themselves. This approach can be frustrating for supervisors who know exactly how the conflict should end, are anxious to get it over with, and want to hurry things along by dictating the resolution. There will be times when this is exactly what supervisors will have to do. In fact this approach is explained in the next section. However, it is always better to help employees arrive at their own resolutions. In this way, they learn how to resolve conflicts so that the next time they can do so without involving the supervisor. This, of course, is one of the goals of effective conflict management.

Ask the Supervisor to be the "Judge"

When the previous options have not worked, supervisors have no choice but to take off their referee's hat and don their judge's robes. Organizational leaders should do everything they can to help their personnel learn how to resolve conflict at the lowest possible level and without involving others. However, unresolved conflict can be tolerated only so long before it must be firmly dealt with. Unresolved conflict has a tendency to fester and grow. Further, people engaged in conflict often try to recruit other employees to their side. When this happens, the whole organization can find itself in an old-fashioned feud. To prevent a conflict from spreading, organizational leaders must occasionally play the role of judge.

Leaders will know when the time has come to don their judge's robes. One obvious time is when they have conducted a mediation session but to no avail. If two parties come to the end of a mediation session and still refuse to resolve their differences, the leader's role changes from referee to judge. When this happens, organizational leaders should explain that since the parties involved have been unable or unwilling to resolve their differences, the resolution will be prescribed for them. Even though this option amounts to a type of binding arbitration, it is still a resolution response because it gets the parties involved back to work with nothing more serious than hurt feelings. However, any time organizational leaders are forced to decide how a conflict will be resolved the employees involved should suffer appropriate consequences (e.g. a low rating on their next performance appraisal for the criterion covering conflict resolution).

Negative Responses to Conflict

Increasingly, organizational leaders are being forced to deal with negative responses to conflict. There are two categories of negative responses: 1) avoidance, and 2) violence. Avoidance responses include internalization, flight, and suicide. Violent responses include unarmed assault, armed assault, and murder. Because of the increased incidence of negative responses to workplace conflict, it is important that organizational leaders and employees become adept at conflict resolution.

Avoidance Responses to Conflict

Conflict is not necessarily bad. Disagreements over ideas can lead to better ideas as long as those involved can disagree without being disagreeable. However, some people are so averse to conflict that even intellectual disagreements over ideas are abhorrent to them. Most people dislike conflict, but being conflict averse goes well beyond just not liking it. Conflict aversion is a fear of conflict that is so strong it can lead to counterproductive, self-damaging behaviors including internalization, flight, and, in extreme cases, suicide. These behaviors are known as avoidance responses.

People who internalize conflict respond to the frustration and anger they feel by keeping it bottled up inside. They have ideas to present, potential solutions to offer, and their side of the argument to espouse, but they cannot make themselves engage.   Instead they keep their ideas, concerns, and fears bottled up inside, silently stewing, frustrated by the opinions of others and even more frustrated by their own unwillingness to join in.   People who internalize conflict are like a teapot that has no vent.   Stress, frustration, and anger build up until, eventually, something has to give.   In some cases, those who internalize conflict eventually explode and respond with violence, against others or themselves.   However, in most cases they simply absorb the stress and frustration until their health—mental and physical—suffers.

Another avoidance response to conflict is flight.   With this response, conflict-averse people not only do not participate in conflict, they run away from it.   Running away can take more than one form.   In some cases, running away from conflict means just that—running away.   Some conflict-averse people will physically remove themselves from the situation as soon as conflict occurs.   People who respond in this way are so averse to conflict that they simply cannot stand to be around it.   Hence, whenever conflict arises they leave.   This is the most extreme of the flight responses.

Running away can also take the form of mental escape.   Rather than leave the room physically when conflict arises, some people leave mentally.   They simply tune out and think about something else while the conflict swirls around them.   Not only do they not participate in the conflict, they do not even listen to it.   Flight amounts to any response that takes the individual away from the conflict, mentally or physically.

The problem with the flight response is that the team loses the intelligence, experience, and intuition of the individual who takes flight, an employee who might have a better idea, different perspective, or valuable input to offer.   In a competitive environment this is a problem.   In order to excel, organizations need all of their personnel to be actively engaged in the continual-improvement process.   Conflict-averse personnel who take flight—mentally or physically—at the first sign of conflict are not engaged.   Hence they cannot do their part to help the organization excel.

The most extreme of the flight responses is suicide. Thankfully, suicide is the rarest of the flight responses, but, nevertheless, it does happen. It is difficult for even the most talented psychologists to pinpoint the exact reason why any person commits suicide. In fact, there is seldom just one reason behind this tragic act. Rather, those who commit suicide are often responding to a multitude of factors that have come together in a certain way and at a certain time that makes coping with them overwhelming. Conflict at work is more likely to be the straw that finally breaks the camel's back than the single root cause of a suicide. However, it is not uncommon for workplace conflict to be a factor in a suicide.

Violent Responses to Conflict

Violent responses to workplace conflict include unarmed assault, armed assault, and murder. Unarmed assault occurs when the conflict escalates to the point that one of the parties attacks the other. Pushing, shoving, and fist fights are the most common manifestations of unarmed assault. When one or both of the parties in conflict resorts to using a potentially lethal weapon, the fight has escalated to armed assault. Armed assault can quickly become murder. As extreme as this response sounds, it is not uncommon to turn on the nightly news and find that an employee has acted out his anger by shooting up the workplace, killing one or more colleagues.

I once had to deal with a murder in the workplace. In my position as vice-president of a state college, I was responsible, among other things, for the college's six branch campuses. The college had a contract with a well-known vendor to provide, stock, and service soda and snack machines on all of our campuses. The employee of the vendor who stocked and serviced the machines for one of our campuses had had disagreements with his supervisor. Over time these disagreements escalated, and the disgruntled employee resigned. Unfortunately, his resignation would not be his last act.

Using his knowledge of his former employer's procedures, the disgruntled former employee placed a telephone call and identified himself as an official of the college. He asked that a specific machine at the campus in question be repaired, claiming it was out of service. Because he had recently left the company, he expected his former supervisor to make the service call. Several minutes before the scheduled time for the service call, the disgruntled former employee came to the campus and hid himself beside the machine that was to be serviced. When the service technician walked in the break room, his former colleague jumped out of his hiding place and started shooting. Hit several times, the technician died shortly thereafter. As it turned out, the technician who was murdered was not the culprit's former supervisor—the intended target. Another individual had volunteered to make the service call.

This tragic event traumatized people in both organizations—the college and the vendor—as well as family members and others who knew both parties. The negative impact workplace violence can have on an organization cannot be overstated. Violence at work creates an environment of fear, anger, frustration, and grief. It can have employees constantly looking over their shoulders worrying about when the next incident might occur rather than focusing on performance and improvement. In fact, it is not uncommon for employees involved even tangentially in an incident of workplace violence to suffer post-traumatic stress syndrome, a psychological disorder associated with combat veterans.

RESOLVING CONFLICT BETWEEN EMPLOYEES

Ideally, employees would settle their disputes without involving others, but this is the opposite of what often happens. Employees in conflict like to pull others into their squabble and have their teammates choose sides. When this happens, a limited conflict can quickly become broad-based. Because of this, conflict resolution is an important skill for employees. The good news is that, like any other skill, it can be learned. When it comes to employees learning conflict resolution skills, organizational leaders have to be teachers, mentors, and role models. Since conflict between employees can quickly spread as others choose sides, it is important for organizational leaders to be observant and intercede when necessary to get it resolved promptly and positively.

When organizational leaders observe employees involved in conflict and they are obviously not resolving it themselves, take action right away. Never wait to see what might happen. Bring the employees together in a private setting and give them an opportunity to state their grievances without interruption, contradiction, or judgmental comments from you or each other. Treat the employees with respect and let them know their conflict will be taken seriously. The message they need to get from organizational leaders is this: "You are both important to the team. The team needs you to get past this conflict and work together cooperatively. Let's talk about how we can make that can happen."

Let each party know that the goal of the meeting is resolution and cooperation. Then let each party state his case without interruptions or contradictions from the other. Apply the following strategies to move them toward resolution and cooperation:

1. Help participants identify the source of the conflict

2. Let participants know you expect all issues to be discussed in a mature and positive manner

3. Let participants know they are responsible for resolving the conflict

4. Let participants propose solutions and then discuss their proposals

5. Guide participants toward a positive resolution.

Help Participants Identify the Source of the Conflict

Employees in conflict tend to attribute the trouble to malice and bad intentions on the part of the other party. The attitude of many people toward conflict can be summarized as follows: "If you disagree with me not only are you wrong, you are bad." Consequently, it is important to show employees that there are a number of predictable factors other than malice and bad intentions that can cause workplace conflicts. These factors include communication problems, differing points of view, insufficient resources, territoriality, and differing agendas. It is important for organizational leaders to help employees see that their conflict might be based—not always but often—on factors that are logical and perfectly understandable rather than on malice and bad intentions.

Poor communication plays a part in most workplace conflicts. Even if poor communication is not the root cause of the problem, it is usually a contributing cause. Having listened to both parties state their positions, does it appear that poor communication is contributing to the conflict? When employees realize that they disagree because of poor communication they have a less explosive, easier to accept cause of conflict than the causes that people tend to attribute to others who disagree with them (e.g. bad intentions, malice, greed, power, ego, ignorance, etc.). If poor communication appears to be a contributing factor, organizational leaders should point this fact out to both parties and help facilitate better communication.

People can have widely differing points of view concerning the same issue. For example, think of a candidate in a presidential election. Some people will think he is wonderful while others will think he's the worst person who ever ran for office. How can people see the same individual so differently? It's simple—they have different perspectives. Some people are liberal while others are conservative. Some people are extroverts while others are introverts. Some people are big-picture oriented while others are detail-oriented.

People can have different points of view about the same issue, and often do. When someone has a different point of view, the human tendency is to ascribe the difference to something bad or wrong in the individual. Organizational leaders will have to help employees in conflict realize that having a different point of view does not make a person bad. It does not even make her wrong. In fact, differing points of view about the same matter can lead to better decisions and better solutions if they are handled in a mature, positive manner.

Expect a Mature and Positive Discussion of the Conflict

At this point in the process, it is a good idea to give each party in the conflict a copy of the organization's mission statement. Remind them that the mission represents the reason for their employment, and that their job is to help the organization accomplish its mission. Personal agendas have no place in the discussion. Explain that you have brought the two parties together to have a mature and positive discussion about issues, and that everything said during the discussion should be viewed in the context of how it helps the organization accomplish its mission. This is an effective way to say, "It's not about you—it's about us." Often, when employees get this message the conflict evaporates and nothing further need be done. However, in those cases when the discussion does need to continue, the context has been converted from petty bickering to a mature discussion.

Hold Employees Responsible for Resolving their Conflicts

Often when team members bring their disagreements to you, they are trying to do a *hand-off.* In other words, they are trying to hand off their problem to you and have you solve it. Do not give in to the temptation to do this. All this will accomplish is the transfer of blame from the employees who are in conflict to you. Do not let this happen. The organizational leader's role is more that of the referee than the judge in this situation. Let participants know that they are responsible for resolving the conflict. Your role is to facilitate the process. Leaders who are too quick to settle conflict rather than helping employees settle it themselves are going to spend a lot of time engaged as referees. The better employees become at settling their own conflicts in positive ways the better they and the team will perform.

Ask Participants to Propose Solutions

The best solutions to conflict are those that: 1) come from the participants themselves, and 2) contribute to helping the organization accomplish its mission. Once you have helped both employees in the conflict identify its source, established the ground rules for a mature, positive discussion, and reminded participants of their responsibility in resolving the conflict, ask them to propose solutions—one at a time and in turn. Hear both employees out and do not allow interruptions, comments, or judgmental behavior from one when the other is proposing a solution. Your main task in this step is to get proposed solutions on the table so that the context of the discussion switches from conflict to solutions.

Guide Participants toward a Solution

The organizational leader's main task in this step is to guide the participants toward the best possible solution. An effective way to do this is to use the organization's mission or the team's as the basis for conducting a quick cost-benefit analysis of proposed solutions. The best solution is the one that most effectively serves the applicable mission. Never make the mistake of trying to find a compromise solution that will please both parties. Compromise is for politics, not business. The most popular solution is not always the best solution from a performance perspective.

DEALING WITH PERSONAL PROBLEMS AT WORK

Many organizations tell employees to leave their personal problems at home when they come to work. This is management's way of telling employees that the company's performance should not be hindered by their personal problems. Although the principle is understandable, just telling employees to leave their personal problems at home is no guarantee that they will, or even that they can. This is one of those situations in which organizational leaders must strive to maintain an appropriate balance between the work they are responsible for and the employees who do the work.

When team members experience personal problems that affect their work, the organizational leader's job is to be a supervisor, not an amateur psychologist. The key words in the previous sentence are *"...that affect their work."* Unless an employee's work performance is hindered by his personal problems, those problems are not the business of executives, managers, and supervisors. What makes an employee's personal problems the business of organizational leaders is the adverse effects they have on the employee's work and performance. In other words, performance is the issue—not the personal problems per se.

When an employee's personal problems begin to adversely affect his performance at work, organizational leaders should document the work-related problems and monitor the situation for a short period of time. If leaders are patient for a few days, the situation might clear itself up and the employee's work performance might correct itself without intervention. However, there is an important caveat to this principle. If there is evidence that the employee's downturn at work is related to drinking or drugs, organizational leaders must act immediately. They should go directly to their organization's Human Resources Department and let HR officials know about their concerns.

On one hand, organizational leaders must never accuse an employee of abusing alcohol or drugs, no matter how convinced they are that this is happening. On the other hand, leaders must never let an impaired employee conduct any work-related tasks in which the impairment could lead to an injury or the destruction of property. Whenever an employee's abilities seem to be impaired, get Human Resources professionals involved immediately and do not allow the employee to perform any work tasks until given a release by the Human Resources Department.

When organizational leaders notice a down turn in an employee's work, the first step is to simply talk with her. Explain the problems that have been observed and documented. Focus on the evidence of declining performance, not on suspicions of the reasons, and keep the discussion on a professional level. The best approach is for organizational leaders to explain why they think there is a problem, solicit feedback from the employee, and listen. Remember, one learns more from listening than from talking. Once the employee has stated her case, ask her to propose a solution, and remember, even if the employee brings up personal problems, leaders should stick to job- performance issues.

Executives, managers, and supervisors should not allow themselves to get pulled into a discussion of an employee's personal problems. While personal problems might make declining work performance understandable, they do not make it acceptable. Work with the employee to develop a plan for improving performance. Set specific goals and time frames. Do not try to be an armchair psychologist. Instead, be a leader, mentor, teacher, coach, and role model.

DEALING WITH ANGRY PEOPLE AT WORK

It is important for organizational leaders to learn how to deal effectively with angry people, and to teach employees this skill. Whether the angry person is a customer, colleague, employee, or team member, organizational leaders must become good role models at doing three things: 1) staying calm as they deal with angry people; 2) taking the steps necessary to help calm angry people; and 3) transitioning angry people from a negative state of mind (anger mode) to a positive state of mind (solution mode).

Staying Calm When Confronted by an Angry Person

When dealing with angry people, some individuals respond by fighting fire with fire. They react to anger by returning it in kind. Although this response is understandable, it is inappropriate. A good rule of thumb for leaders to remember and pass along to employees is this: *When dealing with an angry person, if you lose your temper, you lose period.* Organizational leaders who respond to an angry person with anger of their own have started down a one way street to a bad destination. Anger that is answered with anger is likely to escalate until it blows up.

Try the following strategies for staying calm when confronted by an angry person. First, take a few deep breaths to settle down your breathing and keep it normal. Second, ignore the anger and listen in between the lines for the substance of the problem. The more angry people become, the less able they are to clearly articulate what's bothering them. Angry people tend to exaggerate, leave out pertinent information, and generally make more noise than sense.

The key to staying calm in such situations is to learn to ignore all of the *irrelevant noise* generated by the anger while focusing instead on listening for useful facts. When conducting seminars on this topic, I use the following example from the medical profession to explain the concept of ignoring the noise of anger while listening, instead, for its cause. A man gets a splinter in his forearm and cannot get it out. After a couple of days his arm becomes infected. The area around the splinter becomes swollen, red, and extremely painful—so painful that the man decides to go to the emergency room. At the hospital, the emergency room physician looks at the man's arm to determine the problem. He has two choices: 1) he can treat the swelling, redness, and infection around the splinter; or 2) he can ignore the swelling, redness, and infection, find the splinter, and remove it. If he chooses the first option, the splinter will still be in the man's arm and the infection will just worsen. If he chooses the second option, the arm will begin to heal the moment the splinter is removed. This is because the first option treated only the symptoms of the problem while the second option eliminated its source.

This is how it is when dealing with an angry person. If you get hung up focusing on the anger, you will miss the cause of the problem. Take a couple of deep breaths, ignore the anger, and listen for the source of the problem. The harsh words, exaggerations, and even threats associated with anger are like the swelling, redness, and infection in the man's arm. If the physician in this example allowed himself to get distracted by the swelling, redness, and infection in his patient's arm, he might never have located and removed the splinter, which was the source of the problem.

Take Steps to Calm the Angry Person

Organizational leaders who can stay calm when confronted by an angry person can begin taking the steps necessary to calm that person. What follows are several strategies that can be used to help calm an angry person:

- *Listen and let the angry person vent without interruption.* Angry people are like teakettles. If not given the opportunity to vent, they might explode. Consequently, one of the most effective strategies for dealing with an angry person is to simply sit back, listen without interrupting, and let her vent. While listening, look directly at the person who is venting and give her an affirming expression that says, "I'm listening and I care about what you have to say." Avoid non-verbal cues such as shaking your head in disagreement, moving away defensively, crossing your arms, rolling your eyes, or making negative facial gestures. Just listen non-judgmentally and with body language that conveys interest.

- *Acknowledge the anger.* Do not interrupt while the angry person is venting, but when his tirade seems to have run its course, acknowledge the anger. You can do this by saying something as simple as one of the following: 1) "You're really angry about this aren't you? or 2) "I can see you are really angry about this." Most people, if given an opportunity to vent without interruption or contradiction will typically calm down once their anger is acknowledged. If this does not happen, continue to listen and acknowledge the anger.

- *Use a simple apology as a bridge.* When dealing with angry people, the goal is to help them make the transition from anger mode to solution mode. A well-crafted apology can be an effective way to initiate the transition. "Well-crafted" means that the apology is brief, direct, and solution oriented. It does not go on too long or become maudlin. An example of a well-crafted apology is as follows: "I am sorry this happened. Let's see what you and I can do to correct the problem." Notice that immediately after making a very brief and direct apology, you transition to the solution mode. When the apology is stated like this, the formerly angry person is enlisted as a partner in solving the problem.

- *Paraphrase and repeat back.* Once the person in question has transitioned out of anger mode, let her begin to propose solutions. Once again listen attentively and do not interrupt. After a solution is proposed, paraphrase and repeat it back. This will let the person in question know she has been listened to. It will also give her an opportunity to correct your perception if it is not accurate.

- *Ask open-ended questions to clarify and to solicit additional information.* If what the person in question proposes is not clear or is not well thought out, use open–ended questions to clarify and to solicit additional information. An open-ended question cannot be answered "yes" or "no." Such questions begin with the following types of phrases: "Tell me about…," "What do you think about…," or, "What are your thoughts on…" Open-ended questions can be used to guide people through a mental cost/benefit analysis when their proposed solutions are unrealistic or poorly formulated.

- *Confirm the solution.* Once a realistic solution has been arrived at, confirm it with the person in question. Do not assume that he understands the solution without first confirming it and all of its ramifications. A good solution is one that, once put in place, will stay in place. It eliminates the source of the problem that caused the anger in the first place or it reveals to the formerly angry person that the problem was caused by a miscommunication or misunderstanding, as is often the case. Never gloss over issues that might allow surprises to crop up after a solution has been decided on. Make sure the individual involved understands all of the ramifications of the solution before finally accepting it.

When employees become adept at conflict management the organization benefits in a variety of ways. Effective conflict management encourages peak performance and continual improvement in employees because it allows them to stay focused on doing their jobs rather than fighting internal battles. Consequently, teaching employees to be good conflict managers is an important responsibility for organizational leaders. The most effective way to help employees develop the skills they need for managing conflict is by role modeling those skills as you help prevent and resolve conflict.

GROUP TRAINING ACTIVITIES

1. Assume that two employees in your team are in conflict. Both are good employees, and both have a lot of influence with their fellow team members. The group's assignment is to develop a brief plan or checklist showing how this situation should be handled.

2. One of your best employees stomps into your office, red-faced and obviously angry. She yells, "This place is hopeless—I don't know why I even try to get anything done. Half of the department comes to work late and the rest are retired on the job." The group's assignment is to explain how this situation should be handled.

Seventeen

EMPLOYEE COMPLAINTS

Best Practice Number 17: Use employee complaints as opportunities for improvement and to help employees learn how to solve their own problems.

Employees will complain—count on it. In fact, some people are habitual complainers. However, habitual complainers are the exception, not the rule. Often when employees complain it is because they have a problem that affects their performance and need help in solving it. Consequently, listening to complaints is important for organizational leaders who want to help employees achieve peak performance and improve continually. On the other hand, listening to complaints from employees can be time consuming and intrusive. At times it can even be annoying. For this reason, some organizational leaders make the mistake of adopting an *I-don't-want-to-hear-it* attitude. Those who make this mistake run the risk of not hearing things they need to hear. In fact, it is often the things leaders least want to hear that they most need to hear.

RATIONALE FOR HANDLING EMPLOYEE COMPLAINTS EFFECTIVELY

Typically a complaint from an employee is evidence of a problem or a potential problem. By listening, organizational leaders can often turn employee complaints into opportunities for improvement. Whether a complaint turns out to be a problem or an opportunity often depends on how organizational leaders handle it. Consequently, employee complaints should be taken seriously and responded to appropriately. To ignore employee complaints is to risk allowing a small problem to become a large problem. It is also akin to telling employees, "I don't care about your problems."

Organizational leaders who learn to listen attentively sometimes find that the problem behind an employee complaint is really just the tip of the iceberg. A problem that employees think applies to them alone might actually have much broader implications. Because leaders sit on a higher limb in the organization's hierarchical tree, they are in better positions to see the broader implications of problems. Leaders who see the broader implications of a problem can begin taking steps to deal with them even while they work to solve the specific problem raised by the employee who complained. This approach can kill two birds with one stone. First, it can solve the individual employee's specific problem. Second, it can nip a potentially larger problem in the bud before it can blossom into a major problem. I once witnessed an instructive example of this concept while serving as a consultant. My client was a college.

Case of the Faulty Payroll Software

The college had recently made the transition from a manual payroll system to an automated system. The software had been tested, the bugs eliminated, and the first payroll checks printed. Payroll personnel were excited about the new system. It had reduced the time and effort required to print checks by 80 percent. Consequently, when a professor stopped by the payroll office to complain that his check was short by approximately $100, the payroll clerk thought little of it. She simply checked the records, verified his claim, and produced a hand-written check for the missing amount. Problem solved, or was it?

When the head of the payroll department heard about the situation, she became concerned. Unlike the payroll clerk who dealt with the professor, she understood that with an automated system the problem could be broader than just one individual's check. She was pleased that the error affecting the professor in question had been corrected to his satisfaction, but was concerned that his problem might be just the tip of the iceberg. She pulled several payroll records, manually calculated what the amounts should be, and checked these against the actual amounts of the checks that had just been printed. Out of ten records, four were incorrect.

The seeming randomness of the errors only heightened her concern. Confused, she asked the director of the college's computer department for assistance. It took more than an hour of detective work, but the difference between the checks that were correct and those that were incorrect was finally determined. Professors who taught only straight lecture courses or straight laboratory courses had correct checks. But those who taught a combination of the two types of courses were uniformly incorrect. Unfortunately, those with incorrect checks represented almost 40 percent of the faculty.

While the computer department tried to sort out the software bug behind the problem, the payroll department went into overdrive to quickly produce handwritten checks and to notify the faculty members whose checks had been printed in the wrong amounts. Because the head of the payroll department had the presence of mind to look for the broader implications of what seemed to others to be only an isolated issue, she was able to head off a situation that could have become a major problem.

Few things will anger employees faster than incorrect paychecks. The bug in the payroll software was identified and quickly corrected. As a result, future payrolls were completed correctly and without incident. Had the head of the payroll department not alertly sensed the broader implications of the professor's complaint about his paycheck, the college would have had a major problem to deal with.

SIX-STEP PROCEDURE FOR HANDLING EMPLOYEE COMPLAINTS

Consistency is important in handling employee complaints. Organizational leaders who handle some complaints effectively and others haphazardly will soon lose their credibility with employees. Consequently, it is important to have a well-structured, systematic procedure for handling employee complaints. Having such a procedure can serve several purposes. First, it will reassure employees that their complaints are going to be taken seriously and given the attention they deserve. Second, it will lead to more positive resolutions of the complaints. Finally, it will discourage habitual complainers who use complaints as a way to get attention.

The following six-step procedure will help organizational leaders deal with employee complaints in a well-structured, systematic way that promotes consistent, effective solutions and, in turn, leads to improved performance:

- Establish the five-minute rule

- Listen

- Investigate

- Act

- Report

- Follow up

Establish the Five-Minute Rule

One of the reasons organizational leaders are put off by employee complaints is the lack of time. For many leaders, there just never seems to be enough time in the workday to get everything done that needs to be done. Consequently, organizational leaders are sometimes reluctant to listen when an employee wants to take up valuable time making a complaint. I developed the *five-minute rule* to solve or, at least, mitigate this problem. Use of the five-minute rule has already been explained in an earlier chapter, but is reviewed here to show how it is used specifically for handling employee complaints.

The purpose of the five-minute rule is to allow organizational leaders to maintain an open-door policy for employees while minimizing time-consuming intrusions. If it achieves this goal, the five-minute rule will also contribute to facilitating the best possible resolutions to employee complaints. Organizational leaders should apply the five-minute rule as follows:

- All employees are informed that, within reason, they can have five minutes of your time whenever they have a complaint, suggestion, recommendation, or concern to voice.

- Within the allotted five minutes, employees are expected to explain the problem and recommend a proposed solution.

- Solutions proposed must be carefully thought through in advance. Employees are not allowed to propose off-the-cuff solutions. Rather, they are expected to have performed enough of a cost-benefit analysis that they do not propose a $100 solution to a $10 problem. The bottom-line criterion for determining the viability of proposed solutions is found in this question: *How does this solution contribute to improved performance or to making conditions better than they are now?*

Five minutes is plenty of time to explain most employee complaints, provided the employee has thought the problem through sufficiently, identified a viable solution, and subjected the proposed solution to at least a cursory cost-benefit analysis. Not only will the five-minute rule reduce the amount of time organizational leaders must devote to dealing with employee complaints, it will help employees learn to be critical thinkers, innovators, and problem solvers. The better employees become at solving their own problems, the less often they will need to take their complaints to organizational leaders.

Listen

Organizational leaders should listen carefully to employee complaints with their ears, eyes, and experience. The ears will collect the necessary information about the employee's problem. The eyes will assist in this task by observing non-verbal cues. Experience will tell organizational leaders whether there are broader implications to the employee's problem. While listening to employees as they voice their complaints, the following tips may be helpful:

- Maintain eye contact and assume a posture that sends the message, "I am listening."

- Give the employee undivided attention—eliminate distractions.

- Do not interrupt except for necessary clarifications.

- Listen to what is said as well as what is not said.

- Be attentive to the employee's body language and other non-verbal cues such as tone of voice. Ask yourself if the non-verbal cues correspond with what is said verbally.

- Maintain a professional bearing. Do not become angry, defensive, or hostile.

- Try to remember without taking notes or, at least, minimize note taking.

- Paraphrase and repeat back to show that you have heard and understand.

When dealing with employee complaints, nothing is more important than listening attentively and non-judgmentally. Remember, leaders who do not listen well may miss out on information that is vital to the performance of employees, the team, and the organization.

Investigate

The five-minute rule should assure that organizational leaders are able to form a thorough and accurate picture of the employee's problem, at least from the employee's perspective. However, all stories have at least two sides. Consequently, organizational leaders should never act solely on the basis of what they have heard from just one individual, even if the employee in question is well-respected and trusted. Once you have heard the employee's problem and proposed solution, take no action without first investigating the situation. Get all the facts before acting.

The employee may have been sincere and completely honest in explaining the problem and proposing a solution. However, even the best employees see things from their individual perspectives and within the context of their limited experience. There may have been factors of which the employee was unaware. Listening to the employee's complaint and proposed solution is an important first step in solving the problem. But remember, unless the urgency of the situation dictates otherwise, conduct an independent investigation before taking any corrective action.

Act

It is important for organizational leaders to understand that there are times when an employee with a complaint just needs someone to listen. Sometimes employees become frustrated and just need to vent. When this is the case, organizational leaders need take no action beyond just listening. Listening to employees and allowing them to vent is occasionally the only action required. However, when action beyond just listening is required, organizational leaders should move promptly. Once all pertinent information relating to the complaint has been collected, act. The appropriate action will typically be one of the following: 1) solve the problem, 2) work with higher management to solve problems beyond the scope of your authority, 3) put the situation on hold long enough to collect additional information, or 4) take no action.

Some complaints reveal the need for action that can be taken immediately and unilaterally. When this is the case, the organizational leader in question should take the necessary action to solve the problem. Often complaints will reveal the need for action that is beyond the scope of your authority. In such cases, the leader must work with higher management to solve the problem. Advocating with higher management on behalf of employees is one of the most important responsibilities of organizational leaders at the supervisory and mid-management levels.

It is not uncommon for an employee complaint to reveal a problem that cannot be solved by supervisors or managers. This sometimes happens when a corporate policy adopted by higher management results in unintended consequences. The problem in question cannot be solved without revising the policy that is causing it, and only higher management can change the policy. When this situation occurs, organizational leaders must work their way up the chain of command to the responsible person. This part of the process—identifying the individual who can solve the problem—is usually not too difficult. However, identifying the person who can solve the problem and convincing that individual to do it are often two very different undertakings. Convincing the person with authority to take the necessary action is sometimes a challenge, a challenge that can require tact, patience, and perseverance.

In other instances, the investigation into the employee's complaint might verify that a problem does exist, but more information is needed before it can be solved. In these cases, the solution must be put on hold until more information can be collected. When this happens, organizational leaders must make a special effort to avoid dropping the ball. Pressing responsibilities, deadlines, and other factors can cause problems that are put on hold to be forgotten so that they just stay on hold. A problem that is put on hold should stay there only long enough to collect the additional information needed to solve it.

Occasionally the investigation into an employee's complaint will reveal that the appropriate action to take is no action. This can happen when it becomes apparent that the employee making the complaint either withheld pertinent information that casts the problem in a different light, or was unaware of pertinent information. It can also happen when the investigation reveals another side to the story that calls the employee's complaint into question. A final rationale for taking no action occurs when the investigation reveals that the problem in question will solve itself if just left alone. For example, assume that an employee complains about rudeness and laziness on the part of a fellow team member. The leader's investigation reveals that the complaint has merit. However, the investigation also reveals that the offending team member plans to leave the organization in less than a week. Any effort devoted to counseling and training the offending employee would just be wasted. In this case, the better course of action would be to take no action and let the rude employee leave.

Report

A complaint often heard from employees is that they explain their problems to supervisors, but are never told what—if anything—was done. Failure to close the loop on complaints is a serious mistake that can undermine the leader's credibility. If organizational leaders consistently fail to close the loop, employees will eventually view raising issues as a waste of time. If this happens, organizational leaders will soon find themselves missing out on information they need to know. Closing the loop means letting employees who complain know what has been done, will be done, or will not be done.

It takes only a few minutes to let employees know what happened or did not happen as a result of their complaints. However, a word of caution is in order here. If action was taken, organizational leaders should be careful to protect any applicable confidences. For example, if the action taken was to discipline another employee, the individual who complained should be told only that the problem was solved or that appropriate action was taken. Action taken against another employee is confidential. In such cases, it is sufficient to simply tell employees that their complaint was acted on. If no action was taken or if action must be deferred, organizational leaders should meet with the employee who brought the complaint and explain why. Where this becomes particularly important is when no action was taken because the complaining employee provided misleading information. Organizational leaders should make clear that knowingly providing misleading information when lodging a complaint is unacceptable and could result in disciplinary action.

When action is taken as a result of a complaint, part of closing the loop should be to thank the employee. Obviously, employees who knowingly provide misleading information or use their complaints to advance a personal agenda are not to be thanked. But employees who bring legitimate complaints that point out real problems should be thanked. In addition to thanking the employee, leaders should explain how the complaint may have helped improve performance. This will encourage employees to raise issues in the future and to tie those issues to improving performance.

Follow up

Reporting back to employees is not the leader's final responsibility in responding to employee complaints. Leaders should never make the mistake of assuming that just because they took steps to solve a problem that the solution actually worked. A multitude of factors can keep the solution that was implemented from effectively solving the problem. A better approach is to follow up periodically until it is clear that the solution put in place had the desired effect. One way to follow up is to meet with the employee who made the complaint and ask if conditions have improved. It is not uncommon for organizational leaders to find that problems they thought they had solved were, in reality, only partially solved or not solved at all. By following up, organizational leaders can do what is necessary to find a better solution without having to go through the entire process again.

LISTEN INTENTLY TO EMPLOYEE COMPLAINTS

Listening intently is critical when employees voice complaints. No matter how rushed organizational leaders may be, they should stop what they are doing and listen intently when employees have a complaint. There are a number of reasons for this, the most important of which are:

- *The employee might just be frustrated and need an opportunity to vent.* People can be like tea kettles. When the steam starts building, they have to vent or they will blow up. A few minutes spent listening to frustrated employees is sometimes all that is needed to get them back to normal and back to work. On the other hand, failing to listen to angry or frustrated employees may render them unable to focus on doing their best work. In addition, frustrated and angry employees who have no outlet for venting often undermine the work of others. Letting frustrated or angry employees vent can help restore them to normal frame of mind and get them refocused on achieving peak performance and continual improvement.

- *The complaint might be evidence of a bigger problem.* It is not uncommon for employee complaints to uncover problems that are bigger than they might seem at first. To the employee making the complaint the problem might appear one way, but to the leader hearing the problem it might take on added dimensions. Listening intently will help leaders determine if the employee's problem is isolated or if it has broader implications.

- *The complaint might be the employee's way of pressing a hidden agenda.* A hidden agenda is a secret goal an employee has but does not admit to. For example, an employee who wants to be promoted to a certain job might make complaints about another employee who also wants the job. In this case, there is a hidden agenda behind the complaint: discrediting another employee who is viewed as a competitor. Organizational leaders should be ever vigilant to detect personal agendas in employee complaints.

- *The complaint might reveal a legitimate problem.* Problems that adversely affect performance are common in organizations. They occur every day. Policies and procedures put in place by higher management often have unintended consequences when applied on the front line. Consequently, there is a high probability that an employee complaint might reveal a legitimate problem. In other words, when organizational leaders use the employee complaint procedure wisely it can contribute to improved performance, which of course is its purpose in the first place.

How to Listen Intently

Listening intently means more than just giving employees their five minutes to lodge complaints. It means taking the steps necessary to ensure that complaints are accurately heard and fully understood. The following tips will help organizational leaders listen more intently:

- *Maintain eye contact with the employee and assume a posture that sends the message, "I am listening."* It is important that employees know they are being listened to. Employees who know they are being heard will be more forthcoming.

- *Eliminate distractions and give the employee five minutes of undivided attention.* Turn off cell phones, put land lines on hold, and do not allow others to interrupt. Employees who have complaints should get their full five minutes without distractions.

- *Let the employee explain the complaint without interruption.* Do not break the employee's train of thought unless it is necessary to have a given statement clarified. Let the employee have an uninterrupted five minutes if possible.

- *Listen for what is said and what is not said.* This tip is sometimes called listening with the ears of experience. Experience gives organizational leaders a certain amount of intuition, and intuition helps leaders know when something pertinent is not being said. Sometimes what is not said is as important as what is.

- *Read the employee's body language and tone of voice.* People need no training to interpret non-verbal communication. Even a baby that cannot understand a word of verbal speech can read non-verbal cues that tell if its mother is angry, stressed, relaxed, or anxious. Body language, tone of voice, and rate of speech all provide non-verbal cues that can be helpful to organizational leaders who pay attention. The key to using non-verbal cues to enhance communication is to watch for agreement and disagreement between what is said verbally and non-verbally. If the verbal and non-verbal messages agree the employee is probably telling the truth. If they do not, something is wrong. A mismatch does not automatically mean the employee is lying, but it does mean something is amiss. Organizational leaders who notice a mismatch between the verbal and non-verbal should question employees in a straightforward manner. For example, a leader might say: "John, your words say one thing, but your body language says another. What is going on?"

- *Maintain a professional bearing. Do not become angry or hostile.* Often employees with complaints will be agitated, frustrated, or angry. When confronted with anger, some people respond in kind. This is a mistake. Anger that is answered with anger is likely to escalate and can soon get out of hand. Consequently, it is important for organizational leaders to take a few deep breaths and maintain a calm exterior, even when complaining employees do not.

- *Paraphrase and repeat complaints back to employees.* It is important for employees to know that their complaints have been heard and accurately perceived. An effective way to give employees this assurance is to paraphrase what they have said and repeat it back to them. If the paraphrased statement is correct, employees will know they have been heard and understood. If it is not, they can clear up any discrepancies before the session ends. Either way, organizational leaders will know they are acting on an accurate understanding of the problem.

CLARIFYING COMPLAINTS BY ASKING QUESTIONS

Organizational leaders who act on a complaint without fully understanding it can waste a lot of time. One way to ensure a full understanding of a problem is to ask clarifying questions. When handling employee complaints, use questions for the following reasons:

- *To ensure clarity.* Clarification is the act of gaining a full and accurate understanding. When an employee makes a statement that is not clear, the leader should ask for clarification. For example, if an employee complains about the organization's dress code, does he mean it is too strict or not strict enough? A simple question will clarify the complaint.

- *To clear up inconsistencies.* An inconsistency is a difference between what the complaining employee says and what the leader knows to be true. Inconsistencies can mean the employee is frustrated, confused, or ill-informed or they can mean the employee is pressing a hidden agenda or even lying. In either case, leaders should ask questions to clear up the inconsistencies. For example, if an employee claims that a team member is frequently late but this claim is at odds with the leader's experience, there is an inconsistency. Is the complaining employee pressing a hidden agenda, confused, or angry at the other team member? A few questions will clear up the inconsistency.

- *To gain more complete information.* Employees who complain are often frustrated, sometimes angry, and almost always anxious. Consequently, they do not always provide complete information. Without meaning to they might leave out information that is important to the leader. In addition, employees will sometimes withhold pertinent information if it does not support their argument. In any case, organizational leaders need complete and accurate information before acting on an employee complaint. Consequently, it is sometimes necessary to ask questions to gain more information. For example, an employee might complain that she was unable to complete her work on time because she was not given enough support. What kind of support is she talking about? How much support did she need? A few questions could provide more complete information.

- *To determine what action the employee wants taken.* Often a complaining employee just wants to vent. Sometimes it is obvious that this is the case, but sometimes it is not. Leaders who are not sure if an employee is just venting or if he wants some kind of action should ask. For example, the leader might say: "Thanks for letting me know how you feel about this situation. Is there anything you would like me to do?" In this way, leaders can save themselves the time they would spend solving a problem when, in fact, it has already been solved by listening.

Taking the time to ask clarifying questions can prevent a situation in which you waste time dealing with a problem that either does not exist or is not the problem the complaining employee had in mind. On the other hand, it can ensure that you are fully informed before pursuing a complaint further.

DEALING WITH HABITUAL COMPLAINERS

Habitual complainers are employees who complain constantly about everything. This type of employee can be a challenge for busy organizational leaders. The first thing to understand when attempting to deal with habitual complainers is that most of them are looking for attention, not solutions. Habitual complainers tend to be insecure people who want as much of the leader's attention as possible. Since this is the case, the following tips for dealing with habitual complainers can save organizational leaders both time and trouble:

- *Do not give in to frustration.* It is easy to become frustrated when dealing with employees who complain constantly, but giving in to frustration will not help. Habitual complaining can be a sign of a deeper problem. The employee may be seeking attention, trying to establish a special relationship with the leader, or pressing a hidden agenda. For some habitual complainers, getting the leader frustrated is the whole point. For all of these reasons, it is important for organizational leaders to maintain their composure when dealing with habitual complainers.

- *Take pre-emptive action.* If the goal of a constant complainer is to get more attention from the leader, pre-emptive action will sometimes decrease the number of complaints. Pre-emptive action amounts to pro-actively and purposefully giving the employee more attention than usual. The attention might take the form of email notes, brief telephone conversations, or stopping by his office or workstation to say hello. Pre-emptive action takes time, but not nearly as much as dealing with constant complaints. In addition, with pre-emptive action organizational leaders control the situation. It takes much less time to send an email or make a quick phone call than to listen to a never-ending series of complaints.

- *Ask the complainer to put it in writing.* Sometimes it seems that the habitual complainer is doing all the complaining and the leader is doing all the work. If the previous strategies have been tried with no noticeable effect, ask the complainer to put her complaint in writing. This will turn the tables and put the work back where it belongs—with the complainer. Ask for a detailed written explanation of the problem as well as the proposed solution. In many cases, this will discourage habitual complainers because people, as a rule, do not like to write. Even if the habitual complainer does like to write, the ball has still been placed where it belongs—in her court.

- *Confront the complainer with the facts.* When all else fails, leaders should simply confront the habitual complainer with the facts. This should be done with tact, but the message should be clear and direct. Assume that a departmental manager, Jane, is dealing with a habitual complainer, Mark. Jane has attempted to pre-empt Mark's habitual complaining by giving him more attention than usual. Preemption has not worked. Jane has asked Mark to put his complaints in writing. He now spends more time writing out complaints than working. As a final resort, Jane should confront Mark with the facts. That conversation might proceed as follows: "Mark, let's talk about your complaining. Most of your team mates bring a complaint to me about once a month. Their complaints almost always lead to improvements—some large and some small—but improvements nonetheless. I value your team mates and their complaints because I know that before they come to me they have done everything in their power to solve their own problems. They never bring problems to me that they have not tried to solve themselves. Further, the complaints they bring to me are typically of substance. Mark, you on the other hand bring complaints to be constantly, sometimes several per day. Often they turn out to be issues you could and should have dealt with yourself. I do not remember even one of your complaints leading to improved performance for our team. Now that I have you writing down your complaints, you spend more time writing than doing your job. I want you to understand that this situation is unacceptable. It is going to have to change if you want to continue as a member of this team."

GROUP TRAINING ACTIVITY

Discuss in the group how to handle the following situation. For several years, Maria Gonzalez has been one of the most effective members of the team. When she complains, her concerns are almost always legitimate and several of her complaints have led to major improvements in the team's performance. However, lately she seems to complain constantly. To make matters even worse, her more recent complaints have tended to be petty and inconsequential. How should her supervisor deal with this situation?

Eighteen

MENTORING

Best Practice Number 18: Mentor employees to continually improve their performance and encourage them to respond in kind.

Peak performance, continual improvement, and organizational excellence go together; they are inseparable concepts. Organizational excellence cannot be achieved without peak performance and continual improvement, and these two things cannot be achieved without committing to organizational excellence. Consequently, organizations and organizational leaders committed to excellence have every reason to engage in on-going employee development. One of the most effective forms of employee development is mentoring. Effective mentoring can improve the performance of the employee being mentored, the mentor, and, ultimately, the organization. This means that effective mentoring can be a win-win-win proposition.

MENTORING DEFINED

Mentoring is a process in which a more experienced individual helps one who is less experienced develop the knowledge, skills, and attitudes needed to achieve peak performance and, in turn, succeed in an organization. Being a mentor involves being a role model, but the two concepts are not the same. A role model can be anyone who exemplifies admirable qualities that are worthy of being emulated. It is not necessary to know or even meet a role model. Role models can be found in books, movies, television programs, or any other medium that can convey their examples. Employees can have a face-to-face relationship with a role model, but it is not necessary.

Mentors are different. Mentoring requires a face-to-face, one-on-one relationship that is reinforced by frequent contact and effective communication. Mentors invest time, energy, expertise, and caring in helping their protégés learn, grow, and develop. An effective mentoring relationship will help prepare the protégé to perform at peak levels in the organization. When mentoring is done well, both the protégé and the mentor will do better and be better as a result. The process should have a beneficial effect on both parties.

Case: The Effective Mentor

I had my earliest exposure to mentoring in my first job after college. I worked as part of a team led by an individual who had more experience than all of our team members combined. I will call this person James Jones. Jones was an excellent mentor well before the term became part of the language of organizational excellence. This thoroughly experienced and caring professional was willing to share his considerable knowledge and wisdom with those of us who worked on his team, and we all benefitted greatly from it.

Jones held frequent mentoring meetings, which he called "chalk talks." During these meetings, Jones helped the members of his team develop knowledge and skills that would prove invaluable, not just to the performance of our team but to the development of our careers. Jones seemed to care about us as individuals. It was obvious that his concern for us went beyond our ability to help his team be more productive, although that was certainly part of his plan.

Jones knew what it took to succeed in our organization as well as what it took to build a peak-performing team. He was adept at recognizing the individual strengths and weaknesses of our team members. Every time our team met for a chalk talk, Jones had at least one specific performance-improvement suggestion for every participant. Sometimes he made actual assignments for team members to carry out. For example, he once told one of our team members to enroll in a trigonometry course to improve his skills in that critical area of mathematics. Our company was an engineering firm. Consequently, a good command of trigonometry was important to our team members. Jones then tutored our team mate throughout the course. Regardless of the type of self-improvement assignment he might give us, Jones expected us to report on our progress regularly.

One December our company's CEO decided to host a formal Christmas banquet and invite all salaried personnel to attend. Invitations were sent, but in reality attendance was mandatory. The members of our design team were anxious about the banquet. On one hand we wanted to make a good impression on the CEO and the company's senior managers. On the other hand, we were worried that the only impression we would make would be one of social ineptitude. Most of us had just spent several years in college. Consequently, our social graces were of the jeans, tee shirts, and eating-pizza-out-of-the-box variety. Our knowledge of social etiquette would not have impressed a dormitory manager, much less Emily Post.

Other than Jones, not one member of our design team could distinguish a salad fork from a dessert fork or a water glass from a wine glass, nor did anyone on the team own a tuxedo. When we read the term "black tie" in the invitation, a sense of foreboding set in. My team mates and I were convinced that ignorance of social etiquette would result in our making a bad impression. In fact, we began to consider which might be worse—the impression we would make on the CEO by attending or the one we would make by not attending.

As things turned out, we need not have worried. James Jones, as usual, was way ahead of us. Anticipating our predicament, he invited an expert on social etiquette to our next chalk talk. At that meeting, which lasted several hours, we learned how to properly wear a tuxedo, and the best place in town to rent one. We also learned about proper greetings, introductions, cocktail conversation, formal place settings, and table manners. Thanks to James Jones, when the big day arrived, my team mates and I were ready. We were well prepared and even tentatively confident. As a result, the Christmas banquet went well for us. In fact our team made a sufficiently positive impression on the CEO that he complimented James Jones on our manners.

This is just one example of the many ways Jones helped develop the young and inexperienced design professionals on his team. He also helped us develop positive, can-do attitudes, think critically, make appropriate choices, and develop other important skills. His mentoring helped us, but it also helped the team, the company, and Jones himself. Because of James Jones, my team mates and I performed much better than we otherwise would have. We knew this, and that knowledge made us unswervingly loyal to Jones. Frankly, we would have walked through fire for him.

Our gratitude and loyalty caused us to work hard to give James Jones the highest performing team in the company. Jones continued his practice of mentoring team members every time he attained a successively higher position. Because every team he led consistently performed at peak levels, Jones rose steadily through the ranks of the company. He helped others, himself, and our company by mentoring those who worked for him. As this example shows, when it is done well mentoring can be a win-win-win proposition.

RESPONSIBILITIES OF MENTORS

In order to create win-win-win results, it is necessary to understand the responsibilities of mentors. In broad terms, mentors must be willing to give of their time, remain open-minded, give feedback that is constructive and tactful, and listen well. In addition to these things, they must care about the development of their protégés as individuals. In addition to these broad responsibilities, there are several specific responsibilities mentors must be willing to accept:

- Communicating openly, frankly, tactfully, and frequently with protégés.

- Serving as a sounding board and patient, attentive listener for protégés.

- Providing encouragement, recognition, and support for protégés.

- Providing a steady flow of accurate, up-to-date information about opportunities, issues, problems, and options for protégés.

- Being a consistent role model of performance-enhancing attitudes and behaviors for protégés.

- Helping protégés set goals and realistic timetables for achieving them.

- Helping protégés develop effective strategies for achieving goals.

- Helping protégés understand the organization's culture and how to operate successfully in it.

- Introducing protégés to useful contacts.

- Helping protégés develop specific job and career-related knowledge and skills.

ENCOURAGE EMPLOYEES TO MENTOR THEIR SUPERVISORS

Mentoring can actually be a two-way proposition, and should be. Traditional mentoring involves more experienced personnel helping less experienced individuals develop, grow, and succeed. But there is another side to mentoring that gets very little attention—employees mentoring their supervisors in selected areas. The term "supervisors" is used in the broadest sense here. Remember that executives, managers, and supervisors all qualify as supervisors in the broader sense because they all oversee and lead other people.

An example of how an employee might mentor a supervisor can be found in the concept of technical updating. A younger employee whose knowledge of a new and emerging technology is better than that of her supervisor can provide invaluable updating assistance to her. I call this concept *upward mentoring*. It involves making your supervisor better by helping him strengthen areas of weakness. Organizational leaders should empower their employees to mentor them where appropriate, and encourage them to do so.

Although upward mentoring gets only scant attention in professional literature, it is important none-the-less. In fact, it can help solve one of the most difficult problems that organizations face: employees who try to advance their careers by undermining the work of those above them. Too many employees think that in order to move up the career ladder they need to knock their supervisor off of it or climb over his back. This is a mistake. Taking the low road to career advancement always is. Undermining a supervisor might advance an individual's career in the short run, but over time this approach tends to catch up with the culprit, often doing more harm than good. Most people who choose this approach eventually pay a high price for their choice.

Recall the example of James Jones from the previous section. Jones had a number of strengths that served him well as he rose through the ranks of our company. But, as good as he was, Jones also had some weaknesses. Every professional does. During our team's mentoring meetings, Jones would occasionally reveal certain of his weak areas and ask us for help. Of course, those of us he was mentoring would leap at the chance to help him in any way we could. The fact that he was willing to ask for our help only increased his credibility with us and bolstered our confidence, something I'm sure Jones knew it would do.

Jones was willing to candidly admit to some areas of professional weakness. Other supervisors may not be so revealing. People are often reluctant to admit to professional weaknesses, even with colleagues much less with subordinates. Consequently, the relationship aspect of upward mentoring is often different than that of traditional mentoring. An upward mentor is often a silent mentor—someone who quietly helps without advertising the fact. Professional weaknesses in a supervisor can be observed by those who are attentive enough to recognize them. Upward mentoring often amounts to doing things to help improve the performance of a supervisor without that person asking for help and without there being a formal mentoring relationship established. In spite of the sometimes quiet nature of upward mentoring, when done well it can produce win-win-win results.

Upward Mentoring Strategies

Organizational leaders should teach employees the following strategies for helping enhance the performance of their supervisors: 1) be a second pair of eyes and ears for the supervisor; 2) speak positively about the supervisor or do not speak at all; 3) work quietly to enhance the supervisor's image and performance; and 4) point out potholes in the road before the supervisor steps in one.

A Second Pair of Eyes and Ears

Nobody can be everywhere at once. A supervisor, no matter how bright, is not omniscient. Consequently, one way employees can help their supervisors is to serve as a second pair of eyes and ears for them. If there is a controversy brewing that could affect the supervisor or the team's performance, employees should let her know about it. If there is a problem in the team the supervisor is unaware of or does not accurately perceive, employees should discuss the situation with her. If an employee learns that someone above the supervisor in the organization has issues with her or the team, he should let the supervisor know.

Anything employees hear, see, or learn that could potentially help or harm the supervisor, should be passed along to her. If employees have recommendations for dealing with problems or issues, they should ask if the supervisor would like to hear them. If so, they should make the recommendations. It is true that the supervisor will see and hear things employees will not. After all, the supervisor sits on a higher branch in the organizational tree than employees. But it is also true that employees sometimes hear and see things their supervisors don't. When this happens, employees should talk with their supervisor. They should keep her informed of anything that could harm her or the team's performance.

Speak Positively or Remain Silent

In any organization there will be a few people who think they gain some benefit by running down those above them. Organizational leaders should make sure that employees know that doing this is a mistake. Backbiting conversation and gossip serve no positive purpose. Further, those who participate in these things lose credibility, even with people who appear to agree with them. People who hear an employee running down a supervisor will interpret it as disloyalty. Further, they will think "I wonder what he says about me when I'm not present?"

Teach employees they should always speak positively about their supervisor and team mates in public and private. Employees who have problems, complaints, or other issues with their supervisor should take them up in private in face-to-face conversations, and always for the purpose of facilitating improvements. Even when a supervisor is wrong—unless she is engaged in unethical or illegal activities—she deserves this courtesy. This professional approach will help build a positive supervisor/subordinate relationship that, in turn, will contribute to better performance. Once a supervisor knows that a team member is loyal and helpful, he will be more open to that employee's suggestions, recommendations, feedback, and input.

Quietly Enhance the Performance of Supervisors

Every individual has strengths and weaknesses. This is just as true of supervisors, managers, and executives as it is of anyone else. This is why it is important for organizational leaders to tell employees that when they observe an area of weakness in a supervisor, they should work quietly to improve that weakness or to mitigate the negative effects of it. Whatever an employee does to help improve a supervisor's performance should be done quietly and behind the scenes. Employees do not help themselves or their supervisors by publicly pointing out their weaknesses. Doing so might make an employee feel smart, but it will make the supervisor look bad, and that is never a good idea. Employees should be taught to observe this unchanging rule of the workplace: *Getting at odds with their supervisor will not help the team's performance or their career.*

I had an opportunity early in my career to mentor a supervisor, although at the time I did not view it as mentoring. Rather, I just saw it as helping a good supervisor who had a weakness: he could not write well. His letters to customers and memorandums to colleagues suffered from poor grammar, poor sentence structure, and poor spelling. Don't get the wrong impression here. This individual was bright and good at his job. When it came to technical knowledge, none of us could match him. But because his country of origin was China, he struggled with the English language.

After reading only a couple his memorandums, I knew that his limited writing skills were going to hurt his image and that of the team. In fact, they probably already had. This individual was a good supervisor and I wanted to help him, but the situation produced a real dilemma. How do you tell your supervisor his writing is terrible?

It took me a while to determine how to approach the situation. Finally, after much thought, I decided to just wait for an opportune opening. Then, one day while I was in his office, my grammatically-challenged supervisor told me he hated to write. Seeing my chance, I told him that many people struggle with writing but that I was one of those strange people to whom it came easily. I offered to edit the drafts of his letters and memorandums. I would just mark them up for grammar, sentence structure, and spelling and his secretary could clean them up and create final drafts.

My supervisor liked the idea and handed me a draft of a letter on the spot. The time it took me to play my role in this partnership was negligible, just a few minutes per day. But, as it turned out, those few minutes enhanced my supervisor's performance. Nobody but my supervisor and I knew about the arrangement. Everything was done quietly. Even his secretary knew only that he had begun to give her marked up drafts of letters and memorandums that she would correct. My supervisor returned this minor favor many times over and eventually made an important contribution to advancing my career.

Guide Supervisors around Potholes in the Road

Everybody makes mistakes. This fact applies to even the most talented, experienced, and intuitive professionals. The only way to avoid making mistakes is to do nothing. Like everyone, supervisors make mistakes. Since this is the case, one way employees can assist supervisors is by helping them avoid mistakes, especially those that might harm their career, the performance of their team, or the image of the organization. I learned this lesson years ago when a subordinate kept me from making what could have been a serious mistake.

I was preparing for a meeting in which my department might have its budget cut substantially. Our company had lost several large customers and was having to make adjustments. The person responsible for slashing our budget was an executive vice-president who had come up through the ranks from the field of marketing. Although no longer in marketing, his favoritism toward that department was legendary.

Aware of the vice-president's reputation for preferential treatment of the marketing department, I planned to give an impassioned defense of my department during the meeting. I was going to use graphs, charts, and slides to prove that my department was more important than all of the other departments combined—especially marketing. My message would be clear: Not only should my department's budget not be cut, it should receive a well-deserved increase. At least that was my thinking as I prepared for the meeting.

I asked several members of my department to critique a trial run of my presentation. Pulling no punches, I stated my case with the evangelistic zeal of an old-fashioned revivalist. After flipping the last slide, I asked my team members what they thought. At first no one spoke. Everyone waited to see if someone else would break the ice and venture an opinion. Finally one team member spoke up. He said the presentation was right on target, and encouraged me to enter the upcoming budget meeting with both guns blazing. The others in the room quickly agreed. One team member seemed to speak for the entire group when he said, "It's about time somebody told our executive vice-president there is more to this company than marketing."

Then, amid the ensuing trash talk and bravado, a lone voice from the back of the room said, "I don't think that's a good idea." Taken aback, I asked the dissenting team member to expound. He explained that in his opinion my approach might make me feel good for a short time, but that in the long run it would just create powerful enemies for our department. He suggested that it would be better to work on convincing all department heads, including the one from marketing, to be united in approaching the vice-president with a proposal for an equal distribution of the budget cuts on a pro-rata basis. In this way, rather than making enemies we might build partnerships with the other departments. These partnerships might serve us well, not just in the current situation but in the future too.

Although I was still inclined to make my original presentation, I saw the wisdom in this team member's input. After thinking it over for a while, I decided to take his advice and, as it turned out, I'm glad I did. Not only were the other department heads willing to present a united front to our executive vice-president, the marketing manager actually took the lead. Before anyone else could speak, he actually offered to take a larger share of the cuts in his department. Shocking everyone, our usually pro-marketing executive vice-president accepted the marketing manager's magnanimous offer.

I had originally intended to take the floor first and pre-empt any action by our executive vice-president with my impassioned presentation of reality as I saw it. Had I done so, not only would my action have insulted the marketing manager who had come to the meeting prepared to be selfless and equitable, it would have turned the meeting into a battleground. Thanks to the wisdom and sound advice of one of my team members, I got through the meeting without: 1) making a complete fool of myself, and 2) making a powerful enemy. As an added bonus, my department as well as those of my colleagues received less of a budget cut then they otherwise would have. One level-headed team member kept me—his supervisor—from making a serious mistake. This is an illustrative example of upward mentoring at its best.

Organizational leaders should encourage employees to keep their eyes and ears open and use what they hear and see to help their supervisor. Teach them to speak only positive words about their supervisor, and to keep their disagreements private. Teach employees to help improve or mitigate any weaknesses their supervisors might have, and—if possible—to quietly keep them from making mistakes that might harm their career, image, or the performance of their teams. Teach employees to quietly take care of their supervisors in these ways so that their supervisors will, in turn, take care of them. Of course, there will be the occasional exception to this rule. Not all supervisors are ethical, equitable people. But this principle will apply favorably in the majority of cases.

GROUP TRAINING ACTIVITIES

1. Assume that you have just been appointed head of a department that has had productivity problems. Several of your new team members are still new in their jobs and the rest are only mediocre in their job-related knowledge, skills, and attitudes. Explain how you could use mentoring to help improve the performance of your new department.

2. Assume that your supervisor is uncomfortable working with customers, suppliers, and members of the general public. Also assume that working with what she calls "outsiders" is an important part of her job. Explain how you might use upward mentoring to help improve your supervisor in this critical area.

Nineteen

PERSEVERANCE

Best Practice Number 19: Set an example of persevering during times of adversity and encourage employees to follow this example.

For organizational leaders, a career is like a baseball game in that it consists of more than just one inning. In a baseball game each batter comes to the plate several times and even the most talented player strikes out occasionally. In fact, some players will occasionally go into a slump and strikeout consistently for a period of time. But the best players persevere no matter how difficult the game becomes and no matter how many times they strike out. This willingness to persevere in times of adversity is what makes some players champions while others remain mediocre.

One of the reasons champions become champions is because they refuse to give up and they never quit. On the other hand, even champions are human. Like all people, during times of adversity, they can become discouraged. But what separates the best from the mediocre is that the best refuse to give in to discouragement. One of the characteristics of the best organizational leaders is that they view every set back as an opportunity for a comeback.

In a competitive environment, organizations need personnel at all levels to be willing to persevere in spite of obstacles, setbacks, and difficulties. Consequently, having organizational leaders who set a consistent example of persevering during times of adversity is essential to peak performance, continual improvement, and organizational excellence. Perseverance is not a trait people are born with. Rather, it is something they must learn. Fortunately, employees can learn to persevere. The best way to make this happen is for organizational leaders to consistently provide a good example for them to follow.

Every organization experiences adversity. Consequently, having personnel who can stay positive and persevere through the difficulties is essential to achieving and maintaining organizational excellence. Contracts will fall through, workplace tragedies will occur, important personnel will leave, the economy will fluctuate, natural disasters will occur, competitors will gain an advantage in the marketplace, supply shortages will happen, work stoppages will occur, suppliers will fail to deliver, product recalls will be necessary, a new product line will flop, and the list goes on and on. There is never a scarcity of adversity in organizations trying to compete in today's global environment. For this reason, organizations need leaders and employees who understand that adversity comes with a gift in its hand. That gift is the opportunity to: 1) grow stronger by weathering the storm, and 2) get better by learning from the experience.

DON'T QUIT—NEVER GIVE UP

Peak performance is not just a matter of talent. The highway to failure is paved with the unfulfilled potential of talented people who, when faced with adversity and hard work, chose to give up. When the going got tough, they quit. This is unfortunate because victory often goes to the individual or the organization that is willing to simply stay the course a little longer than the competition. Think of America's Olympic women's softball team. It had to work long and hard just to get its sport accepted as an Olympic event. Turned down numerous times, they became frustrated, discouraged, and even angry, but they persevered and refused to quit. As a result, they were eventually successful and softball became an Olympic event. But America's team did not stop there. Having won the battle for Olympic acceptance, America's women went on to win three consecutive gold medals in their sport.

Think of the boxer who loses the first nine rounds of the fight, but perseveres and wins by a knockout in the 10th round. Think of all the times baseball games have been won when the last batter in the bottom of the ninth inning knocks a home run. Think of football games won by a field goal as the clock winds down to zero. Think of great basketball games won at the buzzer by a desperation shot tossed up from mid court. In all of these examples, victory went to the individual or team that persevered, that refused to give up or quit. Sometimes victory is just one step beyond that last step you think you can take. These examples come from the world of sports because the best-known and most dramatic instances of victory through perseverance come from the world of sports. But the never-quit-never-give-up attitude applies just as directly in organizations as in sports. Consequently, it is just as important for personnel in organizations to learn to persevere as it is for athletes.

Strategies for Persevering

Perseverance is about continuing to give your best when what you would really like to do is quit. Persevering is more of a mental than a physical exercise. In fact, perseverance can be thought of as the mental equivalent of physical stamina. Achieving organizational excellence requires people to do a lot of things well, often difficult things. Further, it can take a long time. To complicate matters, the road to excellence is never easy. Once achieved, organizational excellence is difficult to maintain. Market forces, competition, supplier problems, the economy, technological developments, and a variety of other ever-present factors make achieving peak performance a daily and never-ending challenge for employees and organizations.

Consequently, organizations need leaders and employees who can bear up under the pressures of competition and keep going in spite of anxiety, frustration, fear, uncertainty, and fatigue, both mental and physical. The following strategies may be helpful for organizational leaders and employees who are facing adversity:

- When facing an intractable problem and it seems that nothing is working, remember the lesson of the great inventor, Thomas Alva Edison. In trying to invent such useful products as the storage battery and a durable filament for the light bulb, he failed repeatedly. It is said that it took him almost 25,000 attempts to finally succeed with just these two inventions. But when others might have quit, Edison refused to give up. Instead, he persevered, and finally succeeded. The world can be thankful he did.

- When a project seems to go on and on with no end in sight and you feel like giving up, think about how hard you have worked to get to the point where you are now. Consider the advice Vince Lombardi, the hall-of-fame football coach, used to give his players during the golden years of the Green Bay Packers. Paraphrased, Lombardi's message went like this: *The harder you work at accomplishing a goal, the harder it is to give up on achieving it.* In other words, tell yourself "I can't quit now—I've worked too hard to get this far."

- When you fail at something important and discouragement begins to set in remember this: every time you try something and fail, you are better prepared to succeed the next time (think of Thomas Edison and the durable filament for the light bulb). A failed attempt does not become a failure unless you quit. A failed attempt is just another opportunity to try again better prepared the next time.

- When you are unsure of your ability to complete a daunting assignment or when the consequences of failure appear to be dire, focus on what will happen when you succeed rather than what might happen if you fail. Stay focused on the ball that is in play, not on the scoreboard. Then play to win rather than to avoid losing.

FACE ADVERSITY AND OVERCOME IT

There is a tendency to think that success comes easily for those who are the top producers in an organization. In reality, this is hardly ever the case. Further, the concept of the overnight success is typically a myth. Few people who succeed do so overnight. Most so-called over-night successes are people who struggled long and hard to finally succeed. Successful people are rarely strangers to adversity. An excellent example of facing adversity and overcoming it is Franklin Delano Roosevelt, President of the United States during the Great Depression and World War II.

Roosevelt was elected President when the United States was firmly in the grip of the Great Depression. Unemployment was at its highest level in America's history, the nation's banking system had crashed, small businesses were closing daily, people were losing their homes because they could not pay their mortgages, the Midwestern farming states had become a vast dust bowl no longer suited for farming, and many people woke up every morning wondering what, if anything, they would have to eat that day.

Into this bleak picture stepped Franklin Delano Roosevelt, the former governor of New York and a man of great optimism. Soon after taking office he began to use "fireside chats," radio broadcasts in which he reassured Americans that the economy would pick up again and their lives would get better. He spoke to the country in such calm and optimistic terms that Americans began to gain a sense of hope. Then, before any of the President's economic recovery programs had time to produce results, the Japanese attacked Pearl Harbor and the United States found itself embroiled in World War II.

Faced with an even bigger crisis than the Great Depression, President Roosevelt again calmed the anxiety of Americans. In a nationally broadcast address he set a confident and hopeful tone when he said: "All we have to fear is fear itself." Roosevelt used the same calm optimism to face the adversity of World War II that he had used to face the adversity of the Great Depression. The President's optimism during times of unprecedented adversity is a story unto itself, but what is even more instructive about his example is that he held the country together while suffering from a severe case of polio. President Roosevelt—a man who portrayed himself as a robust, vibrant leader—could not even walk. But he hid this fact so well that many Americans were not even aware of it until after his death.

In spite of having to struggle daily against the increasingly debilitating and painful effects of a crippling disease, Franklin Delano Roosevelt remained calm and optimistic in the face of tremendous adversity. He could have simplified his life and eased his daily pain by agreeing to use in public the wheel chair he used in private. But the attitudes of Americans toward people in wheelchairs were less enlightened in those days, not to mention the attitudes of America's enemies. Roosevelt knew that the times and circumstances demanded an image of strength. Consequently, he endured excruciating pain and frustrating inconvenience to provide that example.

Not only did the President fight courageously every day to win the war and revitalize the nation's economy, he did it while supporting himself, when in public, with heavy metal braces that bit painfully into his frail and paralyzed legs. The leg braces, worn under his trousers, and the façade of healthful vigor he felt it necessary to maintain only added to the adversity this courageous man faced every day. But in spite of the pain and inconvenience, Roosevelt maintained the necessary façade from the moment he was elected President of the United States until the day his heart final gave out during a rest-and-recuperation visit to his "Little White House" in Warm Springs, Georgia.

One might wonder why a wealthy President from Hyde Park, New York would have a vacation retreat in rural, poverty-stricken Warm Springs, Georgia. The reason reveals even more about the incredible courage and perseverance of this unique individual. Using his own money, Roosevelt had founded a treatment center at Warm Springs for polio victims. The naturally-occurring warm springs that bubbled up in this tiny, out-of-the-way Georgia town had a stimulating effect on the withered limbs of polio victims, especially children. Although serving as President of the United States during some of America's darkest hours left him no time to undergo the physical therapy offered at his own treatment center, Roosevelt wanted to make sure that future generations of polio victims had a chance to receive the treatments. Thanks to Roosevelt they did.

Organizational leaders facing periods of adversity would do well to remember the example of President Franklin Delano Roosevelt and set a similar example for employees. They should stay positive and optimistic, be calm and reassuring, and focus on solutions rather than problems. No matter how difficult the problems they must face become, organizational leaders should provide a consistent, calm, and resolute example of perseverance that sends the message, "We can get through this."

ACCEPT THAT ADVERSITY IS A NORMAL PART OF LIFE

If achieving organizational excellence and peak performance were easy, all organizations and all employees would achieve these things. Unfortunately, achieving these things is seldom easy. Rather, they are difficult to achieve and even more difficult to maintain. There will always be plenty of obstacles on the road to excellence—inhibitors that undermine performance. It is when dealing with these inevitable obstacles that a willingness to persevere separates an organization from its competition. This is why it is so important that, during hard times, organizational leaders set an example for employees that says, "Adversity is normal—just keep going."

In a competitive environment, adversity is often the rule rather than the exception. Consequently, the individuals most likely to thrive in such an environment are those who can maintain their focus, positive attitude, and solution orientation in spite of the difficulties. People who approach adversity as if it is a one-time event to be survived rather than as the normal state of things will eventually feel overwhelmed and may give up. This is important because in a competitive environment, adversity can be the normal state of things. Even in the best of times there will be periods of adversity. This means that organizational leaders and employees must learn to deal with adversity in a positive way as a normal part of their jobs.

Case: Expecting Adversity

The value of expecting adversity is best illustrated by an example. I am a native Floridian. Consequently, I grew up understanding that hurricanes—although destructive and distressing—are a normal part of June, July, August, and September in most years. Because I understand that the adversity that follows in the wake of a hurricane is normal, the experience is less stressful for me than it is for others who grew up elsewhere and moved to Florida later in life.

My family and I know how to live for days and even weeks in the midst of destruction and without such amenities as electricity, hot meals, hot showers, and so on. This is because we expect these things and deal with them accordingly. We know that if we respond in a certain way, the world will eventually right itself and life will go on. Frankly, in most years we do not take a direct hit from a hurricane, but in those years when we do handling the destruction and inconvenience is just another day at the office for us.

On the other hand, people who are new to Florida tend to approach hurricanes as one-time events to survive. This perspective affects how they prepare for storms and how they respond afterwards. In the wake of today's hurricane, I and other Florida natives simply begin cleaning up and getting prepared for the next one. Newer Florida residents, on the other hand, tend to react in a way that says, "I am glad we survived that one and hope we never have to go through another one." The problem with this approach is that unless they move to another state, they are almost certain to face another hurricane. When this reality sets in, they often become frustrated and overwhelmed. Some simply give up and leave the state.

The way native Floridians deal with hurricanes can be instructive for people who need to learn how to deal with adversity in the workplace. Understanding how native Floridians just keep going when they must deal with the destruction of hurricanes can help organizational leaders and employees understand how to deal with workplace adversity. Some strategies that will help leaders and employees bear up when facing hard times are as follows:

- Understand that adversity is a normal part of life.

- Refuse to get caught up in the here and now of the situation. Look down the road past the difficulties and focus on solutions rather than problems.

- Develop a course of action for getting past the difficulties faced and implement it.

- Prepare physically and mentally for the next crisis and accept that there will be one.

- Stay positive and take adversity in stride.

Not only should organizational leaders internalize these rules of thumb themselves, they should teach them to employees, through both conversation and example.

ACCEPT THAT LIFE CAN BE UNFAIR

One of the factors that can make it difficult for people to deal with adversity in a positive manner is the seeming unfairness of it. People facing adversity often wonder, "Why is this happening to me? It's not fair." While it might be true that the circumstances in question are unfair, getting caught up in the unfairness of adversity is a mistake. Focusing on the unfairness of a situation can cause people to become discouraged and give up. This is a point that organizational leaders should understand and help employees understand.

During times of adversity, it is important for organizational leaders to help employees understand that they are not alone. The maxim about misery loving company certainly applies to people facing adversity. A bad situation can seem less unfair when others are facing it too. If the organization or the team is going through hard times, all personnel are probably affected. Making this point to employees can help them see that they are not alone in dealing with adversity.

Watch people in the aftermath of a natural disaster such as an earthquake, tornado, or hurricane. Amazingly, people who have lost everything can be seen working to help others restore a semblance of normalcy to their wrecked lives. But when people feel isolated in their misery, the unfairness of the situation can give rise to self-pity, frustration, and despair. People who feel this way are especially susceptible to that part of their nature that wants to give up and quit.

This is why it is important for organizational leaders to let employees know that life is not always fair, and they should not expect it to be. Further, no matter how hard good people try to make it otherwise, life is not likely to be fair. Organizational leaders should endeavor to be fair and equitable with employees and colleagues. Organizations should adopt policies, procedures, and practices that ensure as much fairness as possible for their personnel. But never lose sight of the fact that bad things do happen to good people and to good organizations. This fact should be understood by employees as well as everyone else in the organization. When the concept of unfairness is understood and accepted, employees will be better prepared to deal with the adversity they will inevitably face.

HELP SOMEONE ELSE WHO IS FACING ADVERSITY

When facing adversity, it is easy to become self-focused. After all, the fear, frustration fatigue, and uncertainty associated with adversity are felt on a deeply personal level. On the other hand, people who let themselves become self-focused when experiencing adversity are not likely to get through it. Experience shows over and over that one of the most effective ways to deal with adversity is to help someone else who is facing it. This is a strategy that organizational leaders should adopt themselves and teach to employees.

In any organization, one will not have to look far to find someone else who is suffering and needs help. Of course, when the adversity is not work-related, you might have to look a little harder. Sadly, one never has to look too far to find another person who is suffering through some kind of crisis. People in organizations lose loved ones, have children who get into drugs, go through a divorce, become alcoholics or live with one, find themselves estranged from their family, experience financial problems, or face a myriad of other issues. In fact, there are few adversity-free human beings in the world—if any. Reaching out to others who are facing adversity—especially a similar kind of adversity—may be the best way there is to avoid becoming self-focused and giving in to gloom and defeatism.

This concept of helping oneself by helping others should be thoroughly understood by organizational leaders who are trying to encourage perseverance. When the organization goes through hard times, getting its employees to focus on helping each other is an excellent way to lessen everybody's burden and to teach employees how to deal with adversity. Buyouts, downsizings, layoffs, and mergers as well as economic downturns, natural disasters, demographic shifts, market changes, and other adversity-inducing events are a normal part of life for people in organizations. Consequently, helping employees develop the willingness and ability to persevere during hard times is an essential ingredient in the formula for organizational excellence, peak performance, and continual improvement. Organizational leaders who wish to develop a team of peak-performing employees should teach them, especially by example, how to persevere in times of adversity.

GROUP TRAINING ACTIVITY

Assume that the economy has taken a nosedive. Every type of organization—public and private—has been affected. In an attempt to survive the downturn your organization is considering a merger with a competitor. Employees in your organization are worried about what will happen to them as a result of the merger. Which organization will be the headquarters for the new company? Will any employees lose their jobs? Will anyone have to move to the other organization (which is located in another city)? These issues and many others are still undecided. In fact, many of them will not be decided until a comparative performance analysis of the two organizations has been completed. In most cases, the organization and employees that come out best in a given category of performance will fare better in the merger. For this reason, the operations manager for your organization needs his employees to perform at peak levels. Unfortunately, as things stand now, they are so worried about what might happen to them that they cannot concentrate on their work, which is clearly suffering. The group's assignment is to determine how to get the organization's employees focused on the ball rather than the scoreboard. How should the operations manager go about convincing them to do what is necessary to persevere through the adversity they all now face and perform at peak levels?

Twenty

DIVERSITY

Best Practice Number 20: *Become proficient at working in a diverse environment and help employees learn to do the same.*

America is one of the most diverse countries in the world, and this diversity is reflected in organizations. Americans can trace their lineage to virtually every country, race, and culture in the world. Consequently, it is important for people in organizations to be able to work effectively in a diverse environment. The term *diversity* as applied to people in organizations refers to any and all ways they can be different.

There are many ways in which people can be different, but the ways that always seem to command the most attention are race, culture, national heritage, gender, religion, politics, level of education, worldview, and personality. Because people at work can be different from each other in all of these ways, it is important for organizational leaders to teach employees, through words and by example, to work well in a diverse environment.

DIVERSITY DEFINED

Try this experiment. Ask several friends and colleagues what comes to mind when they hear the term *diversity*. Do not be surprised if you find that most people associate the term with racial differences. This limited perception is partially correct, but only partially. Diversity is a much broader concept than just racial differences. As it applies in the workplace, diversity encompasses all of the ways in which people can be different.

What follows is a list of just some ways that people can be different: race, mental ability, physical ability, physical appearance, age, marital status, geographic status, religion, denominations within religions, ethnicity, nationality, worldview, education level, values, political beliefs, interests, personality, cultural background, height, weight, career status, white collar, blue collar, and personal preferences (food, clothing, music, etc.). With a little thought, most people could add other ways that people can be different to this list.

People can be different in a lot of ways. In fact, members of the same family—even identical twins—can be vastly different in terms of their physical abilities, intelligence, personal interests, religion, education, personality, work skills, appearance, attitudes, ambition, political beliefs, personal values, and worldviews. If there can be this many differences between family members, imagine all the ways in which people at work can be different. One fact of life for people in organizations is that they are going to work with team members who are different from them in how they talk, dress, eat, interact, socialize, believe, think, and approach their work. Another fact of life is that people in organizations are not likely to achieve peak performance or continual improvement unless they can work effectively in a diverse environment.

DIVERSITY-RELATED CONCEPTS

In conversations about diversity, certain concepts will surface over and over again. Organizational leaders should be familiar with these concepts themselves and help employees become familiar with them. Important diversity-related concepts include the following:

- Prejudice

- Stereotyping/labeling

- Discrimination

- Tolerance

Prejudice

Prejudice is a predisposition to adopt negative perceptions about groups of people For example, one might be prejudiced against conservatives, liberals, northerners, southerners, easterners, westerners, men, women, whites, blacks, accountants, engineers, Christians, Muslims, Hindus,

Democrats, Republicans, youth, elderly, or any other distinct group of people. People who are prejudiced have learned to harbor negative perceptions of and ill feelings toward a distinct group or groups of people. When you are prejudiced against a given group of people, all members of that group are subject to your negative perceptions and ill feelings. For example, an individual who is prejudiced against teenagers might claim that they all have slouchy posture, bad attitudes, and waste time hanging out at malls. Of course, this description would be accurate for some teenagers but not for all. This some-but-not-all concept is the Achilles heel that undermines the credibility of prejudiced attitudes and practices.

People who are prejudiced tend to divide the world into two distinct groups: "us" and "them." Those who appear to share their values, cultural mores, worldviews, and other pertinent characteristics are part of the "us" group. Everyone else is lumped into the group known as "them." Prejudice reveals itself in the workplace in a number of different ways—all negative. Prejudiced people in the workplace sometimes act out their prejudices through discrimination, stereotyping, and labeling. Others act out their prejudices in less overt, but equally negative ways. For example, an individual who is prejudiced against a given group might refuse to admit to himself that anyone in that group ever had a good idea, did a good job, was worthy of a promotion, or could sufficiently satisfy any given performance measure.

Prejudice can blind organizational leaders to the fact that people they place in a certain group are capable of peak performance and continual improvement. As a result, prejudiced leaders might not invest the time and effort in selected employees that they invest in others. Not only is this wrong from the perspective of equity, it is unwise from the perspective of organizational excellence. An employee's performance on the job is a function of individual talent, attitude, motivation, and other job-related factors rather than such unrelated factors as race, sex, politics, cultural heritage, religion, or worldview. When organizational leaders allow prejudice to influence their actions and decisions, they limit their ability to help the organization excel and to help develop peak-performing employees. In addition, they pass on their prejudice to employees who, in turn, follow their lead and act out their newly learned prejudice.

Stereotyping/Labeling

Stereotyping is a negative by-product of prejudice. It is the act of generalizing certain characteristics to all members of a given identifiable group. For example, you may have heard so-called *blond jokes*. What all blond jokes have in common is the assertion that blonds are dumb. In order to "get" a blond joke, one must accept this assertion. Jokes that apply to all people in a given group in this way are stereotypical in nature.

It was stereotyping that for years denied even the best African-American college quarterbacks opportunities to lead football teams at the professional level. For decades outstanding college quarterbacks who happened to be black were automatically converted to receivers and defensive backs when drafted by professional football teams. Outstanding black athletes were stereotyped in such a way that relegated them to playing only certain positions in the National Football League.

The stereotype behind this travesty was that blacks were not smart enough to lead teams at the professional level. Now that African-American quarterbacks are common in professional football, people who are too young to have experienced this stereotype have trouble believing it ever existed. But, of course, it did. The same kind of stereotype once applied to football coaches at the college and professional levels. Now that some of the most successful coaches who ever walked the sidelines are black, the stereotype has been discarded and forgotten. However, what should not be forgotten is how wrong the stereotype was because it shows how illogical and damaging stereotyping can be.

Labeling is an extension of stereotyping in that it involves attributing a certain characteristic to a distinct group of people and then using that characteristic to label all people in that group. For example, people who are talented in the fields of science, math, or computers are often labeled as "geeks." This label is supposed to conjure up an image of a socially inept person who can solve quadratic equations but cannot tie his shoes. Another example of this concept is when people from the south are labeled as rednecks. This label is supposed to bring to mind an image of an illiterate individual who chews tobacco and is still saving his Confederate dollars.

While there may be some academically gifted individuals who are socially inept and some southerners who are still waiting for the South to rise again, to lump all scholars and all southerners into homogeneous groups in this way is not just illogical, it is narrow minded. Prejudiced behavior such as stereotyping and labeling harm both the victims and the perpetrators. Just because some people in an identifiable group exhibit certain characteristics hardly means that all people in that group share those characteristics. After all, some people in almost any group will exhibit certain characteristics that prejudiced people tend to attribute to just one select group.

To understand how illogical the practices of stereotyping and labeling can be, take the example of referring to southerners as rednecks. Some of America's most brilliant scholars, poets, musicians, artists, scientists, and political leaders have been men and women from the South. In fact, several have been president of the United States, including George Washington, who is still referred to as "the father of our country." The same can be said for the practice of stereotyping and labeling any group. An objective look by anyone who is not prejudiced will reveal the fallacy of stereotyping and labeling.

Organizational leaders who allow stereotyping and labeling to influence their decisions do their victims, the organization, and themselves a great disservice. Try to imagine a baseball coach leaving his best hitter on the bench because of stereotypical thinking that is based on prejudice. In essence, this is what organizational leaders do when they allow prejudiced practices such as stereotyping and labeling to influence their decisions. Leaders in organizations that excel make their decisions on the basis of factors that affect performance. In other words, all decisions are based on what course of action is most likely to enhance performance. This focus on performance rather than prejudice is essential in achieving organizational excellence. It is also essential in helping employees overcome prejudiced behaviors they have learned.

Discrimination

Leaders in organizations must constantly discriminate between best and worst practices, high and low-performing employees, efficient and wasteful processes, and other factors that affect performance. Someone with discriminating taste is said to be a person who recognizes good food, good wine, good styling, and good design. Someone with a discriminating mind is said to be a person who is able to separate fact from opinion. Obviously, there are types of discrimination that are appropriate. However, discrimination—as it applies in the context of diversity—is not one of them.

Diversity-related discrimination is a negative concept. In this context, discrimination means putting prejudice into action. It means allowing diversity-related characteristics such as race, gender, culture, religion, and worldview to influence one's actions and decisions, a practice that is illegal, unethical, and counterproductive. Diversity-related discrimination can quickly and effectively undermine an organization's performance and the morale of its employees. Wherever it exists, discrimination is an obstacle to the achievement of organizational excellence because it undermines teamwork, employee performance, and morale.

Discrimination and Teamwork

In most organizations, work is done in teams. Almost without fail work in organizations is interdependent. This means the work of one employee depends on or is affected by the work of another. Think of a football team. Every time the ball is snapped, eleven people on the offensive team have their individual assignments that must be carried out properly if the ball is to be advanced. In addition to carrying out their individual assignments, each team member is responsible for cooperating with and supporting his team mates.

Take, for example, when the quarterback throws a pass. Before the ball is thrown, the offensive line is responsible for protecting the quarterback from the rush of the defensive line and other players who might blitz. In order to do this well, the offensive linemen must cooperate with each other in mutually-supportive ways. Then, if the ball is caught, these same linemen immediately switch their support to the receiver and cooperate in trying to help him score by providing down-field blocks. Consider what would happen if the offensive linemen decided they would not block for the quarterback because he is an easterner or would not hustle downfield to block for the receiver because he is a westerner. Teamwork would be undermined and an attitude of us-against-them would set in. This lesson about how discrimination can undermine teamwork is one that organizational leaders should teach to employees.

Discrimination and Employee Performance

In order for an organization to excel, its leaders must manage and supervise in ways that encourage, support, and facilitate peak performance and continual improvement in employees. Achieving peak performance on a consistent basis requires focus, motivation, and energy on the part of employees. Few things will undermine the efforts of organizational leaders to promote peak performance faster or more effectively than diversity-related discrimination. This is because employees who feel discriminated against will quickly lose their focus as well as their motivation. Further, their energy will be drained by their efforts to fight the discrimination.

Because discrimination affects its victims on such a basic and personal level, employees simply cannot give their best efforts when focused on the discriminatory practices of others. The more energy employees must invest in fighting discrimination, the less they will have to invest in improving their performance. Employees can spend their time trying to continually improve performance or they can spend it fighting discrimination, but they cannot do both. There is not sufficient time in the work day or energy in the employee.

Discrimination and Morale

Of the various factors that can affect employee performance, few if any, are more important than morale. Morale refers to the spirit of employees—how they feel about themselves, the team, and the organization. Employees with high morale exhibit such characteristics as trust, loyalty, pride, and faith in the organization. Because of this, they are more likely to commit to peak performance and continual improvement. High morale is synonymous with team unity and employee commitment. On the other hand, employees with low morale will achieve neither peak performance nor continual improvement, at least not consistently. In fact, the opposite typically happens. Low morale typically results in poor performance.

Obviously maintaining the highest possible morale must be a goal of organizational leaders who are committed to excellence and hope to develop peak performing employees. Morale is a function of various factors, one of the most important being employee perceptions of how they are treated by organizational leaders and team mates. Employees want to be appreciated, respected, and recognized for their contributions. Employees with low morale typically feel as if the organization does not care about them and does not appreciate, respect, or properly recognize them. It should come as no surprise then that discrimination results in low morale.

Discrimination is certainly evidence that the organization cares little for selected employees, but discrimination goes well beyond just not caring. In fact, it is an oppressive practice that involves denying opportunities to some employees while providing them to others without factoring performance into the equation. Such a practice is not just illegal and unethical, it is counterproductive. Employees who believe they are being discriminated against are likely to suffer from low morale, and low morale is the enemy of peak performance. Worse yet, low morale is contagious. Like chickenpox it spreads through contact. Employees suffering from low morale will soon spread their *disease* to other employees. The inevitable result of declining morale is declining performance.

Tolerance

The diversity-related concepts explained so far—prejudice, stereotyping, labeling, and discrimination—are all negative. The concept explained in this section—tolerance—is positive, at least for as far as it goes. Tolerance is a willingness to remain open to people who are different in some way (e.g. race, gender, national origin, education level, political orientation, point of view, etc.). People who are tolerant do not automatically reject another person, opinion, or perspective on the basis of diversity factors. As a result, tolerant people are more likely to make decisions on the basis of performance than on diversity factors.

Tolerance is a step in the right direction in that it moves people away from prejudice, stereotyping, labeling, and discrimination. But for organizations trying to excel in a global environment and develop peak-performing employees, it is not enough. There are two diametrically opposed problems that can occur with tolerance: 1) in some cases it does not go far enough, and 2) in other cases it goes too far. Organizational leaders should be familiar with both of these shortcomings, as well as how to prevent their occurrence. They should also be prepared to teach these things to employees.

When Tolerance Does Not Go Far Enough

It is often said that diversity is an organizational asset. In fact, some organizations adopt such slogans as "…our diversity is our strength." A more accurate rendering of this philosophical ideal would be that diversity CAN be an organizational asset. It is a concept with enormous potential for good, but potential does not become reality without a concerted effort to make it so. The hard truth about diversity is that it is an organizational asset only when handled well. Organizations that do a poor job of handling diversity run the risk of turning the workplace into a collection of warring factions divided on the basis of factors unrelated to performance. When it comes to making diversity an asset, tolerance is a step in the right direction but it is not enough.

In actual practice, tolerance all too often amounts to diverse people just putting up with each other for the sake of harmony. But harmony is not the goal, and putting up with others is a far cry from embracing them. Too often the unstated message behind tolerance in the workplace is, *I will put up with you but only because I have to.* By definition there is a begrudging aspect to tolerance. Consequently, it can take an organization only so far down the road toward excellence. Organizations that want to enjoy the potential benefits of diversity must go beyond just tolerating it to embracing it. This is an important point that organizational leaders should teach employees.

Embracing diversity is tolerance taken to a higher level. People who embrace diversity do not just put up with others who are different, they seek them out. People who embrace diversity understand that human differences—race, gender, background, experiences, education—can produce differences in perspectives, points of view, and opinion. Further, they understand that one of the best ways to solve problems and improve decisions is to get people with different perspectives, backgrounds, and experiences focused on the issue in question.

The opinions of employees are informed by their individual backgrounds and experiences. This is why different people can look at the same problem and see different causes and solutions. One person, no matter how talented, can see a problem from just one perspective—her own. But a diverse group of people will view the problem from a variety of perspectives. This diversity of perspectives invariably leads to better decisions, better ideas, and better solutions. These, in turn, lead to better performance. Organizational leaders can promote the concept of embracing diversity in a number of ways including:

- Talking with employees about the concept and making sure they understand how it can affect performance

- Insisting on diversity in the makeup of teams

- Seeking out a broad base of opinions before making decisions

- Encouraging employees to break out of their comfort zones and seek out team mates who are different from them

- Recognizing and rewarding employees on the basis of performance

- Setting an example of embracing diversity

When Tolerance Goes Too Far

Tolerance is a practice that can enhance an organization's performance, especially when it is taken to the level of embracing diversity. When promoting tolerance among employees organizational leaders should keep its potential impact on performance foremost in their minds. This is important because when it comes to tolerance, some organizational leaders lose their way. It is not uncommon for organizational leaders to be so anxious to prove they are tolerant that they tolerate things they shouldn't. One of the things overly tolerant organizational leaders should not tolerate but sometimes do is behavior that undermines performance. Not only does this take tolerance too far, it is can quickly undermine the credibility of the concept.

The race, gender, background, religion, or education level of unproductive and counterproductive employees should never be used as an excuse for ignoring poor performance. Unproductive work practices and counterproductive behavior in the workplace are wrong, and should not be tolerated. Tolerance is not intended to mean and should never be allowed to mean giving problem employees a free pass on the basis of diversity-related factors. Tolerance should be practiced because it is the right thing to do from the perspectives of both ethics and performance. The following example will illustrate this point.

John was a new supervisor in an organization that placed a high priority on tolerance. Higher management in John's firm provided training for all supervisors that stressed the importance of valuing diversity in all of its forms. Consequently, John was determined to be a tolerant supervisor. At first, things went well with John's new team. Team members appreciated the fact that John seemed to be sincere in seeking out diverse opinions; treating all members of his team with dignity, respect, and equity; recognizing team members appropriately for their work; and interacting well with team members of both genders and all races.

Things in John's team might have continued in a positive manner indefinitely had it not been for Marie. Marie was assigned to the team after John had been the supervisor for just four months. With her arrival, morale on John's team began to fall apart. Marie had a lax attitude about arriving at work on time. In fact, she typically arrived late three days out of five. In addition, she vigorously resisted working late when it was occasionally necessary. Predictably, it was not long before the members of John's team were grumbling about Marie and wondering why John was tolerating her counterproductive work habits.

At first John's team members gave him the benefit of the doubt. They were sure John would pull Marie aside and take corrective action. When this did not happen, members of the team began to approach John and complain. Each time this happened, John's response was the same: "Why are you complaining? I am just being tolerant. After all, Marie is a minority." Predictably this explanation satisfied no one. When, in spite of their complaints, Marie's counterproductive behavior was allowed to continue, other team members began coming to work late. In addition, they started making excuses when John needed them to work late or take on special projects.

When John began to discipline the male members of his team for infractions that Marie committed on a regular basis, morale plummeted. John's misguided attempts at tolerance were being interpreted by everyone on the team except Marie as bias, and they were right. When the performance of John's team fell to an unprecedented low point, higher management was forced to take action, and John's short-lived career as a supervisor came to an end.

PREJUDICE IS A LEARNED BEHAVIOR

Prejudice in the workplace is unethical and counterproductive. In spite of this, there are still some people who refuse to embrace or even tolerate diversity. People who are uncomfortable working in a diverse environment are not necessarily bad people. But they are people who have learned some bad attitudes and behaviors. This concept of learned behavior is important for organizational leaders to understand because it applies to them personally as well as to the employees they will teach to embrace diversity.

People are not born prejudiced, but many learn to be. To test this theory, consider the example of young children. Left to themselves, little children will gladly play with each other without concern for race, gender, or other differences. They are just happy to have play mates. It is only as they grow older that they learn to adopt negative attitudes toward people who are different from them. These negative attitudes can harden into prejudice. It is important to understand that prejudice is a learned behavior because what is learned can be unlearned. If people can learn negative behaviors they can also learn to replace them with positive behaviors.

Case: An Example of Learned Prejudice

An example from my military service demonstrates that learned prejudice can be unlearned and replaced with an attitude of embracing diversity. I went through Marine Corps boot camp at Parris Island, South Carolina with two men who appeared to be as different as two people could possibly be, at least on the surface. One was an African-American from a large city in the north. The other was a Caucasian from a small community in the rural south. When they were unceremoniously thrown together in boot camp, these two recruits were deeply suspicious of and even hostile toward each other.

Growing up, the African-American recruit had learned that all white people from the rural south hated blacks and were members of the Ku Klux Klan. The Caucasian recruit had learned that all inner-city blacks hated whites and were members of drug gangs. These misguided stereotypes got the two recruits off to a bad start. Their interaction began with insults, escalated into arguments, and culminated in a fight. The fight turned out to be a life-changing experience for both recruits.

Because the Marine Corps knows that its members will eventually have to depend on each other in combat, it has become proficient in turning recruits of different races, cultures, backgrounds, and perspectives into mutually-respectful, mutually-supportive team members. Nothing in the unique psyche of the Marine Corps is more important than individual Marines being able to depend on each other in life-or-death situations. In combat, Marines work in teams. These teams go by various names such as fire teams, squads, platoons, companies, battalions, regiments, and divisions. Regardless of the size and nature of the team, Marines must know without the slightest doubt that they can count on each other.

To build this type of trust, Marine Corps drill instructors apply a variety of methods, beginning on the first day of boot camp. In the case of the two feuding recruits, our drill instructors used what they called the "buddy system." Rather than separate the two antagonists, our drill instructors required them to work together as a team on everything. It was like throwing two angry pit bulls into the same cage. They had to eat together, bunk together, march together, exercise together, run the Confidence Course (a major obstacle course) together, and solve field problems together. If one of them made a mistake or did not measure up to expectations, both of them were punished. For example, if one of them did not complete the Confidence Course in the required time, they both had to re-run it.

At first, sparks flew between these two recruits, each determined to outdo the other in every aspect of the training. However, after enduring hours of *attitude-adjustment activities*—extra push ups, pull ups, sit-ups, running, marching, guard duty, rifle cleaning, toilet scrubbing, and rope climbing—it began to dawn on the two recalcitrant recruits that working together might not be such a bad idea. Their first steps in the right direction were tentative at best. Animosity that is grounded in lifelong stereotypes does not go away overnight. Finally, while spending yet another evening in the sand pit sweating through round after round of extra pushups, the two exhausted recruits—lungs on fire, arms arching, and energy spent—reluctantly admitted to themselves that they would never get through boot camp unless they put their prejudice aside and worked together.

Once these two recruits—outwardly so different—began to work together, an interesting thing happened. They found to their surprise that they actually had much in common. Both had been abandoned by their fathers at an early age. Both had been forced to drop out of high school to help support their families. Both saw the Marine Corps as their ticket to a better life and, hence, both needed to succeed. Both excelled at the physical aspects of boot camp, both liked to march, and both were good at close-order drill. When our platoon finally took its turn at the rifle range, it turned out that they were both excellent shots. In fact, once these two former enemies began to work cooperatively, they learned that their similarities outnumbered their differences.

By the time our recruit platoon completed the crucible that was Parris Island, these newly minted Marines—one an inner-city black from the north and the other a white farmer from the rural south—were inseparable friends. In fact, they were more than friends. They were brothers who would lay down their lives for each other without hesitation. Our drill instructors at Parris Island knew something that all organizational leaders should learn: no matter how different people might appear on the outside, in certain fundamental ways they are more alike than different. The key is getting them to focus on their similarities instead of the differences.

UNLEARNING PREJUDICE AND EMBRACING DIVERSITY

As has already been explained, prejudice, stereotyping, labeling, and discrimination are learned behaviors. They are not genetic. This is actually good news because what can be learned can be unlearned, just ask a former smoker. The comparison with smoking is appropriate because giving up long-held prejudices can be as hard as giving up smoking or any other bad habit. It requires commitment, persistence, and a willingness to change. Further, it requires replacing a bad habit with something better.

Effective strategies for unlearning prejudice and embracing diversity include: 1) focus on character rather than race, gender, culture, or other differences; 2) look for common ground; 3) focus on what really matters; and 4) relate to people as individuals. These strategies can be used by organizational leaders for overcoming their own prejudices and for helping employees overcome theirs. Stating these four strategies is easier than applying them. Remember, breaking bad habits requires persistence, patience, and concerted effort. There will be ups and downs, progress and backsliding—this is to be expected. However, once started down the right path, organizational leaders and employees should keep going and refuse to look back.

Focus on Character Rather than Race, Gender, Culture, or other Differences

The various ways people can be different—race, gender. culture, age, religion, politics, nationality—are the wrong things to consider when forming opinions of people. A better approach is to focus on the traits that really make people who they are, those known as character traits. Character traits that are especially important in a work setting include the following:

- Honesty and integrity
- Selflessness

- Dependability and trustworthiness

- Initiative

- Tolerance/sensitivity

- Perseverance

Race, gender, culture, and the other ways people can be outwardly different are not character traits. They are determined by birth, and do not make people who they are. Character traits, on the other hand, have the element of choice. People can choose to be honest, selfless, dependable, and so on. There are people of every race, both genders, and all cultures who are honest, dependable, and selfless, and, of course, the obverse is also true. It is character, not race, gender, or culture that makes people who they are.

Look for Common Ground

In the earlier example from Parris Island, the two Marine recruits eventually found that they had more commonalities than differences. This is typically the case, even when the people in question appear on the surface to have nothing in common. Even people from different countries who speak different languages, are of different races, and have different cultural backgrounds have more similarities than differences. People tend to share the same desires, hopes, fears, and needs regardless of their apparent differences. The key to finding common ground with other people is to look past the surface-level differences and get to know them well enough to see the similarities.

Case: Common Ground Trumps Differences

A woman pushed her baby stroller through the park on a beautiful Spring day. She was obviously wealthy. Her clothing was expensive and well-tailored. Her stroller was the best model available from the most exclusive store in town. Her jewelry was simple, but elegant. A nanny followed close behind her. From the other direction came a woman of obviously different circumstances. Her clothes, though clean, were second hand and patched in places. She, too, had a small baby, but she carried hers, obviously unable to afford a stroller. The two women could not have presented a more stark contrast. They appeared to have nothing in common.

As they came abreast of one another though, the two women smiled tentatively and then, with some hesitation, stopped. Pleasant words were exchanged about their babies, and soon the two women were seated beside each other on a park bench feeding their babies and sharing the special intimacies of new mothers. They talked for almost a half hour before exchanging hugs and promising to meet in the park the next day. Two women from drastically different circumstances—women who appeared to have nothing in common—were able to transcend the socio-economic chasm that separated their daily lives and become friends. Why? Because they looked past their surface-level differences and found something they had in common, something very special that transcended socio-economic status. This is what people in organizations must learn to do if diversity is going to be an asset in an organization.

Focus on What Really Matters

When an organization must compete in a global environment, what is really important quickly becomes apparent. What organizations striving for excellence need from their personnel is peak performance. Once this fact is grasped, the pathway to a whole new perspective opens up. This new perspective is based on an acknowledgement that what really matters are not such factors as race, gender, age, and culture, but talent, motivation, attitude, and teamwork.

I learned an invaluable lesson about focusing on what really matters as a result of playing organized sports. Growing up at a time when athletes were expected to fit certain stereotypes—short hair, conservative dress, no smoking, sport-appropriate body type—it came as a shock to find that some of the best baseball, football, and basketball players did not fit the mold. There were baseball players with long, shaggy hair who could knock the ball a mile. There were football players who lit up cigarettes all week and then lit up the field on Friday nights. There were tall students who could not step on a basketball court without tripping over their own feet, and short students who could average 30 points a game.

My friends and I soon learned that what mattered in high school sports were not the stereotypical traits that were widely accepted at the time, but talent, motivation, attitude, and teamwork. We also learned that these traits came in a lot of different packages. It did not take long for us to realize that the athletes we wanted as team mates were not those who looked like poster boys for the stereotypes of the day, but those who could produce. We wanted the top performers. In baseball, we wanted players who could hit, field, throw, and steal bases. In football, we wanted players who could run, pass, catch, block, and tackle. In basketball we wanted players who could pass, defend, rebound, and score.

This is precisely how it should be in the workplace. People who make the organization more competitive by performing at peak levels should be the winners in organizations. These are the people who should be appropriately rewarded and recognized, regardless of such factors as race, gender, age, culture, politics, religion, or any of the other ways people can be different. Organizations that allow decisions to be made on the basis of factors unrelated to performance are fated to suffer from self-inflicted mediocrity.

Relate to People as Individuals

One of the things that makes overcoming prejudice difficult is that prejudiced people can always find someone of another race, gender, age, or culture who fits their stereotypes; someone they can use to validate their prejudice. There are usually *some* people in any group who will actually display the characteristics that prejudiced people attribute to the whole group. This is one of the ways that people develop their prejudices—by attributing characteristics or behaviors they see in a few members of a group to everyone in the group.

The truth is that whenever people attribute any characteristic to everyone in a given group, they are automatically wrong. People, no matter how they might be categorized, are individuals. As was explained earlier in this chapter, even identical twins can be vastly different in a variety of ways. Consequently, the only dependable, fair, and equitable way to relate to people is as individuals rather than as members of racial, gender, age, cultural, political, or religious groups.

In the workplace, there are people of different races, ages, genders, and cultures who are positive, talented, motivated, team players who perform at peak levels. There are also those who do not measure up in any of these areas. In both cases, their work-related behavior is the result of their individual character, not their race, age, gender, or cultural background. People who make an effort to relate to others as individuals will find it difficult to maintain the prejudices they have been taught by society. As a result, they will become better team players and more valuable assets to their organizations.

GROUP TRAINING ACTIVITY

Work with the members of the group to list as many stereotypes and corresponding labels as possible. Then discuss how these stereotypes might affect productivity on the job. Discuss how relating to the stereotyped and labeled people as individuals might change a prejudiced person's perspective about them.

ABOUT THE AUTHOR

David Goetsch is Vice-President of Northwest Florida State College where he is also professor of management and business as well as the College's lead corporate trainer. He is also a private corporate trainer and consultant to business, industry, government, and non-profit organizations. Having authored more than 70 books in the fields of business, leadership, management, and supervision, Dr. Goetsch is one of the most widely published college professors and corporate trainers in the United States. Six of his books are bestsellers and four of them have been translated into foreign languages (Korean, Indonesian, Malaysian, and Hindi). As a corporate trainer, Dr. Goetsch provides customized training, consulting services, strategic planning assistance, and management coaching to more than 100 client firms.

CONTACTING THE AUTHOR

Dr. Goetsch welcomes feedback from readers. He may be contacted at the following email address or telephone number:

ddsg2001@cox.net

850-678-4040

INDEX

V

W